NARCOTICS ANONYMOUS

1st Edition: 1st Printing, March 1983

2nd Edition: 1st Printing, July 1983
2nd Printing, Sept. 1983
3rd Printing, Oct. 1983
4th Printing, Jan. 1984
5th Printing, Mar. 1984

3rd Edition: (new & revised)
1st Printing, October 1984
2nd Printing, February 1985

Library of Congress Catalog No. 83-70346
ISBN 0-912075-02-3

World Service Office, Inc.
16155 Wyandotte Street
Van Nuys, CA 91406
(818) 780-3951

PRINTED IN THE UNITED STATES OF AMERICA

NARCOTICS ANONYMOUS

APPROVED
LITERATURE

12 Steps and 12 Traditions
reprinted for adaption
by permission of
A.A. World Services, Inc.

CONTENTS

BOOK II

continued

BOOK II *Continued*

*We cannot change the nature of
the Addict or Addiction . . .
We can help to change the old lie
"Once an addict, always an addict,"
by striving to make recovery more
available.
God, help us to remember this difference.*

OUR SYMBOL

Simplicity is the keynote of our symbol; it follows the simplicity of our Fellowship. We could find all sorts of occult and esoteric connotations in the simple outlines, but foremost in our minds were easily understood meanings and relationships.

The outer circle denotes a universal and total program that has room within for all manifestations of the recovering and wholly recovered person.

The square, whose lines are defined, is easily seen and understood; but there are other unseen parts of the symbol. The square base denotes Goodwill, the ground of both the fellowship and the member of our society. Actually, it is the four pyramid sides which rise from this base in a three dimensional figure that are the Self, Society, Service and God. All rise to the point of Freedom.

All parts thus far are closely related to the needs and aims of the addict seeking recovery and the purpose of the fellowship seeking to make recovery available to all. The greater the base, as we grow in unity in numbers and in fellowship, the broader the sides and the higher the point of freedom. Probably the last to be lost to freedom will be the stigma of being an addict. Goodwill is best exemplified in service and proper service is "Doing the right thing for the right reason." When this supports and motivates both the individual and the fellowship, we are fully whole and wholly free.

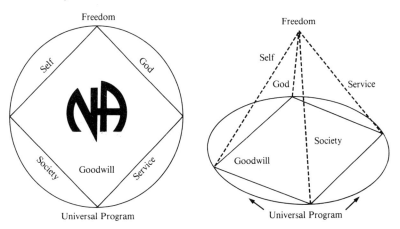

FOREWORD

*"The full fruit of a labor of love lives in the harvest,
and that always comes in its right season. . . ."*

The material for this book was drawn from the personal experiences of addicts within the Fellowship of Narcotics Anonymous. This Basic Text is based on an outline derived from the pamphlet (our "white book"), *Narcotics Anonymous*. The first eight chapters are based on the topic headings in the "white book" and carry the same title. We have included a ninth chapter, 'Just for Today,' and a tenth chapter, 'More Will Be Revealed.'

Following is a brief history of the book:

Narcotics Anonymous was formed in July 1953, with the first meeting held in Southern California. The Fellowship grew erratically, but quickly spread to various parts of the United States. From the beginning the need was seen for a "book on recovery" to help strengthen the Fellowship. The pamphlet, "Narcotics Anonymous," was published in 1962.

However, the Fellowship still had little structure and the 1960's were a period of struggle. Membership grew rapidly for a time, and then began to decline. The need for a more specific direction was readily apparent. N.A. demonstrated its maturity in 1972, when a World Service Office was opened in Los Angeles. The W.S.O. has brought the needed unity and sense of purpose to the Fellowship.

The opening of the W.S.O. brought stability to the growth of the Fellowship. Today, there are many thousand recovering addicts in hundreds of meetings all across the United States and in many foreign countries. Today, the World Service Office truly serves a worldwide Fellowship.

Narcotics Anonymous has long recognized the need for a complete Basic Text on addiction — a book about addicts, by addicts and for addicts.

This effort was strengthened after the formation of W.S.O. with the publication of *The N.A. Tree*, a pamphlet on service work. This pamphlet was the original "service manual" of the Fellowship. It has been followed by subsequent and more comprehensive volumes, and now the *N.A. Service Manual*.

The manual outlined a service structure which included a World Service Conference. The W.S.C., in turn, included a Literature Committee. With the encouragement of W.S.O., several members of the Board of Trustees and the Conference, work began. As the cry for literature, particularly a comprehensive text, became more widespread, the W.S.C. Literature Committee developed. In October 1979, the first World Literature Conference was held at Wichita, Kansas, followed by conferences at Lincoln, Nebraska; Memphis, Tennessee; Santa Monica, California; Warren, Ohio; and Miami, Florida. The W.S.C. Literature Subcommittee, working in conference and as individuals, have collected hundreds of pages of material from members and groups throughout the Fellowship. This material has been laboriously catalogued, edited, assembled, dismembered and reassembled. Dozens of area and regional representatives working with the Committee have dedicated thousands of man-hours to produce the work here presented. But more importantly, those members have conscientiously sought to insure a "group-conscience" text.

In keeping with the spirit of anonymity, we, the W.S., Literature Subcommittee, feel it appropriate to express our special gratitude and appreciation to the Fellowship as a whole, especially the many of you who contributed material for inclusion in the book. We feel that this book is a synthesis of the collective Group Conscience of the entire Fellowship and that every single idea submitted is included in the work, in some form or another.

This volume is intended as a textbook for every addict seeking recovery. As addicts, we know the pain of addiction, but we also know the joy of the recovery we have found in the Fellowship of Narcotics Anonymous. We believe the time has come to share our recovery, in written form, with all who desire what we have found.

Appropriately, this book is devoted to informing every addict: JUST FOR TODAY, YOU NEVER HAVE TO USE AGAIN!

Therefore,

"With gratitude in our cleanliness, we dedicate our N.A. book to the loving service of our Higher Power. That through the development of a conscious contact with God, no addict seeking recovery need die without having had a chance to find a better way of life."

We remain trusted servants.

In gratitude and loving service,

LITERATURE SUBCOMMITTEE
WORLD SERVICE CONFERENCE
NARCOTICS ANONYMOUS

INTRODUCTION

This book is the shared experience of the fellowship of Narcotics Anonymous. We welcome you to read this text, hoping that you will choose to share with us in the new life we have found. We have by no means found a "cure" for addiction. We offer only a proven plan for daily recovery.

In N.A., we follow a program adapted from Alcoholics Anonymous. More than one million people have recovered in A.A., most of them just as hopelessly addicted to alcohol as we were to drugs. We are grateful to the A.A. fellowship for showing us the way to a new life.

The Twelve Steps of Narcotics Anonymous, as adapted from A.A., are the basis of our recovery program. We have only broadened their perspective. We follow the same path with a single exception; our identification as addicts is all-inclusive in respect to any mood-changing, mind-altering substance. "Alcoholism" is too limited a term for us; our problem is not a specific substance, it is a disease called "addiction." We believe that as a fellowship, we have been guided by a Greater Consciousness, and are grateful for the Direction that has enabled us to build upon an already-proven program of recovery.

We have come to Narcotics Anonymous by various means and believe that our common denominator is that we failed to come to terms with our addiction. Because of the degree and variety of addiction found within our fellowship, we have approached the solution contained within this book in general terms. We pray that we have been searching and thorough, so that every addict who reads this volume will find the hope we have found.

Based on our experience, we believe that every addict, including the "potential" addict, suffers from an incurable disease of body, mind and spirit. We were in the grip of a hopeless dilemma, the solution of which is spiritual in nature. Therefore, this book will deal with spiritual matters.

We are not a religious organization. Our program is a set of spiritual principles through which we are recovering from a seemingly hopeless state of mind and body. Throughout the compiling of this work, we have prayed:

"GOD, grant us knowledge that we may write according to Your Divine precepts, instill in us a sense of Your purpose, make us servants of Your will and grant us a bond of selflessness that this may truly be Your work, not ours, in order that no addict, anywhere, need die from the horrors of addiction."

Everything that occurs in the course of N.A. service must be motivated by the desire to more successfully carry the message of recovery to the addict who still suffers. It was for this reason that we began this work. We must always remember that as individual members, groups, and service committees, we are not, and should never be, in competition with each other. We work separately and together to help the newcomer and for our common good. We have learned, painfully, that internal strife cripples our fellowship; it prevents us from providing the services necessary for growth.

It is our hope that this book will help the suffering addict find the solution we have found. Our purpose is to remain clean, just for today, and to carry the message of recovery.

Thank you,

LITERATURE SUBCOMMITTEE
WORLD SERVICE CONFERENCE
NARCOTICS ANONYMOUS

Many books have been written about the nature of addiction. This book primarily concerns itself with the nature of recovery. If you are an addict and have found this book, please give yourself a break and read it!

BOOK ONE

NARCOTICS ANONYMOUS

Chapter One

WHO IS AN ADDICT?

Most of us do not have to think twice about this question. WE KNOW! Our whole life and thinking is centered in drugs in one form or another, the getting and using and finding ways and means to get more. We use to live and live to use. Very simply an addict is a man or woman whose life is controlled by drugs. We are people in the grip of a continuing and progressive illness whose ends are always the same: jails, institutions and death.

Those of us who have found the program of Narcotics Anonymous do not have to think twice about the question: Who is an addict? We know! The following is our experience.

As addicts, we are people whose use of any mind-altering, mood-changing substance causes a problem in any area of life. Addiction is a disease which involves more than simple drug use. Some of us believe that our disease was present long before the first time we used.

Most of us did not consider ourselves addicted before coming to the Narcotics Anonymous program. The information available to us came from misinformed people. As long as we could stop using for a while, we thought we were all right. We looked at the stopping, not the using. As

1

our addiction progressed, we thought of stopping less and less. Only in desperation did we ask ourselves, "Could it be the drugs?"

We did not choose to become addicts. We suffer from a disease which expresses itself in ways that are anti-social and make detection, diagnosis and treatment difficult.

Our disease isolated us from people except for the getting, using and finding ways and means to get more. Hostile, resentful, self-centered and self-seeking, we cut ourselves off from the outside world. Anything not completely familiar became alien and dangerous. Our world shrank and isolation became our life. We used in order to survive. It was the only way of life we knew.

Some of us used, misused and abused drugs and still never considered ourselves addicts. Through all of this, we kept telling ourselves, "I can handle it." Our misconceptions about the nature of addiction conjured up visions of violence, street crime, dirty needles and jail.

When our addiction was treated as a crime or moral deficiency, we became rebellious and were driven deeper into isolation. Some of the highs felt great, but eventually the things we had to do in order to support our using reflected desperation. We were caught in the grip of our disease. We were forced to survive any way we could. We manipulated people and tried to control everything around us. We lied, stole, cheated and sold ourselves. We had to have drugs, regardless of the cost. Failure and fear began to invade our lives.

One aspect of our addiction was our inability to deal with life on its terms. We tried drugs and combinations of drugs in an effort to cope with a seemingly hostile world. We dreamed of finding a magic formula that would solve our ultimate problem — ourselves. The fact was that we could not successfully use any mind-altering or mood-changing substance, including marijuana and alcohol. Drugs ceased to make us feel good.

At times, we were defensive about our addiction and justified our right to use, especially when we had "legal prescriptions." We were proud of the sometimes illegal and often bizarre behavior that typified our using. We "forgot" the times we sat alone consumed by fear and self-pity. We fell into a pattern of selective thinking. We only remem-

2

bered the "good" drug experiences. We justified and rationalized the things we had to do to keep from being sick or going crazy. We ignored the times when life seemed to be a nightmare. We avoided the reality of our addiction.

Higher mental and emotional functions, such as conscience and the ability to love, were sharply affected by our use of drugs. Living skills were reduced to the animal level. Our spirit was broken. The capacity to feel human was lost. This seems extreme, but many of us have been in this state.

We were constantly searching for "the answer"—that person, place or thing that would make everything all right. We lacked the ability to cope with daily living. As our addiction caught up with us, many of us found ourselves in and out of institutions.

These experiences indicated there was something wrong with our lives. We wanted an easy way out and some of us thought of suicide. Our attempts were usually feeble, and only helped to contribute to our feelings of worthlessness. We were trapped in the illusion of "what if," "if only" and "just one more time." When we did seek help, we were really only looking for the absence of pain.

We have regained good physical health many times, only to lose it by using again. Our track record shows that it is impossible for us to use successfully. No matter how well we may appear to be in control, using drugs always brings us to our knees.

Like other incurable diseases, addiction can be arrested. We agree that there is nothing shameful about being an addict, provided we accept our dilemma honestly and take positive action. We are willing to admit without reservation that we are allergic to drugs. Common sense tells us that it would be insane to go back to the source of our allergy. Our experience indicates that medicine cannot "cure" our illness.

Although physical and mental tolerance play a role, many drugs require no extended period of use to trigger allergic reactions. Our reaction is what makes us addicts, not how much we use.

Many of us did not think we had a problem until the drugs ran out. Even when others told us we had a problem, we were convinced that we were right and the world was wrong. We used this belief to justify our

3

self-destructive behavior. We developed a point of view that enabled us to pursue our addiction without concern for our own well-being or that of others. We began to feel the drugs were killing us long before we could ever admit it to anyone else. We noticed that if we tried to stop using, we couldn't. We suspected we had lost control over the drugs and had no power to stop.

Certain things followed as we continued to use. We became accustomed to a state of mind common to addicts. We forgot what it was like before we started using; we forgot the social graces. We acquired strange habits and mannerisms. We forgot how to work; we forgot how to play; we forgot how to express ourselves and show concern for others. We forgot how to feel.

While using, we lived in another world. We experienced only periodic jolts of reality or self-awareness. It seemed we were at last two people instead of one, like Dr, Jekyll and Mr. Hyde. We ran around trying to get our lives together before our next run. Sometimes we could do this very well, but later, it was less important and more impossible. In the end, Dr. Jekyll died and Mr. Hyde took over.

Each of us has a few things we can say we never did. We cannot let these things become excuses to use again. Some of us feel lonely because of differences between us and other members, and this makes it difficult to give up old connections and old habits.

We all have different tolerances for pain. Some addicts needed to go to greater extremes than others. Some of us found we had had enough when we realized that we were getting high too often and it was affecting our daily lives.

At first, we were using in a manner which seemed to be social or at least controllable with little indication of the disaster which the future held for us. At some point, our using became uncontrollable and antisocial. This began when things were going well and we were in situations that allowed us to use frequently. This was usually the end of the good times. We may have tried to moderate, substitute, or even stop using, but we went from a state of drugged success and well-being to complete spiritual, mental and emotional bankruptcy. This rate of decline varies from addict to addict. Whether it is years or days, it is all downhill. Those of us who don't die from the disease will go on to prison, mental institutions or complete demoralization as the disease progresses. Drugs had given us the feeling that we could handle whatever situation might develop. We became aware, however, that drugs were largely responsible for having gotten us into our very worst predicaments. Some of us may spend the rest of our lives in jail for a drug-related crime or a crime commited while using. We had to reach our bottom before we became willing to stop. We were much more motivated to seek help in the latter stage of our addiction. It was easier for us to see the destruction, disaster and delusion of our using. It was harder to deny our addiction when problems were staring us in the face.

Some of us first saw the effects of addiction on the people with whom we were close. We were very dependent on them to carry us emotionally through life. We felt angry, disappointed and hurt when they had other interests, friends and loved ones. We regretted the past, dreaded the future, and we weren't too thrilled about the present. After years of searching, we were more unhappy and less satisfied than when it all began.

Our addiction had enslaved us. We were prisoners of our own mind, condemned by our own guilt. We had given up ever stopping. Our attempts to stay clean had always failed, causing us pain and misery.

As addicts, we have an incurable disease called addiction which is chronic, progressive and fatal. However, it is a treatable disease. We feel that each individual alone has to answer the question, "Am I an addict?" How we got the disease is of no immediate importance to us. We are concerned with recovery.

We begin to treat our addiction by not using. Many of us sought answers but failed to find any workable solution until we found each other. Once we identify ourselves as addicts, help becomes possible. We can see a little of ourselves in every addict and a little bit of them in us. This insight lets us help one another. Our futures seemed hopeless until we found clean addicts who were willing to share with us. Denial of our addiction was what had kept us sick, and our honest admission enabled us to stop using. The people of Narcotics Anonymous told us that they

5

were recovering addicts who had learned to live without drugs. If they could do it, so could we.

The only alternatives to recovery are jails, institutions, dereliction and death. Unfortunately, our disease makes us deny our addiction. If you are an addict, you too can find a new way of life through the N.A. program that would not otherwise be possible. We have become very grateful in the course of our recovery. Our lives have become useful, through abstinence and by working the Twelve Steps of Narcotics Anonymous.

We realize that we are never cured and carry the disease within us all our lives. We have a disease from which we do recover. Each day we are given another chance. We are convinced that there is only one way for us to live, and that is the N.A. way.

Chapter Two

WHAT IS THE N.A. PROGRAM?

N.A. is a non-profit fellowship or society of men and women for whom drugs had become a major problem. We are recovering addicts who meet regularly to help each other stay clean. This is a program of complete abstinence from all drugs. There is only "one" requirement for membership, the honest desire to stop using. There are no musts in N.A., but we suggest that you keep an open mind and give yourself a break. Our program is a set of principles, written so simply that we can follow them in our daily lives. The most important thing about them is that "they work."

There are no strings attached to N.A. We are not affiliated with any other organizations, we have no leaders, no initiation fees or dues, no pledges to sign, no promises to make to anyone. We are not connected with any political, religious, or law enforcement groups, and are under no surveillance at any time. Anyone may join us regardless of age, race, color, creed, religion or lack of religion.

We are not interested in what or how much you used or who your connections were, what you have done in the past, how much or how little you have, but only in what you want to do about your problem and how we can help. The newcomer is the most important person at any meeting, because we can only keep what we have by giving it away. We have learned from our group experience that those who keep coming to our meetings regularly stay clean.

N arcotics Anonymous is a fellowship of men and women who are learning to live without drugs. We are a non-profit society. and have no dues or fees of any kind. Each of us has paid the price of membership. We have paid dearly with our pain for the right to recover.

We are addicts, surviving against all odds, who meet regularly together. We respond to honest sharing and listen to the stories of our members for the message of recovery. We realize that, at last, there is hope for us.

We make use of the tools that have worked for other recovering addicts who have learned to live without drugs in Narcotics Anonymous. The Twelve Steps are positive tools that make recovery possible. Our primary purpose is to stay clean and to carry the message to the addict who still suffers. We are united by our common problem of addiction. By meeting, talking with, and helping other addicts, we are able to stay clean. The newcomer is the most important person at any meeting because we can only keep what we have by giving it away.

Narcotics Anonymous has had many years of experience with literally hundreds of thousands of addicts. This mass of intensive first-hand experience in all phases of illness and recovery is of unparalleled therapeutic value. We are here to share freely with any addicts who want it.

Our message of recovery is based on our own experience. Before coming to the fellowship, we exhausted ourselves trying to "use" successfully, or trying to find out what was wrong with us. After coming to N.A., we found ourselves among a very special group of people who have suffered like us and found recovery. In their experiences, freely shared, we found hope for ourselves. If the Program worked for them, it would work for us.

The only requirement for membership is a desire to stop using. We have seen the Program work for any addict who honestly and sincerely wants to stop. We don't have to be clean when we get here, but after the first meeting, we suggest that newcomers keep coming back and come back clean. We don't have to wait for an overdose, or jail sentence, to get help from Narcotics Anonymous, nor is addiction a hopeless condition from which there is no recovery.

We meet addicts like ourselves who are clean. We watch and listen to them and realize that they have found a way to live and enjoy life without drugs. We don't have to settle for the limitations of the past. We can examine and re-examine all our old ideas and constantly improve on them or replace them with new ones. We are men and women who have discovered and admitted that we are powerless over our addiction. When we use, we lose.

When we discovered that we cannot live with or without drugs, we sought help through N.A. rather than prolong our suffering. The Program works a miracle in our lives. We become different people. The steps and abstinence give us a daily reprieve from our self-imposed life sentences. We become free to live.

We want the place where we recover to be a safe place, free from outside influences. For the protection of the fellowship, we insist that no drugs or paraphernalia be brought to any meeting.

We feel totally free to express ourselves within the fellowship, because no law enforcement agencies are involved. Our meetings have an atmosphere of empathy. In accordance with the principles of recovery, we try not to judge, stereotype or moralize with each other. We are not recruited and it doesn't cost anything. N.A. does not provide counseling or social services.

Our meetings are a process of identification, hope and sharing. The heart of N.A. beats when two addicts share their recovery. What we do becomes real for us when we share it. This happens on a larger scale in our regular meetings. A meeting is two or more addicts gathered together to help each other stay clean.

At the beginning of the meeting, we read N.A. literature which is available to anyone. Some meetings have speakers, topic discussions or both. Closed meetings are for addicts or those who think they might have a drug problem; open meetings welcome anyone wishing to experience our Fellowship. The atmosphere of recovery is protected by our Twelve Traditions. We are fully self-supporting through voluntary contributions from our members. Regardless of where the meeting takes place, we remain unaffiliated. Meetings provide us with a place to be with fellow addicts. All we need are two addicts, caring and sharing, to make a meeting.

We let new ideas flow into us. We ask questions. We share what we have learned about living without drugs. Though the principles of the Twelve Steps may seem strange to us at first, the most important thing about them is that they work. Our Program is, in fact, a way of life. We learn the value of such spiritual principles as surrender, humility and service from reading the N.A. literature, going to meetings, and working the steps. We find that our lives steadily improve, if we maintain abstinence from mind-altering, mood-changing chemicals and work the Twelve Steps to sustain our recovery. Living this Program gives us a relationship with a Power greater than ourselves, corrects defects, leads us to help others, and where there has been wrong, teaches us the spirit of forgiveness.

Many books have been written about the nature of addiction. This book concerns itself with the nature of recovery. If you are an addict and have found this book, please give yourself a break and read it.

Chapter Three

WHY ARE WE HERE?

Before coming to the fellowship of N.A., we could not manage our own lives. We could not live and enjoy life as other people do. We had to have something different and we thought we had found it in drugs. We placed their use ahead of the welfare of our families, our wives, husbands, and our children. We had to have drugs at all costs. We did many people great harm but most of all we harmed ourselves. Through our inability to accept personal responsibilities we were actually creating our own problems. We seemed to be incapable of facing life on its own terms.

Most of us realized, that in our addictions, we were slowly committing suicide, but such cunning enemies of life are narcotics and sedation that we had lost the power to do anything about it. Jail did not help us at all. Medicine, religion and psychiatry seemed to have no answers for us that we could use. All these methods having failed for us, in desperation, we sought help from each other in Narcotics Anonymous.

After coming to N.A. we realized we were sick people who suffered from a disease like Alcoholism, Diabetes or Tuberculosis. There is no known "cure" for these—all, however, can be arrested at some point and "recovery" is then possible.

In N.A. we follow a program borrowed from Alcoholics Anonymous.

In the last forty years, more than one million people have recovered in A.A., most of them just as hopelessly addicted to alcohol as we were to drugs. We are deeply grateful to the A.A. Fellowship for pointing the way for us to a new way of life.

We are addicts seeking recovery. We used drugs to cover up our feelings, and did whatever was necessary to get them. Many of us woke up sick, unable to make it to work, or went to work loaded. Many of us stole to support our habit. We hurt the ones we loved. We did all these things and told ourselves, "We can handle it." We were looking for a way out. We couldn't face life on its own terms. In the beginning, using was fun. For us it became a habit and finally was necessary for survival. The progression of the disease was not apparent to us. We continued on the path of destruction, unaware of where it was leading us. We were addicts and did not know it. Through drugs we tried to avoid reality, pain and misery. When the drugs wore off, we realized that we still had the same problems and that they were becoming worse. We sought relief by using again and again—more drugs, more often.

We sought help and found none. Often doctors didn't understand our dilemma; they tried to help by giving us medication. Our husbands, wives and loved ones gave us what they had and drained themselves in the hope that we would stop using or get better. We tried substituting one drug for another, but this only prolonged our pain. We tried limiting our usage to "social" amounts without success. There is no such thing as a "social addict." Some of us sought an answer through churches, religions or cultism. Some sought a cure by geographic change, blaming our surroundings and living situations for our problems. This attempt only gave us a chance to take advantage of new people. Some of us sought approval through sex or change of friends. This approval-seeking carried us further into our addiction. Some of us tried marriage, divorce or desertion. Regardless of what we tried, we could not escape from our disease.

We reached a point in our lives where we felt like a lost cause. Our worth to our jobs, families and friends was little or none. Many of us were unemployed and unemployable. Any form of success was frightening and unfamiliar. We didn't know what to do. As the self-loathing grew, we needed to use more and more to mask our feelings. We were sick and tired of pain and trouble. We were frightened and ran from the fear. No matter how far we ran, we always carried the fear with us. We were hopeless, useless and lost. Failure had become our way of life and self-esteem was nonexistent. Perhaps the most painful of all was the desperation of loneliness. Isolation and the denial of our addiction kept us moving along this downhill path. Any hope of getting better disappeared. Helplessness, emptiness and fear became our way of life. We were complete failures. Personality change was what we really needed. Change from self-destructive patterns of life became necessary. When we lied, cheated or stole, we degraded ourselves in our own eyes. We had had enough of self-destruction. We experienced how powerless we really are. When nothing relieved our paranoia and fear, we hit bottom and became ready to ask for help.

We were searching for an answer when we reached out and found Narcotics Anonymous. We came to our first N.A. meeting in defeat and didn't know what to expect. After sitting in a meeting, or several meetings, we began to feel that people cared and were willing to help. Although our minds told us we would never make it, the people in the Fellowship gave us hope by insisting we could recover. We found that no matter what our past thoughts or actions were, others had felt and done the same. Surrounded by fellow addicts, we realized that we were not alone. Recovery is what happens in our meetings; each of our lives is at stake. We found that by putting recovery first, the Program works.

We faced three disturbing realizations:

1. We are powerless over addiction and our lives are unmanageable;
2. Although we are not responsible for our disease, we are responsible for our recovery;
3. We can no longer blame people, places and things for our addiction. We must face our problems and our feelings.

The ultimate weapon for recovery is the recovering addict. We concentrate on recovery and how we feel, not what we have done in the past. Old friends, places and ideas are often a threat to our recovery. We

13

need to change our playmates, playgrounds and playthings.

When we realized we are not able to manage on our own, some of us immediately began experiencing depression, anxiety, hostility and resentment. Petty frustrations, minor setbacks and loneliness often made us feel that we were not getting any better. We found that we suffered from a disease, not a moral dilemma. We were critically ill, not hopelessly bad. Our disease can only be arrested through abstinence.

Today we experience a full range of feelings. Before coming into the fellowship, we either felt elated or depressed with very little in between. Our negative sense of self has been replaced by a positive concern for others. Answers are provided and problems are solved. It is a great gift to feel human again.

What a change from the way we used to be! That's how we know that the N.A. program works. It is the first thing that ever convinced us that we needed to change ourselves, instead of trying to change the people and situations around us. We discover new opportunities. We find a sense of self-worth. We learn self-respect. This is a program for doing just those things. By working the steps, we come to accept a Higher Power's will; this acceptance leads us to recovery. We lose our fear of the unknown. We are set free.

Chapter Four

HOW IT WORKS

If you want what we have to offer, and are willing to make the effort to get it, then you are ready to take certain steps. These are suggested only, but they are the principles that made our recovery possible.

1. *We admitted that we were powerless over our addiction, that our lives had become unmanageable.*
2. *We came to believe that a power greater than ourselves could restore us to sanity.*
3. *We made a decision to turn our will and our lives over to the care of God as we understood him.*
4. *We made a searching and fearless moral inventory of ourselves.*
5. *We admitted to God, to ourselves, and to another human being the exact nature of our wrongs.*
6. *We were entirely ready to have God remove all these defects of character.*
7. *We humbly asked Him to remove our shortcomings.*
8. *We made a list of all persons we had harmed, and became willing to make amends to them all.*
9. *We made direct amends to such people wherever possible, except*

when to do so would injure them or others.

10. *We continued to take personal inventory, and when we were wrong promptly admitted it.*

11. *We sought through prayer and meditation to improve our conscious contact with God, as we understood Him, praying only for knowledge of His will for us, and the power to carry that out.*

12. *Having had a spiritual awakening as a result of those steps, we tried to carry this message to addicts and to practice these principles in all our affairs.*

This sounds like a big order, and we can't do it all at once, we didn't become addicted in one day, so remember—EASY DOES IT.

There is one thing more than anything else that will defeat us in our recovery, this is an attitude of indifference or intolerance toward spiritual principles. Although there are no musts in N.A., there are three things that seem indispensable. These are, Honesty, Open-mindedness, and Willingness to try. With these we are well on our way.

We feel that our approach to the problem of addiction is completely realistic, for the therapeutic value of one addict helping another is without parallel. We feel that our way is practical, for one addict can best understand and help another addict. We believe that the sooner we face our problems within our society, in everyday living, just that much faster do we become acceptable, responsible, and productive members of that society.

The only way to keep from getting or continuing a habit is not to take that first fix, pill or drink. If you are like us you know that one is too many and a thousand never enough. We put great emphasis on this for we know that when we use drugs in any form, or substitute one for another, we release our addiction all over again or create a new one.

The substitution of alcohol has caused a great many addicts to form a new addiction pattern, which in its progression brings as many problems as before. We seem to forget that alcohol is one of the oldest known drugs. It would appear that we are people with addictive personalities who are strongly susceptible to alcoholic addiction.

These are some of the questions we have asked ourselves: Are we sure

16

we want to stop using? Do we understand that we have no real control over drugs? Do we recognize that in the long run, we didn't use drugs— they used us? Did jails and institutions take over the management of our lives at different times? Do we fully accept the fact that our every attempt to stop using or control our using failed? Do we know that our addiction changed us into something we didn't want to be: dishonest, deceitful, self-willed people at odds with ourselves and our fellow man? Do we really believe that, as drug users, we have failed?

When we were using, reality became so painful that oblivion was preferable. We tried to keep other people from knowing about our pain. We isolated ourselves, and lived in prisons built out of our loneliness. Through this desperation we sought help in Narcotics Anonymous. When we come to Narcotics Anonymous we are physically, mentally, and spiritually bankrupt. We have hurt long enough that we are willing to go to any length to stay clean.

Our only hope is to live by the example of those who have faced our dilemma, and have found a way out. Regardless of who we are, where we came from, or what we have done, we are accepted in Narcotics Anonymous. Our addiction gives us a common ground for understanding one another.

As a result of attending a few meetings, we begin to feel like we finally belong. It is in these meetings that we are introduced to the Twelve Steps of Narcotics Anonymous. We learn to work them in the order they are written and to use them on a daily basis. The steps are our solution. They are our survival kit. They are our defense, for addiction is a deadly disease. Our steps are the principles that make our recovery possible.

STEP ONE

"We admitted that we were powerless over our addiction, that our lives had become unmanageable."

It doesn't matter what or how much we used. In Narcotics Anonymous staying clean has to come first. We realize that we cannot use drugs and live. When we admit our powerlessness and the inability to manage our own lives, we open the door to recovery. No one could convince us that we were addicts. It is an admission that we had to make for ourselves. When some of us have doubts, we ask ourselves this question: "Can I control my use of any form of mind or mood-altering chemicals?"

Most will see that control is impossible the moment it is suggested. Whatever the outcome, we find that we cannot control our using for any length of time.

This would clearly suggest that an addict has no control over drugs. Powerlessness means using against our will. If we can't stop, how can we tell ourselves we are in control? The inability to stop using, even with the greatest willpower and the most sincere desire, is what we mean when we say, "We have absolutely no choice." However, we do have a choice after we eliminate all the things we have been telling ourselves to justify our using.

We didn't stumble into this fellowship brimming with love, honesty, open-mindedness or willingness. We reached the point where we could no longer continue because of physical, mental, and spiritual pain. When we were beaten, we became willing.

Our inability to control our usage of drugs is a symptom of the disease of addiction. We are powerless not only over drugs, but our addiction as well. We need to admit this in order to recover. Addiction is a physical, mental and spiritual disease, affecting every area of our lives.

The physical aspect of our disease is the compulsive use of drugs: the inability to stop using once we have started. The mental aspect of our disease is the obsession, or overpowering desire, which leads us to using even when it has destroyed our lives. The spiritual part of our disease is our total self-centeredness. We felt that we could stop whenever we wanted to, despite all evidence to the contrary. Denial, substitution, rationalization, justification, distrust of others, guilt, embarrassment, dereliction, degradation, isolation, and loss of control are all results of our disease. Our disease is progressive, incurable and fatal. Most of us are relieved to find out we have a disease instead of a moral deficiency.

We are not responsible for our disease, but we are responsible for our recovery. Most of us tried to stop using on our own, but we were unable to live with or without drugs. Eventually we realized that we were powerless over our addiction.

Many of us tried to stop using on sheer willpower, and this turned out to be a temporary solution. We saw that willpower alone would not work for any length of time. We tried countless other remedies — psychiatrists, hospitals, recovery houses, lovers, new towns, new jobs. Everything we tried, failed. We began to see that we had rationalized the most outrageous sort of nonsense in order to justify the mess drugs had made of our lives.

Until we let go of all our reservations, the foundation on which our recovery is based is in danger. Reservations, no matter what they are, rob us of obtaining all the benefits this program has to offer. In ridding ourselves of all reservations, we surrender. Then, and only then, can we be helped to recover from the disease of addiction.

Now, the question is: "If we are powerless, how can Narcotics Anonymous help?" We begin by asking for help, and this is accomplished by working the Twelve Steps. The foundation is the admission that we, of ourselves, have no power over addiction. When we can accept this, we have completed the first part of Step One.

A second admission must be made before the foundation is complete. If we stop here, we will know only half the truth. We are great ones for manipulating the truth. We might say on one hand, "Yes, I am powerless over my addiction," and on the other hand, "When I get my life together, I can handle drugs." Such thoughts and actions led us back to active addiction. It never occurred to us to ask, "If we can't control our addiction, how can we control our lives?" We felt miserable without drugs.

Unemployability, dereliction and destruction are easily seen as characteristics of an unmanageable life. Our families generally are disappointed, baffled and confused by our actions and often have deserted or disowned us. Becoming employed, socially acceptable and reunited with our families does not make our lives manageable. Social acceptability does not equal recovery.

We have found that we had no choice except to completely change our old ways of thinking or go back to using. When we give our best, it works for us as it has worked for others. When we could no longer stand our old ways, we began to change. From that point forward, we can see that every clean day is a successful day, no matter what happens. Surrender means not having to fight anymore. We accept our addiction and life the way it is. We become willing to do whatever is necessary to stay clean, even the things we don't like doing.

Until we took Step One, we were full of fear and doubt. At this point, many of us felt lost and confused. We felt different. Upon working this step, we affirmed our surrender to the principles of Narcotics Anonymous, and only then did we begin to overcome the alienation of addiction. Help for addicts begins only when we are able to admit complete defeat. This can be frightening, but it is the foundation on which we have built our lives.

Step One means that we do not have to use, and this is a great freedom. It took a while for some of us to realize how unmanageable our lives had become; for others of us, this was the only thing of which we could be sure. We knew in our hearts that drugs had the power to change us into something that we didn't want to be.

Being clean and working this step, we are released from our chains. However, none of the steps work by magic. We do not just say the words of this step; we learn to live them. We see for ourselves that the Program has something to offer us.

We have found hope. We find that we can learn to function in the world we live in. We, too, can find meaning and purpose in life and be rescued from insanity, depravity and death.

When we admit our powerlessness and inability to manage our own lives, we open the door for a Power greater than ourselves to help us. It is not where we were that counts, but where we are going.

STEP TWO

"We came to believe that a Power greater than ourselves could restore us to sanity."

The Second Step is necessary if we expect to achieve any sort of ongoing recovery. The First Step leaves us with the need to believe in something that can help us with our powerlessness, uselessness, and helplessness.

The First Step has left a vacuum in our lives. We need to find something to fill that void. This is the purpose of the Second Step.

Some of us didn't take this step seriously at first; we passed over it with a minimum of concern, only to find the next steps would not work until we worked this one. Even when we admitted we needed help with our drug problem, many of us would not admit to the need for faith and sanity.

We have a disease: progressive, incurable and fatal. One way or another we went out and bought our destruction on the time plan! All of us, from the junkie snatching purses to the sweet little old ladies hitting two or three doctors for legal prescriptions, have one thing in common: we seek our destruction a bag at a time, a few pills at a time, or a bottle at a time until we die. This is at least part of the insanity of addiction. The price may seem higher for the addict who prostitutes for a fix than it is for the addict who merely lies to a doctor, but ultimately both pay with their lives. Insanity is repeating the same mistakes and expecting different results.

Many of us realize when we get to the Program that we have gone back time and again to using, even though we knew that we were destroying our lives by doing so. Insanity is using day after day knowing that only physical and mental destruction comes when we do. The most obvious insanity of the disease of addiction is the obsession to use drugs.

Ask yourself this question: Do I believe it would be insane to walk up to someone and say, "May I please have a heart attack or a fatal accident?" If you can agree that this would be an insane thing, you should have no problem with the Second Step.

The first thing we do in this Program is stop using. At this point we begin to feel the pain of living without drugs or anything to replace them. This pain forces us to seek a Power greater than ourselves that can relieve our obsession to use.

The process of coming to believe is something that we seem to experience in similar ways. One thing most of us lacked was a working relationship with a Higher Power. We begin to develop this relationship by simply admitting to the possibility of a Power greater than ourselves. Most of us have no trouble admitting that addiction had become a destructive force in our lives. Our best efforts resulted in ever greater destruction and despair. At some point we realized we needed the help of some Power greater than our addiction. Our understanding of a Higher Power is up to us. No one is going to decide for us. We can call it the group, the program, or we can call it God. The only suggested guidelines are that this Power be loving, caring and greater than ourselves. We don't have to be religious to accept this idea. The point is that we open our minds to believe. We may have difficulty with this, but by keeping an open mind, sooner or later, we find the help we need.

We talked and listened to others. We saw other people recovering, and they told us what was working for them. We began to see evidence of some Power that could not be fully explained. Confronted with this evidence, we began to accept the existence of a Power greater than ourselves. We can use this Power before we begin to understand it.

As we see "coincidences" and miracles happening in our lives, our acceptance becomes trust. We grow to feel comfortable with our Higher Power as a source of strength. As we learn to trust this Power, we begin to overcome our fears of life.

The process of coming to believe is a restoration to sanity. The strength to move into action comes from this belief. We need to accept this step to start us on the road to recovery. When our belief has grown, we are ready for Step Three.

STEP THREE

"We made a decision to turn our will and our lives over to the care of God as we understood Him."

As addicts, we have turned our will and our lives over many times to a destructive power. Our will and our lives were controlled by drugs. We were trapped by our need for the instant gratification that drugs gave us. During that time, our total being — body, mind and spirit — was dominated by drugs. For a time it was pleasurable, then the euphoria began to wear off, and we saw the ugly side of addiction. We found that the higher our drugs took us, the lower they brought us. We faced two choices: either we suffered the pain of withdrawal or took more drugs.

For all addicts, the day comes when there is no longer a choice; we had to use. Having given our will and lives to our addiction, in utter desperation we looked for another way. In Narcotics Anonymous, we decide to turn our will and our lives over to the care of God as we understand Him. This is a giant step. We don't have to be religious; anyone can take it. All that is required is willingness. All that is essential is that we open the door to a Power greater than ourselves.

Our concept of God comes not from dogma but from what we believe ourselves, what works for us. Many of us understand God to be simply whatever keeps us clean. The right to a God of your understanding is total and without any catches. Because we have this right, it is necessary to be honest about our belief if we are to grow spiritually.

We found that all we needed to do was to try. When we gave our best effort to the Program, it worked for us as it has worked for countless others. The Third Step does not say, "We turned our will and our lives over to the care of God." It says, "We made a decision to turn our will and our lives over to the care of God as we understood Him." We made the decision; it was not made for us by the drugs, our families, a probation officer, judge, therapist or doctor. We made it. For the first time since that first high, we have made a decision for ourselves.

The word "decision" implies action. This decision is based on faith. We have only to believe that the miracle we see working in the lives of clean addicts can happen to any addict with the desire to change. We simply realize there is a force for spiritual growth that can help us become more tolerant, patient, and useful in helping others. Many of us have said, "Take my will and my life. Guide me in my recovery. Show me how to live." The relief of "letting go and letting God" helps us develop a life worth living.

Surrendering to the will of our Higher Power gets easier with daily practice. When we honestly try, it works. Many of us start our day with a simple request for guidance from our Higher Power.

Although we know that "turning it over" works, we may still take our will and life back. We may even get angry because God permits it. At times during our recovery, the decision to ask for God's help is our greatest source of strength and courage. We cannot make this decision often enough. We surrender quietly and let the God of our understanding take care of us.

At first, our heads reeled with the questions: "What will happen when we turn our life over? Will be become 'perfect'?" We may have been more realistic than this. Some of us had to turn to an experienced N.A. member and ask, "What was it like for you?" The answer will vary from member to member. Most of us feel open-mindedness, willingness and surrender are the keys to this step.

We have surrendered our will and our lives to the care of a Power greater than ourselves. If we are thorough and sincere, we will notice a change for the better. Our fears are lessened and faith begins to grow as we learn the true meaning of surrender. We are no longer fighting fear, anger, guilt, self-pity or depression. We realize that what brought us to this Program is still with us today and will continue to guide us if we allow it. We are slowly beginning to lose the paralyzing fear of hopelessness. The proof of this step is in the way we live.

We have come to enjoy clean living and want more of the good things that the N.A. fellowship holds for us. We know now that we cannot pause in our spiritual program; we want all we can get.

We are now ready for our first honest self-appraisal, and we begin with Step Four.

STEP FOUR

"We made a searching and fearless moral inventory of ourselves."

The purpose of a searching and fearless moral inventory is to sort through the confusion and the contradiction of our lives so that we can find out who we really are. We are starting a new way of life and need to be rid of the burdens and traps which have controlled us and prevented our growth.

As we approach this step, most of us are afraid that there is a monster inside us that, if released, will destroy us. This fear can cause us to put off our inventory or may even prevent us from taking this crucial step at all. We have found that fear is lack of faith, and we have found a loving, personal God to whom we can turn. We no longer need to be afraid.

We have been experts at self-deception and rationalization; by writing our inventory, we can overcome these obstacles. A written inventory will unlock parts of our subconscious which remain hidden when we simply think about or talk about who we are. Once it is all down on paper, it is much easier to see, and much harder to deny our true nature. Honest self-assessment is one of the keys to our new way of life.

Let's face it; when we were using, we were not honest with ourselves. We are becoming honest with ourselves when we admit that addiction has defeated us and that we need help. It took a long time to admit that we were beaten. We found that we do not recover physically, mentally or spiritually overnight. Step Four will help us toward our recovery more than we imagine. Most of us find that we were neither as terrible, nor as wonderful, as we supposed. We are surprised to find that we have good points in our inventory. Anyone who has some time in the Program and has worked this step will tell you that the Fourth Step was a turning point in their life.

Some of us make the mistake of approaching the Fourth Step as if it were a confession of how horrible we are — what a bad person we have been. In this new way of life, a binge of emotional sorrow can be dangerous. This is not the purpose of the Fourth Step. We are trying to free ourselves of living in old, useless patterns. We take the Fourth Step to gain the necessary strength and insight which enables us to grow. We may approach the Fourth Step in a number of ways.

It is advisable that before we start, we go over the first three steps with a sponsor.

These steps are the preparation necessary to have the faith and courage to write a fearless inventory. We get comfortable with our understanding of these steps. We allow ourselves the privilege of feeling good about what we are doing. We have been thrashing about for a long time and have gotten nowhere. Now we are going to start this step, not letting it frighten us. We simply put it on paper, to the best of our present ability.

We must be done with the past, not cling to it. We want to look our past in the face, see it for what it really was and release it so we can live today. The past, for most of us, has been a ghost in the closet. We have been afraid to open that closet for fear of what that ghost may do to us. We do not have to do this alone. Our will and our life are now in the hands of our Higher Power.

Writing a thorough and honest inventory seemed impossible. It was, as long as we were operating under our own power. We take a few quiet moments before writing and ask for the strength to be fearless and thorough.

In Step Four, we begin to get in touch with ourselves. We write about our liabilities such as guilt, shame, remorse, self-pity, resentment, anger, depression, frustration, confusion, loneliness, anxiety, betrayal, hopelessness, failure, fear and denial.

We write on paper what is bothering us here and now. We have a tendency to think negatively, so putting it on paper gives us a chance to look more positively at what is happening.

Assets must also be considered if we are to get an accurate and complete picture of ourselves. This is very difficult for most of us because it is hard for us to accept that we have good qualities. However, we all have assets, many of them newly found in the Program, such as being clean, open-mindedness, God-awareness, honesty with others, acceptance, positive action, sharing, willingness, courage, faith, caring, gratitude, kindness and generosity. Also, our inventories usually include a lot of material on relationships.

We review our past performance and our present behavior to see what we want to keep and what we want to be rid of. No one is forcing us to give up our misery. This step has the reputation of being difficult; in reality, it is quite simple.

We write our inventory for ourselves without considering with whom we might share it. We work Step Four as if there were no Step Five. We can write alone or near other people; whatever is more comfortable to the writer is fine. We can write as long or as short as needed. Someone with experience can help with this. The important thing is to write a moral inventory. If the word "moral" bothers us, we may call it a positive/negative inventory.

The way to write an inventory is to write it! Thinking about an inventory, talking about it, theorizing about the inventory will not get it written. We sit down with a notebook, ask for guidance, pick up our pen and start writing. Anything we think about is inventory material. When we realize how little we have to lose, and how much we have to gain, we begin this step.

A basic rule of thumb is that we can write too little, yet we can never write too much. The inventory will fit the individual. Perhaps this seems difficult or painful. It may appear impossible. We may fear that being in touch with our feelings will trigger an overwhelming chain reaction of pain and panic. We may feel like avoiding an inventory because of a fear of failure. When we ignore our feelings, the tension becomes too much for us. The fear of impending doom is so great it overrides our fear of failure.

An inventory becomes a relief to do because the pain of doing it is less than the pain of not doing it. We learn that pain can be a motivating factor in recovery. Thus, facing it becomes unavoidable. Every topic of step meetings we attend seems to be on the Fourth Step or doing a daily inventory. Through the inventory process, we are able to deal with all the things that can build up. The more we live our Program, the more God seems to position us to have things surface, so we can write about them. We begin enjoying our recovery because we have a way to resolve the shame, guilt, or resentment.

We are also able to be rid of the stress trapped inside. Writing will lift the lid from our pressure cooker to see whether we want to serve it up, put the lid back on it, or throw it out. We no longer have to stew in it.

We sit down with paper and pen and ask for our God's help in revealing the defects that are causing pain and suffering. We pray for the courage to be fearless and thorough so that this inventory may help us to put our lives in order. When we pray and take action, it always goes better for us.

We are not going to be perfect. If we were perfect, we would not be

27

human. The important thing is that we do our best. We use the tools available to us, and we develop the ability to survive our emotions. We do not want to lose any of what we have gained; we want to continue in the Program. It is our experience that no matter how searching and thorough, no inventory is of any lasting effect unless it is promptly followed by an equally thorough Fifth Step.

STEP FIVE

"We admitted to God, to ourselves, and to another human being the exact nature of our wrongs."

The Fifth Step is the key to freedom. It allows us to live clean in the here and now. Sharing the exact nature of our wrongs sets us free to live. After taking a thorough Fourth Step, we have to deal with what we have found in our inventory. We are told that if we keep these defects inside us, they will lead us back to using. Holding on to our past would eventually sicken us and keep us from taking part in this new way of life. If we are not honest when we take a Fifth Step, we will have the same negative results that dishonesty brought us in the past.

Step Five suggests that we admit to God, to ourselves, and to another human being the exact nature of our wrongs. We have looked at our wrongs, have seen patterns on paper, and have begun to see deeper aspects of our disease. Now we sit down with another person and share our inventory out loud.

Our Higher Power will be with us when we do this, and will help to free us from the fear of facing ourselves and another human being. It seemed unnecessary to some of us to admit the exact nature of our wrongs to our Higher Power. "God already knows that stuff," we rationalized. Although He already knows, the admission must come from our own lips to be truly effective. Step Five is not simply a reading of Step Four.

For years, we avoided seeing ourselves as we really were. We were ashamed of ourselves and felt isolated from the rest of the world. Now that we have the shameful part of our past trapped, we can sweep it out of our lives if we face and admit it. It would be tragic to have it all written down and then shove it in a drawer. These defects grow in the dark, and die in the light of exposure.

Before coming to Narcotics Anonymous, we felt that no one could ever relate to us or understand the things we had done. We feared that if we ever revealed ourselves as we were, we would surely be rejected. Most addicts are uncomfortable about this. We recognize that we have been unrealistic in feeling this way. Our fellow members do understand us.

We must carefully choose the person who is to hear our Fifth Step. We must make sure they know what we are doing and why we are doing it. Although there is no hard rule about whom we should choose, it is important that we trust the person. Only complete confidence in the person's integrity and discretion can make us willing to be thorough in this step. Some of us take our Fifth Step with a total stranger, although some of us feel more comfortable choosing a member of Narcotics Anonymous. We know that another addict would be less likely to judge us with malice or misunderstanding.

Once we make up our minds and are actually alone with the person we have chosen to accept our confidence, we proceed, with their encouragement. We want to be definite, honest and thorough, realizing that this is a life and death matter.

Some of us have attempted to hide part of our past, and in doing so, have tried desperately to find easier ways of dealing with our inner feelings. We may think that we have done enough by writing everything down, and this is a mistake we cannot afford. This step will expose our motives and our actions for what they really are. We cannot expect these things to reveal themselves.

Our embarrassment is eventually overcome and we can avoid future guilt.

We do not procrastinate. We must be exact. We want to tell the simple truth, cut and dried, as quickly as possible. There is always a danger that we will exaggerate our wrongs, and an equal danger that we will minimize or rationalize away our part in past situations. If we are anything like we were when we first entered the N.A. fellowship, we still want to "sound good."

Addicts tend to live secret lives. For many years, we covered low self-esteem by hiding behind phony images that we hoped would fool people. Unfortunately, we ended up fooling ourselves more than anyone. Although we often appeared attractive and confident on the outside, we were really hiding a shaky, insecure person on the inside. The masks have to go. We share our inventory as it is written, skipping nothing. We continue to approach this step with honesty and thoroughness until we finish. It is a great relief to get rid of all our secrets and to share the burden of our past.

Usually, as we share this step, the listener will share some of his or her story too, and we will find out that the things about ourselves that we thought were so awful or different were not all that unique. We see, by the acceptance of our confidant, that we can be accepted just the way we are.

We may never be able to remember all of our past mistakes. We do, however, give it our best and most complete effort. We begin to experience real personal feelings of a spiritual nature. Where once we had spiritual theories, we now begin to awaken to spiritual reality. This initial examination of ourselves usually reveals some things about us that we don't particularly like. However, facing these things and bringing them out in the open makes it possible for us to deal with them constructively. We cannot make these changes alone. We will need the help of God, as we understand Him, and the fellowship of Narcotics Anonymous.

STEP SIX

"We were entirely ready to have God remove all these defects of character."

Why ask for something that we are not ready for? This would be asking for trouble. So many times we addicts have sought the rewards of hard work without the labor. Willingness is what we strive for in Step Six. How sincerely we work this step will be proportionate to our desire for change.

Do we really want to be rid of our resentments, our anger, our fear?

30

Many of us cling to our fears, doubts, and self-loathing or hatred of others because there is a certain distorted security in familiar pain. It seems safer to hold on to what we know than to let go of it for the unknown.

Letting go of character defects should be done decisively. We suffer because their demands weaken us. Where we were proud, we now find that we cannot get away with arrogance. Those of us who are not humble are humiliated. If we are greedy, we find that we are never satisfied. Where before we could get away with fear, anger, dishonesty or self-pity, we now see where they cloud our ability to think logically. Selfishness becomes an intolerable, destructive chain that ties us to our bad habits. Our defects drain us of all our time and energy.

We examine the Fourth Step inventory and get a good look at what these defects are doing to our lives. We begin to long for freedom from these defects. We pray or otherwise become willing, ready and able to let God remove these destructive traits. We need a personality change if we are to stay clean. We want to change.

We should approach old defects with an open mind. We are aware of them and yet we still make the same mistakes and are unable to break the bad habits. We look to the fellowship for the kind of life we want for ourselves. We ask our friends, "Did you let go?" Almost without exception the answer is, "Yes, to the best of our ability." When we see how our defects exist in our lives and accept them, we can let go of them and get on with our new life. We learn that we are growing when we make new mistakes instead of repeating old ones.

When we are working Step Six, it is important to remember that we are human and should not place unrealistic expectations on ourselves. This is a step of willingness. That is the spiritual principle of Step Six. It is as if to say that we are now willing to move in a spiritual direction. Being human we will, of course, wander.

Rebellion is a character defect that spoils us here. We need not lose faith when we become rebellious. The indifference or intolerance that rebellion can bring out in us has to be overcome by persistent effort. We keep asking for willingness. We may be doubtful still that God will see fit

31

to relieve us or that something will go wrong. We ask another member who says, "You're right where you're supposed to be." We renew our readiness to have our defects removed. We surrender to the simple suggestions that the Program offers us. Even though we are not entirely ready, we are headed in that direction.

Eventually faith, humility and acceptance replace pride and rebellion. We come to know ourselves. We find ourselves growing into a mature consciousness. We begin to feel better as willingness grows into hope for relief. Perhaps for the first time, we see a vision of our new life. With this in sight, we put our willingness into action by moving on to Step Seven.

STEP SEVEN

"We humbly asked Him to remove our shortcomings."

Having decided we want God, as we understand Him, to relieve us of the useless or destructive aspects of our personalities, we have arrived at the Seventh Step. We couldn't handle the ordeal of life all by ourselves. It wasn't until we made a real mess of our lives that we realized we couldn't do it alone. By admitting this, we achieved a glimpse of humility. This is the main ingredient of Step Seven. Humility has a lot to do with getting honest with ourselves, which is something we have practiced from Step One. We accepted our addiction and powerlessness. We found a strength beyond ourselves and learned to rely on it. We examined our lives and discovered who we really are. To be truly humble is to accept and honestly try to be who we are. None of us are perfectly good or perfectly bad. We are people who have assets and liabilities and most important of all, we are human.

Humility is as much a part of staying clean as food and water are to staying alive. As our addiction progressed, we devoted our energy toward satisfying our material desires. All other needs were beyond our reach. We always wanted gratification of our basic desires.

Character defects are those things which cause pain and misery all of our lives. If they really contributed to our health and happiness, we would not have come to such a state of desperation. We had to become ready to have God remove these defects.

The Seventh Step is an action step, and it is time to ask God for help and relief. We have to understand that our way of thinking is not the only way; other people can give us direction. When someone points out a shortcoming, our first reaction may be one of defensiveness. We must realize that we are not perfect. There will always be room for growth. If we truly want to be free, we will take a good look at what is pointed out to us. If the shortcomings we discover are real and we have a chance to be rid of them, we will surely experience a sense of well-being.

Some will want to get on their knees for this step. Some will be very quiet, and others will put forth a great emotional effort to show intense willingness. The word humble applies because we approach this Power greater than ourselves to ask for the freedom to live without the limitations of our past ways. Many of us are willing to do it without reservations, on pure blind faith, because we are sick of what we have been doing and how we are feeling. Whatever works, we go all the way.

This is our road to spiritual growth. We change every day to gradually, carefully and simply pull ourselves out of the isolation and loneliness of addiction into the mainstream of life. This comes not from wishing, but from action and prayer. The main objective of Step Seven is to get out of ourselves and strive for achieving the will of our Higher Power.

If we are careless and fail to grasp the spiritual meaning of this step, we may have difficulties and stir up old troubles. One danger is in being too hard on ourselves.

Sharing with other addicts in recovery helps us to not become morbidly serious about ourselves. Accepting the defects of others can help us become humble enough to be relieved of our own defects. God often works through those who care enough about our recovery to help make us aware of our shortcomings.

We have noticed that humility plays a big part in this Program and our new way of life. We take our inventory; we become ready to let God remove our defects of character; we humbly ask Him to remove our shortcomings. This is our road to spiritual growth and we will want to continue. We are ready for Step Eight.

STEP EIGHT

"We made a list of all persons we had harmed and became willing to make amends to them all."

This step is the test of our new-found humility. Our purpose is to achieve freedom from the guilt we have carried so far, so that we can look the world in the eye with neither aggressiveness nor fear.

Are we willing to make a list to clear away the fear and guilt that our past holds for us? Our experience tells us that we must become willing before this step will have any effect.

The Eighth Step is not easy; it demands a new kind of honesty about our relations with other people. The Eighth Step starts the procedure of forgiving others and possibly being forgiven by them, forgiving ourselves, and learning how to live in the world. By the time we reach this step, we have become ready to understand rather than to be understood. We can live and let live easier when we know the areas in which we owe amends. It seems hard now, but once we have done it, we will wonder why we did not do it long ago.

We need some real honesty before we can make an accurate list. In preparing to make the Eighth Step list, it is helpful to define harm. One definition of harm is physical or mental damage. Another definition of harm is inflicting pain, suffering or loss. The damage may be caused by something that is said, done or left undone, and the harm resulting from these words or actions may be either intentional or unintentional. The degree of harm can range from making someone feel mentally uncomfortable to inflicting bodily injury or even death.

A problem many of us have with the Eighth Step and the admission of the harm is the belief that we were victims, not victimizers, in our addiction. Avoiding this rationalization is crucial to the Eighth Step. We must separate what was done to us from what we did. We cut away all our justifications and all our ideas of being a victim. We often feel that we only harmed ourselves, yet we usually list ourselves last, if at all. This step is doing the legwork to repair the wreckage of our lives.

It will not make us better people to judge the faults of another. It will

34

make us feel better to clean up our lives by relieving ourselves of guilt. By writing our list, we can no longer deny that we did harm. We admit that we hurt others, directly or indirectly, through some action, lie, broken promise, neglect or whatever.

We make our list, or take it from our Fourth Step, and add any additional people we can think of. We face this list honestly, and openly examine our faults so that we can become willing to make amends.

We may not know who it was we wronged. Just about anyone we came in contact with risked being harmed. Many members mention their parents, spouses, children, friends, lovers, other addicts, casual acquaintances, co-workers, employers, teachers, landlords or total strangers. We may find it beneficial to make a separate list of people to whom we owe financial amends. We may also place ourselves on the list because while practicing our addiction, we have slowly been killing ourselves.

As with each step, we must be thorough. Most of us fall short of our goals more often than we exceed them. At the same time, we cannot put off completion of this step just because we are not sure we are done. We are never done.

The final difficulty in working the Eighth Step is separating it from the Ninth Step. Projecting about actually making amends can be a major obstacle both in making the list and in becoming willing. We do this step as if there were no Ninth Step. We do not even think about making the amends but just concentrate on exactly what the Eighth Step says which is to make a list and to become willing. The main thing this step does for us is to help build an awareness that, little by little, we are gaining new attitudes about ourselves and how we deal with other people.

Listening carefully to other members share their experience with this step can clean up any confusion we may have about our list and the benefits of it. Also, our sponsors may share with us how it worked for them. Asking questions during a meeting can give us the benefit of Group Conscience.

The Eighth Step is a big change from a life dominated by guilt and remorse. Our futures are changed because we don't have to avoid those we have harmed, and as a result of this step, we've received a new freedom which contributes to the end of isolation. As we realize our need to be forgiven, we tend to be more forgiving. At least, we know we are no longer intentionally making life miserable for people in our recovery. The Eighth Step is an action step. Like all the steps, it offers immediate benefits. We are now free to begin our amends in Step Nine.

STEP NINE

"We made direct amends to such people wherever possible, except when to do so would injure them or others."

This step should not be avoided. If we do, we are reserving a place in our Program for relapse. Pride, fear and procrastination often seem an impossible barrier; they stand in the way of progress and growth. The important thing is to take action and be ready to accept the reactions of those persons we have harmed. We make amends to the best of our ability.

Timing is an essential part of this step. We should make amends when the first opportunity presents itself, except when to do so will cause more harm. Sometimes we cannot actually make the amends; it is neither possible nor practical. In some cases, amends may be beyond our means. We have found that willingness can serve in the place of action where we are unable to contact the person we have harmed. However, we should never fail to contact anyone because of embarrassment, fear or procrastination.

We want to be free of our guilt, but we don't wish to do so at the expense of anyone else. We might run the risk of involving a third person or some companion from our using days who does not wish to be exposed. We do not have the right or the need to endanger another person. It is often necessary to take guidance from others in these matters.

We recommend turning our legal problems over to lawyers and our financial or medical problems to professionals. Part of learning how to live is not to take on problems and responsibilities that we are not equipped to deal with.

In some old relationships, an unresolved conflict may still exist. We do our part to resolve old conflicts by making our amends. We want to step

36

away from further antagonisms and ongoing resentments. In many instances we can only go to the person and humbly ask for understanding of past wrongs. Sometimes this will be a joyous occasion when some old friend or relative proves very willing to let go of their bitterness. To go to someone who is hurting from the burn of our misdeeds can be dangerous. Indirect amends may be necessary where direct ones would be unsafe or endanger other people. We can only make our amends to the best of our ability. We try to remember that when we make amends, we are doing it for ourselves. Instead of feeling guilty and remorseful, we feel relieved about our past.

We accept that it was our actions that caused our negative attitude. Step Nine helps us with our guilt and others with their anger. Sometimes, the only amend we can make is to stay clean ourselves. We owe it to ourselves and loved ones. We are no longer making a mess in society as a result of our using. The only way we can make amends to some of the people we have harmed is to contribute to society. Now, we are helping ourselves and other addicts achieve cleanliness. This is a tremendous amend to the whole community.

In the process of our recovery we were restored to sanity and part of sanity is effectively relating to others. We less often view people as a threat to our security. Real security will replace the physical ache and mental confusion we have experienced in the past. We approach those we have harmed with humility and patience. Many of our sincere well-wishers would be reluctant to accept our recovery as real. We must remember the pain they have known. In time many miracles will occur. Many of us that were separated from our families succeed in establishing relationships with them. Eventually it becomes easier for them to accept the change in us. Clean time speaks for itself. Patience is an important part of our recovery. The unconditional love we experience will rejuvenate our will to live, and each positive move on our part will be matched by an unexpected opportunity. A lot of courage and faith goes into making an amend, and a lot of spiritual growth results.

We are achieving freedom from the wreckage of our past. We will want to keep our "house in order" by practicing a continuous personal inventory in Step Ten.

STEP TEN

"We continued to take personal inventory, and when we were wrong promptly admitted it."

The Tenth Step frees us from the wreckage of our present. If we do not stay aware of our defects, they can drive us into a corner that we can't get out of clean.

One of the first things we learn in Narcotics Anonymous is that if we use, we lose. By the same token, we won't experience as much pain if we can avoid the things that cause us pain. Continuing to take a personal inventory means that we form a habit of looking at ourselves, our actions, our attitudes and our relationships on a regular basis.

We are creatures of habit and are vulnerable to our old ways of thinking and reacting. At times it seems easier to continue in the old rut of self-destruction rather than to attempt a new and seemingly dangerous route. We don't have to be trapped by our old patterns. Today we have a choice.

The Tenth Step can do this for us; it can help us correct our living problems and prevent their recurrence. We examine our actions during the day. Some of us write about our feelings, explaining how we felt and what part we might have played in any problems which occurred. Did we cause someone harm? Do we need to admit that we were wrong? If we find difficulties, we make an effort to take care of them. When these things are left undone, they have a way of festering.

This step can be a defense against the old insanity. We can ask ourselves if we are being drawn into old patterns of anger, resentment or fear. Do we feel trapped? Are we "setting ourselves up" for trouble? Are we too hungry, angry, lonely or tired? Are we taking ourselves too seriously? Are we judging our insides by the outside appearances of others? Do we suffer from some physical problem? The answers to questions like these can help us to deal with the difficulties of the moment. We no longer have to live with the feeling of a "hole in the gut." A lot of our chief concerns and major difficulties come from our inexperience with living without drugs. Often when we ask an "oldtimer" what to do, we are amazed at the simplicity of the answer.

The Tenth Step can be a pressure relief valve. We work this step while the day's ups and downs are still fresh in our minds. We list what we have done and try not to rationalize our actions. This may be done in writing at the end of the day. The first thing we do is stop! Then we take the time to allow ourselves the privilege of thinking. We examine our actions, our reactions, and our motives. We often find that we've been "doing" better than we've been "feeling." This allows us to find out where we have gone wrong and admit fault before things get any worse. We need to avoid rationalizing. We promptly admit our faults, not explain them.

We work this step continuously. This is a prevention, and the more we do it, the less we will need the corrective part of this step. This is really a great tool. It gives us a way of avoiding grief before we bring it on ourselves. We monitor our feelings, our emotions, our fantasies, and our actions. By constantly looking at these things we may be able to avoid repeating the actions that make us feel bad.

We need this step even when we're feeling good and things are going well. Good feelings are new to us and we need to nurture them. In times of trouble we can try the things that worked before. We have the right not to feel miserable. We have a choice. The good times can also be a trap; the danger is that we may forget that our first priority is staying clean. For us, recovery is more than just pleasure.

We need to keep in mind that everyone makes mistakes. We will never be perfect. However, we can accept this fact by using Step Ten. By continuing a personal inventory we are set free, in the here and now, from ourselves and the past. We no longer are forced to justify our existence. This step allows us to be ourselves.

STEP ELEVEN

"We sought through prayer and meditation to improve our conscious contact with God, as we understood Him, praying only for knowledge of His will for us and the power to carry that out."

The first ten steps have set the stage for us to improve our conscious contact with the God of our understanding. They give us the foundation to achieve our long-sought positive goals. Having entered into this phase of our spiritual program through practicing our previous ten steps, most of us find that we can welcome the exercise of prayer and meditation. We have found that our spiritual condition is the basis for a successful recovery that offers unlimited growth.

Many of us really begin to appreciate the fact that we have been clean for awhile when we get to the Eleventh Step. In the Eleventh Step, the life we've been practicing begins to take on a deeper meaning. By the surrender of our control, we gain a far greater power.

The nature of our belief will determine the manner of our prayers and meditations. We need only to make sure we have a system of belief which works to provide for our needs. Results count in recovery. As has been noted elsewhere, our prayers seemed to work as soon as we entered the Program of Narcotics Anonymous and surrendered to our disease. The conscious contact described in this step is the direct result of living these steps. We use this step to improve and maintain our spiritual condition.

When we first came into the Program, we received help from some Power greater than ourselves. This was set in motion by our surrendering to the Program. The purpose of the Eleventh Step is to increase our awareness of that Power and to improve our ability to use it as a source of strength in our new lives.

The more we improve our conscious contact with our God through prayer and meditation, the easier it is to say, "Your will, not mine, be done." We can ask for God's help when we need it and our lives get better. The experiences some people talk about in regard to meditation no more apply to us than do their individual religious beliefs. Ours is a spiritual, not religious, program. By the time we get to the Eleventh Step, the factors that could cause problems have usually been dealt with by the actions we have taken in the preceding steps. Our deepest longings and images of the kind of people we would like to be are but fleeting glimpses of God's will for us. Often our outlooks are so limited we can only see our immediate wants and needs.

It is easy to slip back into our old ways. We have to learn to maintain our new lives on a spiritually sound basis to insure our continued growth and recovery. God will not force His goodness on us, but we will receive it if we ask. We usually feel the difference at the time and see the change in our lives later. When we finally get our own selfish motives out of the way, we begin to find a peace we never imagined. Enforced morality lacks the power that comes to us when we choose to live a spiritually-oriented life. Most of us pray when we are hurting. We learn that if we pray regularly we won't be hurting as often, or as intensely.

Outside of Narcotics Anonymous, there are any number of different groups practicing meditation, but nearly all of them are connected with a particular religion or philosophy. An endorsement of any one of these methods would be a violation of our Traditions and a restriction on individuals' freedom to have a God of their own understanding. Meditation allows us to develop spiritually in our own way. Some of the things that didn't work for us before might work today. We take a fresh look each day with an open mind. We now know that if we pray to do God's will, we will receive what is really best for us, regardless of what we think. This knowledge is based on our belief and experience as recovering addicts.

Prayer is communicating our concerns to a Power greater than ourselves. Sometimes when we pray, a remarkable thing happens; we find the means, the ways and the energies to perform tasks far beyond our capacities. We grasp the limitless strength provided for us through our daily prayer and surrender so long as we keep faith and renew it.

For some, prayer is asking for God's help, and meditation is listening for God's answer. We learn to be careful of praying for specific things. We pray that God will show us His will and that He will help us carry that out. In some cases He makes His will so obvious to us that we have little difficulty seeing it. In others, our egos are so self-centered that we won't accept God's will for us without another struggle and surrender. If we pray for God to remove any distracting influences, the quality of our prayers usually improves and we feel the difference. Prayer takes practice and it may be well to remind ourselves that skilled people were not born with their skills. It took lots of effort on their part to develop them. Through prayer we seek conscious contact with our God. In meditation we achieve this contact and the Eleventh Step helps us to maintain it.

We may have been exposed to and practiced many religious and meditative disciplines before coming to Narcotics Anonymous. Some of us were devastated and completely confused by these practices, and we were sure that it was God's will for us to use drugs to reach "higher consciousness." Many of us find ourselves in very strange states as a result of these practices. We never suspected the damaging effects of our addiction as the root of the difficulty and pursued to the end whatever path offered hope.

In quiet moments of meditation, God's will can become evident to us. Quieting the mind through meditation brings an inner peace which brings us into contact with the God within. A basic premise of meditation is that it is difficult, if not impossible, to obtain conscious contact unless our mind is still. The usual, never-ending succession of thoughts has to cease for progress to be made. So our preliminary practice is aimed at stilling the mind, and letting the thoughts that arise die a natural death. We leave our thoughts behind, as the meditation part of the Eleventh Step becomes a reality for us.

Emotional balance is one of the first results of meditation, and our experience bears this out.

Some of us have come into the Program broken, and hung around for awhile, only to find God or salvation in one kind of religious cult or another. It is easy to float back out the door on a cloud of religious zeal and forget we are addicts with an incurable disease.

It is said that for meditation to be of value, the results must show in our daily lives, and this is implicit in the Eleventh Step: ". . . His will for us and the power to carry it out." For those of us who do not pray, meditation is our only way of working this step.

We find ourselves praying because it brings us peace and restores our confidence and courage. It helps us to live a life free of fear and distrust. When we remove our own selfish motives and pray for guidance, we find feelings of peace and serenity that we never knew before. We begin to experience an awareness and an empathy with other people that was not possible before.

As we seek our personal contact with God, we begin to open up like a flower in the sun. We begin to see that God's love has been here all the time, just waiting for us to accept it. We can put in the footwork and accept what's being freely given to us on a daily basis. We find relying on God becomes more comfortable for us.

When we first come to the Program, we usually express a lot of things which seem to be important wants and needs. As we grow spiritually and find out about a Power greater than ourselves, we begin to realize that as long as our spiritual needs are truly met, our living problems are reduced to a point of comfort. When we forget where our real strength lies, we quickly become subject to the same patterns of thinking and action that got us to the Program in the first place. We eventually redefine our beliefs and understanding to the point where we see that our greatest need is for knowledge of God's will for us and the strength to carry that out. We are able to set aside some of our personal preference, if necessary, to do this because we learn that God's will consists of the very things we care most about. God's will for us becomes our own true will for ourselves. This happens in an intuitive manner which cannot be adequately explained in words.

We become willing to let other people be what they are without having to pass judgment on them. The urgency to take care of things isn't there anymore. We couldn't comprehend acceptance in the beginning—now we can.

We know that whatever the day brings, God has given us everything we need for our spiritual well-being. It is all right for us to admit powerlessness because God is powerful enough to help us stay clean and enjoy spiritual progress. God is helping us get our house in order.

We begin to see more and more clearly what is happening, and through constant contact with our Higher Power, the answers we are looking for come to us and we gain the ability to do what we once could not. We respect the beliefs of others. We encourage you to seek strength and guidance according to your belief.

We are thankful for this step because we begin to get what is best for us. The way we have sometimes prayed for our wants often got us into the trap of having to live with them once we got them. We could pray and get something, then have to pray for its removal because we couldn't handle it.

Hopefully, having learned the power of prayer and the responsibility prayer brings with it, we can use the Eleventh Step as a guideline for our daily Program.

We begin to pray only for God's will for us. This way we are getting only what we are capable of handling. We are able to respond to it and handle it because God helps us prepare for it. Some of us simply use our words to give thanks for God's grace.

In an attitude of surrender and humility, we approach this step again and again to receive the gift of knowledge and strength from the God of our understanding. The Tenth Step clears the errors of the present so we may work this step. Without this step, it is unlikely that we could ever experience a spiritual awakening, be able to practice spiritual principles in our lives, or carry a sufficient message to attract others to recovery. There is a spiritual principle of giving away what we have been given in Narcotics Anonymous in order to keep it. By helping others to stay clean, we enjoy the benefit of the spiritual wealth we have found. We must give freely and gratefully that which has been freely and gratefully given to us.

STEP TWELVE

"Having had a spiritual awakening as a result of those steps, we tried to carry this message to addicts and to practice these principles in all our affairs."

We came to Narcotics Anonymous as the end result of the wreckage of our past. The last thing we expected was an awakening of the spirit. We just wanted to stop hurting.

The steps lead to an awakening of a spiritual nature. This awakening within is evidenced by change in our lives. This change makes us better able to live by spiritual principles and to carry our message of recovery and hope to the addict who still suffers. The message, however, is meaningless unless we live it. As we live it, our lives and actions give it more meaning than our words and literature ever could.

The idea of a spiritual awakening takes many different forms in the different personalities we find in the fellowship. However, all spiritual awakenings have some things in common. Among them are an end to loneliness and a sense of direction in our lives. Many of us believe a spiritual awakening is meaningless unless accompanied by an increase in peace of mind and concern for others. In order to maintain peace of mind, we strive to live in the here and now.

Those of us who have made the effort to work these steps to the best of our ability received many benefits. We believe that these benefits are a direct result of living this Program.

When we first begin to enjoy relief from our addiction, we run the risk of assuming control of our lives again. We forget the agony and pain we have known. Our disease controlled all our lives when we were using. It is ready and waiting to take over again. We quickly forget that all our past efforts at controlling our lives failed.

By this time most of us have come to realize that the only way we can keep what was given to us is by sharing this new gift of life with the still-suffering addict. This is our best insurance against relapse to the torturous existence of using. We call it carrying the message and we do it in a number of ways.

In the Twelfth Step, we practice the spiritual principles of giving the N.A. message of recovery in order to keep it. Even a member with one day in the N.A. fellowship can carry the message that this Program works.

When we share with someone new, we may ask to be used as a spiritual instrument of our Higher Power. We don't set ourselves up as gods. We often ask for the help of another recovering addict when sharing with a new person. It is a privilege to respond to a cry for help. We who have been in the pits of despair feel fortunate to help others find recovery.

We help new people learn the principles of Narcotics Anonymous. We try to make them feel welcome and help them learn what the Program has to offer. We share our experience, strength and hope and when possible accompany them to a meeting.

The selfless service of this work is the very principle of Step Twelve.

We received our recovery from the God of our understanding, so we now make ourselves available as His tool to share recovery with those who seek it. Most of us learn in time that we can only carry our message to someone who is asking for help. Sometimes the only message necessary to make the suffering addict reach out is the power of example. An addict may be suffering but unwilling to ask for help. We can make ourselves available to these people, so that when they ask, someone will be there.

Learning the art of helping others when it is appropriate is a benefit of the N.A. Program. Remarkably, the Twelve Steps guide us from humiliation and despair to a state wherein we may act as instruments of our Higher Power. We are given the ability to help a fellow addict when no one else can. We see it happening among us every day. This miraculous turnabout is evidence of spiritual awakening. We share from our own personal experience what it has been like for us. The temptation to give advice is great, but when we do so we lose the respect of newcomers. This clouds our message. A simple, honest message of recovery from addiction rings true.

We attend meetings and make ourselves visible and available to serve the fellowship. We give freely and gratefully of our time, service, and what we have found here. The service we speak of in Narcotics Anonymous is the primary purpose of our groups. Service work is carrying the message to the addict who still suffers. The more eagerly we wade in and work, the richer our spiritual awakening will be.

The first way in which we carry the message speaks for itself. People see us on the street and remember us as devious, frightened loners. They notice the fear leaving our faces. They see us gradually come alive.

Once we find the N.A. way, boredom and complacency have no place in our new life. By staying clean we begin to practice such spiritual principles as hope, surrender, acceptance, honesty, open-mindedness, willingness, faith, tolerance, patience, humility, unconditional love, sharing and caring. As our recovery progresses, they touch every area of our lives because we simply try to live this Program in the here and now.

We find an indescribable joy as we start to learn how to live by the principles of recovery. It is the joy of watching a person two days clean say to a person with one day clean, "An addict alone is in bad company." It is the joy of watching a person who was really struggling to make it, suddenly, in the middle of helping another addict to stay clean, become able to find the words they need to say coming from within.

We feel our lives have become worthwhile. Spiritually refreshed, we are glad to be alive. When using, our lives became an exercise in survival. Now we are doing much more living than surviving. Realizing the bottom line is staying clean, we can enjoy it. We like being clean and enjoy helping to carry the message of recovery to the addict who still suffers. Going to meetings really works.

Practicing spiritual principles in our daily lives leads us to a new image of ourselves. Honesty, humility and open-mindedness help us to treat our associates fairly. Our decisions become tempered with tolerance. We learn to respect ourselves.

The lessons we learn in our recovery are sometimes bitter and painful. By helping others we find the reward of self-respect as we are able to share these lessons with other members of Narcotics Anonymous. We cannot deny other addicts their pain, but we can carry the message of hope that was given to us by our fellow addicts in recovery. We share the principles of recovery as they have worked in our lives. God helps us as we help each other. Life takes on a new meaning, a new joy, and a quality of being and feeling worthwhile. We become spiritually refreshed and are glad to be alive. One aspect of our spiritual awakening comes through the new understanding of our Higher Power that we develop by sharing another addict's recovery.

Yes, we are a vision of hope. We are examples of the Program working. The joy we have in living clean is an attraction to the addict who still suffers.

We do recover to live clean and happy lives. Welcome to N.A. The steps do not end here; they are a new beginning.

Chapter Five

WHAT CAN I DO?

Begin your own program by taking Step One from the previous chapter "How It Works." When we fully concede to our innermost selves that we are powerless over our addiction, we have taken a big step in our recovery. Many of us have had some reservations at this point, so give yourself a break and be as thorough as possible from the start. Go on to Step Two, and so forth, and as you go on you will come to an understanding of the program for yourself. If you are in an institution of any kind, you have gone through complete withdrawal and have stopped using for the present. Now, with a clear mind, try this way of life.

Upon release, continue your daily program and contact a member of N.A. Do this by mail, by phone, or in person. Better yet, come to our meetings. Here you will find answers to some of the things that may be disturbing you now.

If you are not in an institution, the same holds true. Stop using for today. Most of us can do for eight or twelve hours what seems impossible for a longer period of time. If the obsession or compulsion becomes too great, put yourself on a five minute basis of not using. Minutes will grow to hours and hours to days, so you will break the habit and gain some peace of mind. The real miracle happens when you realize that the need for drugs has in some way been lifted from you. You have stopped using and started to live.

The first step to recovery is to stop using. We cannot expect the Program to work for us if our minds and bodies are still clouded by drugs. We can do this anywhere, even in prison or an institution. We do it anyway we can, cold turkey or in a detox, just as long as we get clean.

Developing the concept of God as we understand Him is a project we can undertake. We can also use the steps to improve our attitudes. Our best thinking is what got us into trouble. We recognize the need for change. Our disease involves much more than using, and so our recovery must involve much more than simple abstinence. Recovery is an active change of our ideas and attitudes.

The ability to face problems is necessary to stay clean. If we had problems in the past it is unlikely that simple abstinence will provide the solution to them. Guilt and worry can keep us from living in the here and now. The denial of our disease and other reservations keep us sick. Many of us feel that we cannot possibly have a happy life without drugs. We suffer from fear and insanity and feel that there is no escape from using. We may fear rejection from our friends if we get clean. These feelings are common to the addict seeking recovery. We could be suffering from an overly sensitive ego. Some of the most common excuses for using are loneliness, self-pity and fear. Dishonesty, close-mindedness and unwillingness are three of our greatest enemies. Self-obsession is the core of our disease.

We have learned that old ideas and old ways won't help us to stay clean or live a better life. If we allow ourselves to stagnate and cling to "terminal hipness" and "fatal cool," we are giving into the symptoms of our disease. One of the problems is that we found it easier to change our perception of reality than to change reality. We must give up this old concept and face the fact that reality and life go on whether we choose to accept them or not. We can only change the way we react and the way we see ourselves. This is necessary for us to accept that change is gradual and recovery is an ongoing process.

A meeting a day at least the first ninety days is a good idea. There is a special feeling that comes over a person with our disease when they discover that there are other people who share their difficulties, past and present. At first we can do little more than go to meetings. Probably we cannot remember a single word, person or thought from our first meeting. In time, we relax and enjoy the atmosphere of recovery. Meetings strengthen our recovery. We may be scared at first because we don't know anyone. Some of us think we don't need meetings. When we hurt though, we go to a meeting for relief. Meetings keep us in touch with where we've been, but more importantly with where we could go in our recovery. As we go to meetings regularly, we learn the value of talking with other addicts who share our problems and goals. We have to open up and accept the love and understanding we need in order to change. When we become acquainted with the fellowship and its principles and begin to put them into action, we start to grow. We apply our efforts to our most obvious problems and let go of the rest. We do the job at hand and as we progress, new opportunities for improvement present themselves.

Our new friends in the fellowship will help us. Our common effort is recovery. Clean, we face the world together. We no longer have to feel backed into a corner and at the mercy of events and circumstances. It makes all the difference to have friends who care if we hurt. We find our place in the fellowship, and we join a group whose meetings help us in our recovery. We have been untrustworthy for so long that most of our friends and families will doubt our recovery because they think it won't last. We need people that understand our disease and the recovery process. At meetings we can share with other addicts, ask questions and learn about our disease. We learn new ways to live. We are no longer limited to our old ideas.

Gradually, we replace old habits with new ways of living. We become willing to change. We go to meetings regularly, get and use telephone numbers, read literature, and most importantly, we don't use. We learn to share with others. If we don't tell someone we are hurting, they will seldom see it. When we reach out for help, we can receive it.

Another tool for the newcomer is involvement with the fellowship. As we become involved we learn to keep the Program first and take it easy in other matters. We begin immediately by asking for help and trying out the recommendation of the people at the meetings. It is beneficial to allow others in the group to help us. In time, we will be able to pass on what we have been given. We learn that service will get us out of ourselves. Our work can begin with simple things: emptying ashtrays, making coffee, cleaning up, setting up for a meeting, opening the door, chairing a meeting, and passing out literature. Doing these things helps us feel a part of the fellowship.

We have found it helpful to have a sponsor and to use this sponsor. Sponsorship is merely a way of describing the special interest of an experienced member that can mean so much to newcomers after they turn to N.A. for help. Sponsorship is also a two-way street, helping both the newcomer and the sponsor. The sponsor's clean time and experience may well depend on the availability of sponsors in a locality. Sponsorship is also the responsibility of the group for helping the newcomer. It is implied and informal in its approach, but it is the heart of the N.A. way of recovery from addiction—one addict helping another.

One of the most profound changes in our lives is in the realm of personal relationships. Our earliest involvements with others often begin with our sponsor. As newcomers we find it easier if we have someone whose judgment we trust and can confide in. We find trusting others with more experience to be a strength rather than a weakness. Our experience reveals that working the steps is our best guarantee against a relapse. Our sponsors and friends can advise us regarding how to work the steps. We can talk over what the steps mean with them. They can help us to prepare for the spiritual experience of living the steps. Asking God as we understand Him for help improves our understanding of the steps. When we are prepared, we must try out our newly found way of life. We learn that the Program won't work when we try to adapt it to our life. We must learn to adapt our life to the Program.

Today we seek solutions, not problems. We try what we learn on an experimental basis. We keep what we need and leave the rest. We find that by working the steps, communicating with our Higher Power, talking to our sponsors, and sharing with newcomers we are able to grow spiritually.

The Twelve Steps are used as a program of recovery. We learn that we can go to our Higher Power for help in solving problems. When we find ourselves sharing difficulties that used to have us on the run, we experience good feelings that give us the strength to begin seeking God's will for us.

We believe that our Higher Power will take care of us. If we honestly try to do God's will to the best of our ability, we can handle the results of anything that happens. Seeking our Higher Power's will is a spiritual principle found in the steps. Working the steps and practicing the principles simplifies our lives and changes our old attitudes. When we admit that our lives had become unmanageable, we don't have to argue our point of view. We have to accept ourselves as we are. We no longer have to be right all the time. When we give ourselves this freedom, we can allow others to be wrong. Freedom to change seems to come mainly after our acceptance of ourselves.

Sharing with fellow addicts is a basic tool in our Program. This help can only come from another addict. It is help that says, "I have had something like that happen to me, and I did this...." For anyone who wants our way of life, we share experience, strength and hope instead of preaching and judging. If sharing the experience of our pain helps just one person, it will have been worth the suffering. We strengthen our own recovery when we share it with others who ask for help. If we keep what we have to share, we lose it. Words mean nothing until we put them into action.

We recognize our spiritual growth when we are able to reach out and help others. We help others when we participate in Twelve Step work and try to carry the message of recovery to the addict who still suffers. We learn that we keep what we have only by giving it away. Also, our experience shows many personal problems are resolved when we get out of ourselves and offer to help those in need. We recognize that one addict can best understand and help another. No matter how much we give, there is always another addict seeking help.

We cannot afford to lose sight of the importance of sponsorship and of taking a special interest in a confused addict who wants to stop using. Experience shows clearly that those who get the most out of the N.A.

Program are those to whom sponsorship is important. Sponsorship responsibilities are welcomed by us and accepted as opportunities to enrich our personal N.A. experience.

Working with others is only the beginning of service work. N.A. service allows us to spend much of our time directly helping the suffering addicts as well as insuring that Narcotics Anonymous itself survives. This way we keep what we have by giving it away.

Chapter Six

THE TWELVE TRADITIONS
OF NARCOTICS ANONYMOUS

We keep what we have only with vigilance, and just as freedom for the individual comes from the Twelve Steps, so freedom for the groups springs from our Traditions.

As long as the ties that bind us together are stronger than those that would tear us apart, all will be well.

1. *Our common welfare should come first; personal recovery depends on N.A. unity.*
2. *For our Group purpose there is but one ultimate authority — a loving God as He may express Himself in our Group conscience; our leaders are but trusted servants, they do not govern.*
3. *The only requirement for membership is a desire to stop using.*
4. *Each Group should be autonomous, except in matters affecting other Groups, or N.A., as a whole.*
5. *Each Group has but one primary purpose — to carry the message to the addict who still suffers.*
6. *An N.A. Group ought never endorse, finance, or lend the N.A. name to any related facility or outside enterprise, lest problems of money, property or prestige divert us from our primary purpose.*

7. *Every N.A. Group ought to be fully self-supporting, declining outside contributions.*

8. *Narcotics Anonymous should remain forever non-professional, but our Service Centers may employ special workers.*

9. *N.A., as such, ought never to be organized; but we may create service boards or committees directly responsible to those they serve.*

10. *N.A. has no opinion on outside issues; hence the N.A. name ought never to be drawn into public controversy.*

11. *Our public relations policy is based on attraction rather than promotion; we need always maintain personal anonymity at the level of press, radio, and films.*

12. *Anonymity is the spiritual foundation of all our Traditions, ever reminding us to place principles before personalities.*

Understanding these Traditions comes slowly over a period of time. We pick up information as we talk to members and visit various groups. It usually isn't until we get involved with service that someone points out that "personal recovery depends on N.A. unity," and that unity depends on how well we follow our Traditions. Because we hear about "suggested steps" and "no musts" so often, some of us make a mistake and assume that this applies to groups the way it applies to the individual. The Twelve Traditions of N.A. are not negotiable. They are the guidelines that keep our fellowship alive and free.

By following these guidelines in our dealings with others and society at large, we avoid many problems. That is not to say our Traditions eliminate them all. We still have to face difficulties as they arise: communication problems, differences of opinion, internal controversies, and troubles with individuals and groups outside the fellowship. However, when we apply these principles, we avoid some of the pitfalls.

Many of our problems are like those our predecessors had to face. Their hard-won experience gave birth to the Traditions, and our own experience has shown that these principles are just as valid today as they were when these Traditions were formulated. Our Traditions protect us from the internal and external forces which could destroy us. They are truly the ties that bind us together. It is only through understanding and application that they work.

TRADITION ONE

"Our common welfare should come first; personal recovery depends on N.A. unity."

Our First Tradition concerns unity and our common welfare. One of the most important things about our new way of life is being a part of a group of addicts seeking recovery. Our survival is directly related to the survival of the group and of the fellowship. To maintain unity within Narcotics Anonymous it is imperative that the group remain stable, or else the entire fellowship perishes and the individual dies.

It wasn't until we came to Narcotics Anonymous that recovery became possible. This program can do for us what we could not do for ourselves. We became part of a group and found that we could recover. We learned that those who did not continue to be an active part of the fellowship faced a rough road. The individual is precious to the group, and the group is precious to the individual. We never experienced the kind of attention and personal care that we found in the Program. We are accepted and loved for what we are, instead of "in spite" of what we are. No one can revoke our membership or make us do anything we do not choose to do. We follow this way of life by example rather than direction. We share our experience and learn from each other. In our addiction, we consistently placed our personal desires before anything else. In Narcotics Anonymous we found that what is best for the group is usually good for us.

Our personal experiences while using differed from one another. However, as a group we have found many common themes in our addiction. One of these was the need to prove self-sufficiency. We had convinced ourselves that we could make it alone and proceeded to live life on that basis. The results were disastrous, and in the end, each of us had to admit that self-sufficiency was a lie. This admission was the starting point of our recovery and is a primary point of unity for the fellowship.

Not only are these common themes in our addiction, but we find that in our recovery we have much in common. We share a common desire to stay clean. We have learned to depend on a Power greater than ourselves. Our purpose is to carry the message to the addict who still suffers. Our Traditions are the guidelines that protect us from ourselves. They are our unity.

Unity is a must in Narcotics Anonymous. This is not to say that we do not have our disagreements and conflicts; we do. Whenever people get together there are differences of opinion. However, we can disagree without being disagreeable. Time and time again, we have seen that in crises we set aside our differences and work for the common good. We have seen two members who usually do not get along well working together with a newcomer. We have seen a group doing menial tasks to pay rent for their meeting hall. We have seen members drive hundreds of miles to help support a new group. These activities and many others are commonplace in our fellowship. They must be because without these things, N.A. could not survive.

We must live and work together as a group to insure that in a storm our ship does not sink and members perish. With faith in a Power greater than ourselves, hard work, and unity we will survive and continue to carry the message to the addict who still suffers.

TRADITION TWO

"For our Group purpose there is but one ultimate authority, a loving God as He may express Himself in our Group conscience. Our leaders are but trusted servants; they do not govern."

In Narcotics Anonymous, we are concerned with protecting ourselves from ourselves. Our Second Tradition is an example of this. By nature, we are strong-willed, self-centered people, thrust together in N.A.; mismanagers all; not one of us is capable of making consistently good decisions.

In Narcotics Anonymous, we rely on a loving God as He expresses Himself in our group conscience, rather than on personal opinion or ego. In working the steps, we learn to depend on a Power greater than ourselves, and utilize it for our group purposes. We must be constantly on guard that our decisions are truly an expression of God's will. There is often a vast difference between group conscience and group opinion, as dictated by powerful personalities or popularity. Some of our most painful growing experiences have come as a result of decisions made in the name of "group conscience." True spiritual principles are never in conflict; they complement each other. The spiritual conscience of a group will never contradict any of our Traditions. The Second Tradition concerns the nature of leadership in N.A. We have learned that for our fellowship, leadership by example and be selfless service works and that direction and manipulation fail. We choose not to have presidents, masters, or directors. Instead we have secretaries, treasurers and representatives. These titles imply service rather than control. Our experience shows that if a group becomes an extension of the personality of a leader or a certain member, it loses its effectiveness. An atmosphere of recovery in our groups is one of our most valued assets, and we must guard it carefully lest we lose it to politics and personalities.

Those of us who have been involved in service or in getting a group started sometimes have a hard time letting go. Egos and unfounded pride and self-will would destroy a group if given authority. We must instead remember that offices have been placed in trust, that we are trusted servants and that at no time do any of us govern. Narcotics Anonymous is a God-given Program, and we can maintain our group in dignity only with group conscience and God's love.

Some will resist. However, many will become the role models for newcomers to follow while the self-seeking soon find they are on the outside, causing dissension and eventually disaster to themselves. Many of them change; they learn we can only be governed by a loving God as expressed in our group conscience.

TRADITION THREE

"The only requirement for membership is a desire to stop using."

This Tradition is important for both the individual and the group. Desire is the key word; desire is the basis of our recovery. In our stories and in our experience of trying to carry the message of recovery to the addict who still suffers, one painful fact of life has emerged again and again. An addict who does not want to stop using will not stop using. They can be analyzed, counseled, reasoned with, prayed over, threatened, beaten, locked up, or whatever, but they will not stop until they want to stop. The only thing we ask of our members is that they have this desire. Without it they are doomed, but with it miracles will happen.

Desire is our only requirement, and rightly so. Addiction does not discriminate. This Tradition is to insure that any addict regardless of drugs used, race, religious beliefs, sex, sexual preference or financial condition is free to practice the N.A. way of life. That only the desire to stop using is needed insures that no caste system will develop making one addict superior to another. All addicted persons are welcome and equal in obtaining the relief they are seeking from their addiction; every addict can recover in this program on an equal basis. This Tradition guarantees our freedom to recover.

Membership in Narcotics Anonymous is not automatic when someone walks in the door or when the newcomer decides to stop using. The decision to become a part of our fellowship rests with the individual. Any addict who has a desire to stop using can become a member of N.A. We are addicts and our problem is addiction.

The choice of membership rests with the individual. We feel the ideal state for our fellowship exists when addicts can come freely and openly to an N.A. meeting, whenever and wherever they choose, and leave just as freely if they want. We realize that recovery is a reality and that life without drugs is better than we ever imagined. We open our doors to addicts hoping that they can find what we have found, knowing only those who have a desire to stop using and want what we have to offer will join us in our way of life.

TRADITION FOUR

"Each Group should be autonomous, except in matters affecting other Groups, or N.A. as a whole."

The autonomy of our groups is necessary for our survival. A dictionary defines autonomous as "having the right or power of self-government...undertaken or carried on without outside control." This means our groups are self-governing and are not subject to outside control. Every group has had to stand and grow on its own.

One might ask, "Are we truly autonomous? What about our service committees, our offices, activities, hot lines, and all the other things that go on in N.A.?" They are services we utilize to help us in our recovery and to further the primary purpose of our groups. Narcotics Anonymous is a fellowship of men and women, addicts meeting in groups and using a given set of spiritual principles to find freedom from addiction and a new way to live. Those things we mentioned are the result of members caring enough to reach out and offer their help and experience so that our road might be easier.

A Narcotics Anonymous group is any meeting which meets regularly at a specified place and time for the purpose of recovery provided that it follows the Twelve Steps and Twelve Traditions of Narcotics Anonymous. There are two basic types of meetings: those which are opened to the general public and those closed to the public (for addicts only). Meetings vary widely in format from group to group. Some are participation meetings, some speakers, some question and answer, some special problems discussion.

Despite the type or format a group uses for its meetings, the function of a group is always the same: to provide a suitable and reliable environment for personal recovery and to promote such recovery. These Traditions are part of a set of spiritual principles of Narcotics Anonymous, and without them, N.A. does not exist.

We say that for N.A., autonomy is more than this. It gives our groups the freedom to act on their own to establish their atmosphere of recovery, serve their members, and fulfill their primary purpose. It is for these reasons that we guard our autonomy so carefully.

It would seem that we, in our groups, can do whatever we decide regardless of what anyone says. This is partly true. Each group does have complete freedom, except when their actions affect other groups or N.A. as a whole. Like group conscience, autonomy can be a two-edged sword. Group autonomy has been used to justify the violation of the Traditions. If a contradiction exists, we have slipped away from our principles. If we check to make sure that our actions are clearly within the bounds of our Traditions; if we do not dictate to other groups, or force anything upon them; and if we consider the consequences of our action ahead of time, then all will be well.

TRADITION FIVE

"Each group has but one primary purpose, to carry the message to the addict who still suffers."

"You mean to say that our primary purpose is to carry the message? I thought we were here to get clean. I thought that our primary purpose was to recover from drug addiction." For the individual, this is certainly true; our members are here to find freedom from addiction and a new way of life. However, groups aren't addicted and don't recover. All our groups can do is plant the seed for recovery and bring addicts together so that the magic of empathy, honesty, caring, sharing, and service can do their work. The purpose of this Tradition is to insure that this atmosphere of recovery is maintained. This can only be achieved by keeping our groups recovery-oriented. The fact that we, each and every group, focus on carrying the message provides consistency; addicts can count on us. Unity of action and purpose makes possible what seemed impossible for us—recovery.

The Twelfth Step of our personal Program also says that we carry the message to the addict who still suffers. Working with others is a powerful tool. "The therapeutic value of one addict helping another is without parallel." For the newcomers, this is how they found Narcotics Anonymous and learned to stay clean. For the members this reaffirms their commitment to recovery. The group is the most powerful vehicle we have for carrying the message. When a member carries the message, he is somewhat bound by interpretation and personality. The problem with literature is language. The feelings, the intensity, and the strengths are sometimes lost. In our group, with many different personalities, the message of recovery is a recurring theme.

"What would happen if our groups had another primary purpose?" We feel our message would be diluted and then lost. If we concentrated on making money, many might get rich. If we were a social club, we could find many friends and lovers. If we specialized in education, we'd end up with many smart addicts. If our speciality was medical help, many would get healthy. If our group purpose were anything other than to carry the message, many would die and few would find recovery.

What is our message? That an addict, any addict, can stop using drugs, lose the desire to use, and find a new way to live. Our message is hope and the promise of freedom. When it is said and done, our primary purpose can only be to carry the message to the addict who still suffers because that is all we have to give.

TRADITION SIX

"An N.A. Group ought never endorse, finance, or lend the N.A. name to any related facility or outside enterprise, lest problems of money, property or prestige divert us from our primary purpose."

Our Sixth Tradition tells us some of the things we must do to preserve and protect our primary purpose. This Tradition is the basis for our policy of non-affiliation and is extremely important to the continuation and growth of Narcotics Anonymous.

Let's take a look at what this Tradition says. The first thing a group ought never do is endorse. To endorse is to sanction, approve or recommend. Endorsements can be either direct or implied. We see direct endorsements everyday in T.V. commercials. An implied endorsement is one that is not specifically stated.

Many other organizations wish to ride on the N.A. name. To allow them to do so would be an implied endorsement and a violation of this Tradition. Hospitals, drug recovery houses, probation and parole offices are some of the facilities we deal with in carrying the N.A. message. While these organizations are sincere and we hold N.A. meetings in their establishments, we cannot endorse, finance or allow them to use the N.A. name to further their growth. However, we are willing to carry the N.A. principles into these institutions to the addicts who still suffer so that they can make the choice.

The next thing we ought never to do is finance. This is more obvious. To finance means to supply funds or to help support financially.

The third thing warned against is lending the N.A. name to fulfill the purposes of other programs. For example, several times other programs have tried to use Narcotics Anonymous as part of their "services offered" to help justify funding.

This Tradition also tells us "who." A related facility is any place that involves N.A. members. It might be a halfway house, a detox center, a counseling center, a clubhouse or any one of a number of such places. People are easily confused by what is N.A. and what are the related facilities. Recovery houses which have been started or staffed by N.A. members have to take care that the differentiation is clear. Perhaps the most confusion exists when it involves a clubhouse situation. Newcomers and even older members often identify the clubhouse with Narcotics Anonymous. We should make a special effort to let these people know that these are not the same. The second "who" are outside enterprises. An outside enterprise is any agency, business venture, religion, society, organization, related activity, or any other fellowship. Most of these are easy to identify, except for the other fellowships. Narcotics Anonymous is a separate and distinct fellowship in its own right. Our problem is addiction. The other Twelve Step fellowships specialize in other problems, and our relationship with them is one of "cooperation, not affiliation." The use of literature, speakers, and announcements of other fellowships in our meetings constitutes an implied endorsement of an outside enterprise.

This Sixth Tradition goes on to warn us what may happen: "lest problems of money, property or prestige divert us from our primary purpose." These often become obsessions and shut us off from our spiritual aim. For the individual, this type of abuse can be devastating; for the group, it can be disastrous. When we as a group waver from our primary purpose, addicts die who might have found recovery.

TRADITION SEVEN

"Every N.A. group ought to be fully self-supporting, declining outside contributions."

Being self-supporting is an important part of our new way of life. For the individual, this is usually quite a change. In our addictions, we were dependent on people, places and things. We looked to them to support us and supply the things we found lacking in ourselves. As recovering addicts, we find that we are still dependent, but our dependence has shifted from the things around us to a loving God and the inner strength we get in our relationship with Him. We, who were unable to function as human beings, now find anything is possible of us. Those dreams we gave up long ago can now become realities. Addicts as a group have been a burden to society. In N.A., our groups not only stand on their own, but demand the right to do so.

Money has always been a problem for us. We could never find enough to support ourselves and our habits. We worked, stole, conned, begged and sold ourselves; there was never enough money to fill the emptiness inside. In our recovery, money is still often a problem.

We need money to run our group: there is rent to pay, supplies and literature to buy. We take a collection in our meetings to cover these expenses and whatever is left over goes to support our services and to further our primary purpose. Unfortunately, there is little left over once a group pays its way. Sometimes members who can afford it kick in a little extra to help. Sometimes a committee is formed to put on an activity to raise funds. These efforts help and without them, we could not have come this far. N.A. services remain in need of money, and even though it is sometimes frustrating, we really would not have it any other way; we know the price would be too high. We all have to pull together, and in pulling together we learn that we really are part of "something greater than ourselves."

Our policy concerning money is clearly stated: We decline any outside contributions; our fellowship is completely self-supporting. We accept no funding, endowments, loans, and/or gifts. Everything has its price, regardless of intent. Whether the price is money, promises, concessions, special recognition, endorsements, favors, or anything else, it's too high for us. Even if those who would help us could guarantee no strings, we still would not accept their aid. We cannot afford to let our members contribute more than their fair share. We have found that the price paid by our groups is disunity and controversy. We will not put our freedom on the line.

TRADITION EIGHT

"Narcotics Anonymous should remain forever non-professional, but our service centers may employ special workers."

The Eighth Tradition is vital to the stability of N.A. as a whole. In order to understand this Tradition we need to define "non-professional service centers" and "special workers." With an understanding of these terms, this important Tradition is self-explanatory.

In this Tradition we say we have no professionals. By this, we mean we have no staff psychiatrists, doctors, lawyers, counselors, etc. Our program works by one addict helping another. By employing professionals in N.A., we would destroy our unity. We are simply addicts of equal status freely helping one another.

We recognize and admire the professionals. Many of our members are professionals in their own right. It is just that there is no room for professionalism in N.A.

A service center is defined as a place where N.A. service committees operate. The World Service Office or local regional and area offices are examples of service centers. A clubhouse or halfway house, or similar facility, is not an N.A. service center and is not affiliated with N.A. A service center is, very simply, a place where N.A. services are offered on a continuing basis.

"Service centers may employ special workers." This statement means that service centers may employ workers for special skills such as phone answering, clerical work, or printing. Such employees are directly responsible to a service committee. As N.A. grows, the demand for these workers will grow. Special workers are necessary to insure efficiency in an ever-expanding fellowship.

The difference between professionals and special workers should be defined for clarity. Professionals work in specific professions which do not direct services of N.A., but are for personal gain. Professionals do not follow N.A. Traditions. Our special workers, on the other hand, work within our Traditions and are directly responsible always to those they serve, to the fellowship.

In regards to our Eighth Tradition, we do not single out our members as "professional;" by not placing professional status on any member, we insure that we remain "forever non-professional."

TRADITION NINE

"N.A. as such ought never be organized; but we may create service boards or committees directly responsible to those they serve."

This Tradition defines the way our fellowship functions. We must first understand what N.A. is. Narcotics Anonymous is addicts who have the desire to stop using, and have joined together to do so. Our meetings are a gathering of members for the purpose of staying clean and carrying the message of recovery. Our Steps and Traditions are set down in a specific order. They are numbered, not random and unstructured. They are organized, but this is not the type of organization referred to in the Ninth Tradition. For the purpose of this Tradition, "organized" means having management and control. On this basis, the meaning of Tradition Nine is clear. Without this Tradition, our fellowship would be in opposition to spiritual principles. A loving God as He may express Himself in our group conscience is our ultimate authority.

The Ninth Tradition goes on to define the nature of the things that we can do to help N.A. It says that we may create service boards or committees to serve the needs of the fellowship. They exist solely to serve the fellowship. This is nature of our service structure as it has evolved and been defined in the N.A. service manual.

TRADITION TEN

"N.A. has no opinion on outside issues; hence the N.A.
name ought never be drawn into public controversy."

In order to achieve our spiritual aim, Narcotics Anonymous must be known and respected. Nowhere is this more obvious than in our history. N.A. was founded in 1953. For twenty years, our fellowship remained small and obscure. In the 1970's, society realized that addiction had become a worldwide epidemic and began to look for answers. Along with this came change in the way people conceived the addict. This change allowed addicts to seek help more openly. N.A. groups sprang up in many places where we were never tolerated before. Recovering addicts paved the way for more groups and more recovery. Today N.A. is a worldwide fellowship; we are known and respected everywhere.

If an addict has never heard of us, he cannot seek us out. If those who work with addicts are unaware of our existence, they cannot refer them to us. One of the most important things we can do to further our primary purpose is to let people know who, what and where we are. If we do this and keep our reputation good, we will surely grow.

Our recovery speaks for itself. Our Tenth Tradition specifically helps protect our reputation. This Tradition says that N.A. has no opinion on outside issues. We don't take sides. We don't have any recommendations. N.A., as a fellowship, does not participate in politics; to do so would invite controversy. It would jeopardize our fellowship. Those who agree with our opinions might commend us for taking a stand, but some would always disagree.

With a price this high, is it any wonder we choose not to take sides in society's problems? For our own survival, we have no opinion on outside issues.

TRADITION ELEVEN

"Our public relations policy is based on attraction rather than promotion; we need always maintain personal anonymity at the level of press, radio and films."

This Tradition deals with our relationship to those outside the fellowship. It tells us how to conduct our efforts at the public level.* Our public image consists of what we have to offer which is a successful proven way of maintaining a drug-free lifestyle. While it is important to reach as many persons as possible, it is imperative for our protection that we are careful about ads, circulars and any literature that may reach the public's hands.

Our attraction is that we are successes in our own right. As groups gathered together we offer recovery. We have found the success of our program speaks for itself; this is our "promotion."

This Tradition goes on to tell us that we need to maintain personal anonymity at the level of press, radio and films. This is to protect the membership and reputation of Narcotics Anonymous. We do not give our last names nor appear in the media as a member of Narcotics Anonymous. No individual inside or outside the fellowship represents Narcotics Anonymous.

*For detailed examples refer to public information pamphlet.

69

TRADITION TWELVE

"Anonymity is the spiritual foundation of all our Traditions,
ever reminding us to place principles before personalities."

A dictionary definition of anonymity is "a state of bearing no name." In keeping with this, the "I" becomes "we." The spiritual foundation becomes more important than any one particular group or individual. As we find ourselves growing closer together the awakening of humility occurs. Humility is a by-product which allows us to grow and develop in an atmosphere of freedom, and removes the fear of becoming known by our employers, families, or friends as addicts. Therefore, we attempt to rigorously adhere to the principle that "what is said in meetings stays in meetings."

Throughout our Traditions, we speak in terms of "we" and "our" rather than "me" and "mine." By working together for our common welfare we achieve the true spirit of anonymity.

We have heard the phrase "principles before personalities" so often that it is like a cliche. While we may disagree as individuals, the spiritual principle of anonymity makes us all equal as members of the group. No member is greater or lesser than any other member. The drive for personal gain in the areas of sex, property and social position, which brought so much pain in the past, falls by the wayside if the principle of anonymity is adhered to. Anonymity is one of the basic elements of our recovery and so it pervades our Traditions and our fellowship. It protects us from our own defects of character and renders personalities and their differences powerless. Anonymity in action makes it impossible for personalities to come before principles.

Chapter Seven

RECOVERY AND RELAPSE

Many consider continuous abstinence and recovery as noteworthy and therefore synonymous, while relapsers are sort of pushed aside, or worse yet, used as statistics that in no way give a true picture of the entire addiction pattern. We in the recovery program of Narcotics Anonymous have noted with some satisfaction that many of the relapsers when again active in the prime or substitute addiction have dropped many of the parallel behaviors that characterized them in the past. This change alone is significant to us. Honesty of a kind has penetrated their character. Yet there are others, completely abstinent, whose dishonesties and self-deceits still prevent them from enjoying complete recovery and acceptance within society. Complete and continuous abstinence, however, is still the best ground for growth. In close association and identification with others in N.A. groups, our chances for recovery and complete freedom in a changing and creative form are enhanced a hundred fold.

Although all addicts are basically the same in kind, we do, as individuals, differ in degree of sickness and rate of recovery. There may be times when a relapse lays the groundwork for complete freedom. At other times only by a grim and obstinate willfulness to hang on to abstinence come hell or high water until a crisis passes, can that freedom be achieved. An addict, who by any means, can lose even for a time the need or desire to use, and has free choice over impulsive thinking and compulsive action, has reached a turning point that may be the decisive factor in his recovery. The feeling of true independence and freedom hangs here at times in the balance. To step out alone and run our own lives again draws us, yet we seem to know that what we have has come from dependence on a Power greater than ourselves and the giving and receiving of help from others in acts of empathy. Many times in our recovery the old bugaboos will haunt us. Life may again become meaningless, monotonous and boring. We may tire mentally in repeating our new ideas and tire physically in our new activities, yet we know that if we fail to repeat them we will surely take up our old practices. We suspect that if we do not use what we have, we will lose what we have. These times are often the periods of our greatest growth. Our minds and bodies seem tired of it all, yet the dynamic forces of change or true conversion, deep within, may be working to give us the answers that alter our inner motivations and change our lives.

Quality and not quantity is the most important aspect of abstinence. Emotional sobriety in reality is our goal, not mere physical abstinence. To improve ourselves takes effort and since there is no way in the world to graft a new idea on a closed mind, an opening must be made somehow. Since we can do this only for ourselves, we need to recognize two of our seemingly inherent enemies, apathy and procrastination. Our resistance to change seems built in and only a nuclear blast of some kind will bring about any alteration or initiate another course of action. A relapse may provide the charge for the demolition process. A relapse and sometimes subsequent death of someone close to us can do the job of awakening us to the necessity for vigorous personal action.

We have seen addicts come to our fellowship, try our Program and stay clean for a period of time. They lost contact with other recovering addicts and eventually returned to active addiction. They forgot that it is really the first fix, pill, drink, snort or toke that starts the deadly cycle all over again. They tried to control it, to use in moderation, or to use just certain drugs. None of these worked for them.

Relapse is a reality. It can and does happen. Experience shows that those who do not work our Program of recovery on a daily basis may relapse. We see them come back seeking recovery. Maybe they were clean for years before their relapse. If they are lucky enough to make it back, they are shaken badly. They tell us that the relapse was more horrible than before they first found N.A. We have never seen a person relapse who lives the Narcotics Anonymous program.

Relapses are often fatal. We have attended funerals of loved ones who died from a relapse. They died in various ways. Other times we see relapsers lost for years, living in misery. Those who make it to jail or institutions may survive longer and perhaps have a reintroduction to N.A.

In our daily lives we are subject to emotional and spiritual lapses, causing us to become defenseless against the physical relapse of drug use. As an incurable disease, drug addiction is subject to relapse.

We are never forced into relapse. We are given a choice. Relapse is never an accident. Relapse is a sign that we have had a reservation in our program. We slighted our program and left loopholes in our daily lives. Unaware of the pitfalls ahead, we stumbled blindly on in the belief we could make it on our own. Sooner or later we fell back into the illusions that drugs would make life easier. We believed that drugs would change us, and we forgot that these changes are lethal. When we believe that drugs will solve our problems and forget what they can do to us, we are in real trouble. Unless the illusions are shattered that we, in any way can continue to use or stop using on our own, we most certainly sign our own death warrant. For some reason, not taking care of our personal affairs lowers our self-esteem and that sets up a pattern that repeats itself in all areas of our lives. If we begin to avoid our new responsibilities by missing meetings, neglecting Twelve Step work, or not getting involved, our Program stops. These are the kinds of things that lead to relapse. We may sense a change coming over us. Our ability to remain open-minded disappears. We may become angry and resentful toward anyone or anything. We may begin to reject those who were close to us. We isolate ourselves. We become sick of ourselves in a short time. We revert back to our sickest behavior patterns without even having to use drugs.

When a resentment or any other emotional upheaval occurs, failure to practice the steps can result in a relapse.

Obsessive behavior is a common denominator for addictive people.

We have times when we try to fill ourselves up until we are satisfied, only to discover that there is no way to satisfy us. Part of our addictive pattern is that we can never get enough of whatever we think we want. Sometimes we forget and we think that if we can just get enough food or enough sex, or enough money we'll be satisfied and everything will be all right. Self-will still leads us to make decisions based on manipulation, ego, lust or false pride. We don't like to be wrong. Our egos tell us that we can do it on our own, but loneliness and paranoia quickly return. We find that we cannot really do it alone; when we try things get worse. We need to be reminded of where we came from and that it will get progressively worse if we use. This is when we need the fellowship the most.

We don't recover overnight. When we realize that we have made a bad decision or bad judgment, our inclination is to make an attempt to rationalize it. We often become extreme in our self-obsessive attempt to cover our tracks. We forget we have a choice today. We get sicker.

There is something in our self-destructive personalities that cries for failure. Most of us feel that we do not deserve to succeed. This is a common theme with addicts. Self-pity is one of the most destructive of defects. It will drain us of all positive energy. We focus on anything that isn't going our way and ignore all the beauty in our lives. With no real desire to improve our lives, or even to live, we just keep going further and further down. Some of us never make it back.

We must relearn many things that we have forgotten and develop a new approach to life if we are to survive. This is what Narcotics Anonymous is all about. It is about people who care about desperate, dying addicts and who can, in time, teach them how to live without drugs. Many of us had difficulty coming into the fellowship because we did not understand that we have the disease of addiction. We sometimes see our past behavior as part of ourselves and not part of our disease.

We take the First Step. We admit we are powerless over our addiction, that our lives have become unmanageable. Slowly things get better and we start getting our confidence back. Our ego tells us we can do it on our own. Things are getting better and we think we really don't need this program. Cockiness is a red light indicator. The loneliness and paranoia will come back. We find out we can't do it on our own and things get worse. We really take the First Step, this time internally. There will be times, however, when we really feel like using. We want to run, and we feel lousy; we need to be reminded of where we came from and that it will be worse this time. This is when we need the program the most. We realize we must do something.

When we forget the effort and work it took us to get a period of freedom in our lives, lack of gratitude sinks in and self-destruction begins again. Unless action is taken immediately we run the risk of a relapse, which threatens our very existence. Keeping our illusion of reality, rather than using the tools of the program, will return us to isolation. Loneliness will kill us inside and the drugs, which almost always come next, may do the job completely. The symptoms and the feelings we experienced at the end of our using will come back even stronger than before. This impact is sure to destroy us if we don't surrender ourselves to the N.A. program.

Relapse can be the destructive force that kills us or leads us to the realization of who and what we really are. The eventual misery of using is not worth the temporary escape it might give us. For us, to use is to die, often in more ways than one.

One of the biggest stumbling blocks seems to be in placing unrealistic expectations on ourselves or others. Relationships can be a terribly painful area. We tend to fantasize and project what will happen. We get angry and resentful if our fantasies are not fulfilled. We forget that we are powerless over other people. The old thinking and feelings of loneliness, despair, helplessness and self-pity creep in. Thoughts of sponsors, meetings, literature and all other positive input leave our consciousness. We have to keep our recovery first and our priorities in order.

Writing about what we want, what we are asking for, and what we get and sharing this with our sponsor or another trusted person helps us to work through negative feelings. Letting others share with us about their experience gives us hope that it does get better. It seems that being powerless is a huge stumbling block. When a need arises for us to admit our powerlessness, we may first look for ways to exert power against it.

Exhausting these ways, we begin sharing with others and find hope. Attending meetings daily, living a day at a time, and reading literature seems to send our mental attitude back toward the positive. Willingness to try what has worked for others is vital. Even when we feel that we don't want to attend, meetings are a source of strength and hope for us.

It is important to share our feelings of wanting to use drugs. It is amazing how often newcomers think that it is really abnormal for a drug addict to want to use. When we feel the old urges come over us, we think there must be something wrong with us, and that other people in Narcotics Anonymous couldn't possibly understand.

It is important to remember that the desire to use will pass. We never have to use again, no matter how we feel. All feelings will eventually pass.

The progression of recovery is a continuous uphill journey. Without effort we start the downhill run again. The progression of the disease is an ongoing process, even during abstinence.

We come here powerless, and the power we seek comes to us through other people in Narcotics Anonymous, but we must reach out for it. Now clean and in the fellowship, we need to keep ourselves surrounded by others who know us well. We need each other. Narcotics Anonymous is a fellowship of survival, and one of its advantages is that it places us in intimate, regular contact with the very people who can best understand and help us in our recovery. Good ideas and good intentions do not help if we fail to put them into action. Reaching out is the beginning of the struggle that will set us free. It will break down the walls that imprison us. A symptom of our disease is alienation, and honest sharing will free us to recover.

We are grateful that we were made so welcome at meetings that we felt comfortable. Without staying clean and coming to those meetings, we would surely have had a rougher time with the steps. Just one fix, pill, drink, snort, or toke will interrupt the process of recovery.

We all find that the feeling we get from helping others motivates us to do better in our own lives. If we are hurting, and most of us do from time to time, we learn to ask for help. We find that pain shared is pain lessened. Members of the Fellowship are willing to help a relapser recover and have insight and useful suggestions to offer when asked. Recovery found in Narcotics Anonymous must come from within, and no one stays clean for anyone but themselves.

In our disease, we are dealing with a destructive, at times violent, power greater than ourselves that can lead to relapse. If we have relapsed, it is important to keep in mind that we must get back to meetings as soon as possible. Otherwise, we may have only months, days, or hours before we reach a threshold where we are gone beyond recall. Our disease is so cunning that it can get us into impossible situations. When it does, we come back to the program if we can, while we can. Once we use, we are under the control of our disease.

We never fully recover, no matter how long we've been clean. Complacency is the enemy of members with substantial clean time. If we remain complacent for long, the recovery process ceases. The disease will manifest apparent symptoms in us. Denial returns, along with obsession and compulsion. Guilt, remorse, fear and pride may become unbearable. Soon we reach a place where our backs are against the wall. Denial and the First Step conflict in our minds. If we let the obsession of using overcome us, we are doomed. Only a complete and total acceptance of the First Step can save us. We must totally surrender ourselves to the Program.

The first thing to do is to get clean. This makes the other stages of recovery possible. As long as we stay clean, no matter what, we have the greatest possible advantage over our disease. For this we are grateful.

Many of us get clean in a protected environment, such as a rehabilitation center or recovery house. When re-entering the world, we feel lost, confused and vulnerable. Going to meetings as often as available will reduce the shock of change. Meetings provide a safe place to share with others during this time. We begin to live the program; we learn to apply spiritual principles in our lives. We must use what we learn or we will lose it in a relapse.

Many of us would have had nowhere else to go, if we could not have trusted N.A. groups and members. At first, we were both captivated and intimidated by the fellowship. No longer comfortable with our using friends, we were not yet at home in the meetings. We began to lose our fear through the experience of sharing. The more we did this, the more our fears slipped away. We shared for this reason. Growth means change. Spiritual maintenance means ongoing recovery, and isolation is dangerous to spiritual growth.

Those of us who find the fellowship and begin to live the steps develop some kind of relationship with others. As we grow, we learn to overcome the tendency to run and hide from ourselves and our feelings. Being honest about our feelings helps others to identify with us. We find that when we communicate honestly we reach others better. Honesty takes practice and none of us claims to be perfect. When we feel trapped or pressured, it takes great spiritual and emotional strength to be honest. Sharing with others keeps us from feeling isolated and alone. This process is a creative action of the spirit.

When we work the program we are living the steps daily. This gives us experience in applying spiritual principles. The experience we gain with time helps our ongoing recovery. We must use what we learn or we will lose it, no matter how long we have been clean. Eventually we are shown that we must get honest or we will use again. We pray for willingness and humility and finally get honest about our mistaken judgements or bad decisions. We tell those who we hurt that we were to blame and make whatever amends are necessary. Now we are in the solution again. We are working the program. It becomes easier to work the program now. We know that the steps help prevent relapse.

Relapsers may also fall into another trap. We may doubt that we can stop using and stay clean. We can never stay clean on our own. Frustrated, we cry, "I cannot do it!" We beat ourselves as we come back into the program. We imagine that our fellow members will not respect the courage it takes to come back. We have learned the utmost respect for that type of courage. We applaud heartily. It is not shameful to relapse — the shame is in not coming back. We must smash the illusion that we can do it alone.

Another type of relapser does not keep being clean as top priority. Staying clean must always come first. At times, we all experience difficulty in our recovery. Emotional lapses result from not putting into practice what we have learned. Those who make it through these times show a courage not their own. After coming through one of these periods, we can readily agree that it is always darkest before the dawn. Once we get through a difficult time clean, we are given a tool of recovery that we can use again and again.

If we relapse, we may feel guilt and embarassment. Our relapse is embarrassing, but we cannot save our face and our ass at the same time. We find it best to get back on the program as soon as possible. It is better to swallow our pride than to die or go permanently insane.

As long as we maintain an attitude of being thankful for being clean, we find it is easier to remain clean. The best way to express gratitude is by carrying the message of our experience, strength and hope to the still-suffering addict. We are ready to work with any suffering addict.

Living the program on a daily basis provides many valuable experiences. If we are plagued by an obsession to use, experience has taught us to call a fellow recovering addict and get to a meeting.

Using addicts are self-centered, angry, frightened and lonely people. In recovery, we experience spiritual growth. While using we were dishonest, self-seeking and often institutionalized. The program allows us to become responsible and productive members of society.

As we begin to function in society, our creative freedom helps us sort our priorities and do the basic things first. Daily practice of our Twelve Step program enables us to change from what we were to what our Higher Power would have us become. With the help of our sponsor or spiritual advisor, gradually we learn to trust and depend on our Higher Power as we understand it.

Chapter Eight

WE DO RECOVER

Although "Politics makes strange bedfellows," as the old saying goes, addiction makes us one of a kind. Our personal stories may vary in individual pattern but in the end we all have the same thing in common. This common illness or disorder is addiction. We know well the two things that make up true addiction: obsession and compulsion. Obsession — that fixed idea that takes us back time and time again to our particular drug or some substitute, to recapture the ease and comfort we once knew.

Compulsion — that once having started the process with one fix, one pill, or one drink we cannot stop through our own power of will. Because of our physical sensitivity to drugs, we are completely in the grip of a destructive power greater than ourselves.

When at the end of the road we find that we can no longer function as a human being, either with or without drugs, we all face the same dilemma. What is there left to do? There seems to be this alternative: either go on as best we can to the bitter ends — jails, institutions or death; or find a new way to live. In years gone by, very few addicts ever had this last choice. Those who are addicted today are more fortunate. For the first time in man's entire history, a simple way has been proving itself in

81

the lives of many addicts. It is available to us all. This is a simple spiritual — not religious — program, known as Narcotics Anonymous.

When my addictions brought me to the point of complete powerlessness, uselessness and surrender some twenty-six years* ago, there was no N.A. I found A.A. and in that fellowship met addicts who had also found that program to be the answer to their problem. However, we knew that many were still going down the road of disillusion, degradation and death, because they were unable to identify with the alcoholic in A.A. Their identification was at the level of apparent symptoms and not at the deeper level of emotions or feelings, where empathy becomes a healing therapy for all addicted people. With several other addicts and some members of A.A. who had great faith in us and the program, we formed, in July of 1953, what we now know as Narcotics Anonymous. We felt that now the addict would find from the start as much identification as each needed to convince himself that he could stay clean, by the example of others who had recovered for many years.

That this was what was principally needed, has proved itself in these passing years. That wordless language of recognition, belief and faith, which we call empathy, created the atmosphere in which we could feel time, touch reality and recognize spiritual values long lost to many of us. In our program of recovery we are growing in numbers and in strength. Never before have so many clean addicts, of their own choice and in free society, been able to meet where they please, to maintain their recovery in complete creative freedom.

Even addicts said it could not be done the way we had it planned. We believed in openly scheduled meetings; no more hiding as other groups had tried. We believed this differed from all other methods tried before by those who advocated long withdrawal from society. We felt that the sooner the addict could face his problem of everyday living just that much faster would he become a real productive citizen. We eventually have to stand on our own feet and face life on its own terms, so why not from the start. Because of this, of course, many relapsed and many were lost completely. However, many stayed and some came back after their setback. The brighter part is the fact that of those who are now our members, many have long terms of complete abstinence and are better able to

82

*Written in July, 1979.

help the newcomer. Their attitude, based on the spiritual values of our steps and traditions, is the dynamic force that is bringing increase and unity to our program. Now we know that the time has come when that tired old lie, "Once an addict, always an addict," will no longer be tolerated by either society or the addict himself. We do recover.

Recovery begins with surrender. From that point forward, each of us is reminded that a day clean is a day won. In Narcotics Anonymous our attitudes, thoughts and reactions change. We come to realize that we are not alien and begin to understand and accept who we are.

As long as there have been people, addiction has existed. For us, addiction is an obsession to use the drugs that are destroying us followed by a compulsion which forces us to continue. Complete abstinence is the foundation for our new way of life.

In the past, there was no hope for an addict. In Narcotics Anonymous, we learn to share the loneliness, anger and fear that addicts have in common and cannot control. Our old ideas are what got us into trouble. We weren't oriented toward fulfillment; we focused on the emptiness and worthlessness of it all. We could not deal with success, so failure became a way of life. In recovery, failures are only temporary setbacks rather than links in an unbreakable chain. Honesty, open-mindedness and willingness to change are all new attitudes that help us admit our faults and ask for help. We are no longer compelled to act against our true nature and do things we don't really want to do.

Most addicts resist recovery, and the program we share with them interferes with their using. If a newcomer tells us that they can continue to use drugs in any form and suffer no ill effects, there are two ways we can look at it. The first possibility is that they are not an addict. The other is that their disease has not become apparent to them and that they are still denying their addiction. Addiction and withdrawal distort rational thought, and newcomers usually focus on differences rather that similarities. They look for ways to disprove the evidence of addiction or disqualify themselves from recovery.

Many of us did the same thing when we were new, so when we work with others we try not to do or say anything that will give them the excuse to continue using. We know that honesty and empathy are essential. Complete surrender is the key to recovery, and total abstinence is the only thing that has ever worked for us. In our experience, no addict who has completely surrendered to this Program has ever failed to find recovery.

Narcotics Anonymous is a spiritual, not religious program. Any clean addict is a miracle, and keeping the miracle alive is an ongoing process of awareness, surrender and growth. For an addict, not using is an abnormal state. We learn to live clean. We learn to be honest with ourselves and think of both sides of things. Decision-making is rough at first. Before we got clean, most of our actions were guided by impulse. Today, we are not locked into this type of thinking. We are free.

In our recovery, we find it essential to accept reality. Once we can do this, we do not find it necessary to use drugs in an attempt to change our perceptions. Without drugs, we have a chance to begin functioning as useful human beings, if we accept ourselves and the world exactly as it is. We learn that conflicts are a part of reality, and we learn new ways to resolve them instead of running from them. They are a part of the real world. We learn not to become emotionally involved with problems. We deal with what is at hand and try not to force solutions. We have learned that if a solution isn't practical, it isn't spiritual. In the past, we made simple situations into problems; we made mountains out of molehills. Our best ideas got us here. In recovery, we learn to depend on a Power greater than ourselves. We don't have all the answers or solutions, but we can learn to live without drugs. We can stay clean and enjoy life, if we remember to live "Just for Today."

We are not responsible for our disease, only our recovery. As we begin to apply what we have learned, our lives begin to change for the better. We seek help from addicts who are enjoying lives free from the obsession to use drugs. We do not have to understand this Program for it to work. All we have to do is follow direction.

We get relief through the Twelve Steps which are essential to the recovery process, because they are a new, spiritual way of life that allows us to participate in our own recovery.

From "day one," the Twelve Steps become a part of our lives. At first, we may be filled with negativity, and only allow the First Step to take hold. Later, we have less fear and can use these tools more fully and to our greater advantage. We realize that old feelings and fears are symptoms of our disease. Real freedom is now possible.

As we recover, we gain a new outlook on being clean. We enjoy a feeling of release and freedom from the desire to use. We find that everyone we meet eventually has something to offer. We become able to receive as well as to give. Life can become a new adventure for us. We come to know happiness, joy and freedom.

There is no model of the recovered addict. When the drugs go and the addict works the Program, wonderful things happen. Lost dreams awaken and new possibilities arise. Our willingness to grow spiritually keeps us buoyant. When we take the actions indicated in the steps, the results are a change in our personality. It is our action that is important. We leave the results to our Higher Power.

Recovery becomes a contact process; we lose the fear of touching and of being touched. We learn that a simple, loving hug can make all the difference in the world when we feel alone. We experience real love and real friendship.

We know that we are powerless over a disease which is incurable, progressive and fatal. If not arrested, it gets worse until we die. We cannot deal with the obsession and compulsion. The only alternative is to stop using and start learning how to live. When we are willing to follow this course and take advantage of the help available to us, a whole new life opens up. In this way, we do recover.

Today, secure in the love of the fellowship, we can finally look another human being in the eye and be grateful for who we are.

Chapter Nine

JUST FOR TODAY
LIVING THE PROGRAM

Tell yourself:

JUST FOR TODAY my thoughts will be on my recovery, living and enjoying life without the use of drugs.

JUST FOR TODAY I will have faith in someone in N.A. who believes in me and wants to help me in my recovery.

JUST FOR TODAY I will have a program. I will try to follow it to the best of my ability.

JUST FOR TODAY through N.A. I will try to get a better perspective on my life.

JUST FOR TODAY I will be unafraid, my thoughts will be on my new associations, people who are not using and who have found a new way of life. So long as I follow that way, I have nothing to fear.

87

We admit our lives have been unmanageable, but sometimes we have a problem admitting our need for help. Our own self-will leads to many problems in our recovery; we want and demand that things go our way. We should know from our past experience that our way of doing things did not work. The principle of surrender guides us into a way of life in which we draw our strength from a Power greater than ourselves. Our daily surrender to our Higher Power provides the help we need. As addicts we have trouble with acceptance which is critical to our recovery. When we refuse to practice acceptance, we are, in effect, still denying our faith in a Higher Power. Worrying is the practice of lack of faith.

Surrendering our will puts us in contact with a Higher Power which fills the empty place inside that nothing could ever fill before. We learned to trust God for help daily. Living just for today relieves the burden of the past and the fear of the future. We learned to take whatever actions are necessary and leave the results in the hands of our Higher Power.

The Narcotics Anonymous program is spiritual. We strongly suggest that each person make an attempt to find a Higher Power of their understanding. Some of us have profound spiritual experiences, dramatic and inspirational in nature. For others, the awakening is more subtle. We recover in an atmosphere of acceptance and respect for one another's beliefs. We try to avoid the self-deception of arrogance and self-righteousness. As we develop faith in our daily lives, we find that our Higher Power supplies us with the strength and guidance we need.

Each of us is free to work out our own concept of a Higher Power. Many of us were suspicious and skeptical because of disappointments we have had with religion. As new members, the talk of God we heard in meetings repelled us. Until we sought our own answers in this area, we were trapped in the ideas gathered from our past. Agnostics and atheists sometimes start out by just talking to "whatever's there." There is a spirit or an energy that can be felt in the meetings. This is sometimes the newcomer's first concept of a Higher Power. Ideas from the past are often incomplete and unsatisfactory. Everything we know is subject to revision, especially what we know about the truth. We reevaluate our old ideas, so we can become acquainted with the new ideas that lead to a new way of life. We recognize we are human with a physical, mental and spiritual sickness. When we accept that our addiction caused our own hell and that there is a power available to help us, we begin to make progress in solving our problems.

Lack of daily maintenance can show up in many ways. Through open-minded effort we come to rely on a daily relationship with God as we understand Him. Each day most of us ask our Higher Power to help us stay clean, and each night we give thanks for the gift of recovery. As our lives become more comfortable, many of us lapse into spiritual complacency, and risking relapse, we find ourselves in the same horror and loss of purpose from which we have been given only a daily reprieve. This is hopefully when our pain motivates us to renew our daily spiritual maintenance. One way we can continue a conscious contact, especially in hard times, is to list the things for which we are grateful.

Many of us have found that setting aside quiet time for ourselves is helpful in making conscious contact with our Higher Power. By quieting of the mind, meditation can lead us to calmness and serenity. This quieting of the mind can be done in any place, time, or manner according to the individual.

Our Higher Power is accessible to us at all times. We receive guidance when we ask for knowledge of God's will for us. Gradually as we become more God-centered than self-centered, our despair turns to hope. Change also involves the great source of fear — the unknown. Our Higher Power is our source of the courage we need to face this fear.

Some things we must accept, and others we can change. The wisdom to know the difference comes with growth in our spiritual program. If we maintain our spiritual condition daily, we find the pain and confusion easier to deal with. This is the emotional stability that we so badly need. With the help of our Higher Power, we never have to use again.

Any addict clean is a miracle. We keep this miracle alive in ongoing recovery with positive attitudes. If, after a period of time, we find ourselves in trouble with our recovery, we have probably stopped doing one or more of the things which helped us in the earlier stages of our recovery.

Three basic spiritual principles are Honesty, Open-mindedness, and Willingness to try. We say these are the HOW of our program. The initial honesty that we express is the desire to stop using. Next we honestly admit our powerlessness and the unmanageability of our lives.

Rigorous honesty is the most important tool we have in learning to live for today. Although honesty is difficult to practice, it is most rewarding. Honesty is the antidote to our diseased thinking. Our newly found faith serves as a firm foundation for courage in the future.

What we knew about living when we got here had almost killed us. Managing our own lives got us to the program of Narcotics Anonymous. We came in, knowing very little about how to be happy and enjoy life. A new idea cannot be grafted onto a closed mind. Being open-minded allows us to hear something that might save our lives. It allows us to listen to opposing points of view, and come to conclusions of our own. Open-mindedness leads us to the very insights that have eluded us during our lives. It is this principle that allows us to participate in a discussion without jumping to conclusions or predetermining right and wrong. We no longer need to make fools of ourselves by standing up for nonexistent virtues. We have learned that it is O.K. to not know all the answers, for then we are teachable and can learn to live our new life successfully.

Open-mindedness without willingness, however, will get us nowhere. We must be willing to do whatever is necessary to recover. We never know when the time will come when we must put forth all the effort and strength we have just to stay clean.

Honesty, open-mindedness and willingness to try, work hand-in-hand. The lack of one of these principles in our personal program can lead to relapse, and will certainly make recovery difficult and painful when it could be simple. This program is a vital part of our everyday living. If it were not for this program most of us would be dead or institutionalized. Our viewpoint changes from that of a loner to that of a member. We emphasize setting our house in order because it brings us relief. We trust in our Higher Power for the strength to meet our needs.

One way to practice the principles of HOW is by taking a daily inventory. Our inventory allows us to recognize our daily growth. We shouldn't forget about our assets in striving to eliminate our defects. The old self-deception and self-centeredness can be replaced with spiritual principles.

Staying clean is the first step in facing life. When we practice acceptance, our lives are simplified. When problems arise, we hope to be well equipped with the tools of the program. We honestly have to surrender our own self-centeredness and self-destructiveness. In the past we believed desperation would give us the strength to survive. Now we accept responsibility for our problems and see that we're equally responsible for our solutions.

As recovering addicts, we have a lot to be grateful for. As our defects are removed, we are free to become all we can. We emerge as new individuals with an awareness of ourselves and the ability to take our places in the world.

In living the steps, we begin to let go of our self-obsession. We ask a Higher Power to remove our fear of facing ourselves and life. We redefine ourselves by working the steps and using the tools of recovery. We see ourselves differently. Our personalities change. We become feeling people, capable of responding appropriately to life. We put spiritual living first and learn to use patience, tolerance and humility in our daily affairs.

Other people in our lives help us develop trust and loving attitudes; we demand less and give more. We anger more slowly and forgive more easily. We learn about love from members of Narcotics Anonymous. Through the love we receive in our fellowship we begin to feel lovable ourselves, a feeling totally alien to our old egocentric selves.

Ego used to control us in all sorts of subtle ways. Anger is our reaction to our present reality. Resentments are reliving of past experiences again and again in our minds, and fear is our response to the future. We need to become willing to let God remove these defects that burden our spiritual growth.

New ideas are available to us through the sharing of our living experience. Rigorously practicing the few simple guidelines in this chapter, we recover daily. The principles of the program shape our personalities.

From the isolation of our addiction, we find a fellowship of people with the common bond of recovery. N.A. is like a lifeboat in a sea of isolation, hopelessness and destructive chaos. Our faith, strength and hope come from people sharing their recovery and from our relationship with the God of our own understanding. At first it feels awkward to share our feelings. Part of the pain of addiction is being cut off from this sharing experience. If we find ourselves in a bad place or we sense trouble coming, we call someone or get to a meeting. We learn to seek help before making difficult decisions. By humbling ourselves and asking for help, we can get through the toughest of times. I can't, we can! In this way we find the strength we need when we need it the most. We form a mutual bond as we share our spiritual and mental resources.

Sharing in regularly scheduled meetings and one-on-one with recovering addicts helps us to stay clean. Attending meetings reminds us what it is like to be new and of the progressive nature of our disease. Attending our home group provides encouragement from the people we get to know. This sustains our recovery and helps us in our daily living. When we honestly tell our own story, someone else may identify with us. Serving the needs of our members and making our message available gives us a feeling of joy. Service gives us opportunities to grow in ways which touch all parts of our lives. Our experience in recovery may help them deal with their problems—what worked for us might work for them. Most addicts are able to accept this type of sharing, even from the very beginning. The get-togethers after our meetings are good opportunities to share things we didn't get to discuss during the meeting. This is also a good time to talk one-on-one with our sponsors. Things we need to hear will surface and become clearer to us.

By sharing the experience of our recovery with newcomers, we help ourselves to stay clean. We share comfort and encouragement with others. Today we have people in our lives who stand with us. Getting away from our self-centeredness gives us a better perspective on life. By asking for help, we can change. Sharing is risky at times, but by becoming vulnerable we are able to grow.

Some will come to Narcotics Anonymous still trying to use people to help them continue their habit. Their closed mind is a barrier against change. A spirit of open-mindedness, coupled with an admission of powerlessness, is a key that will unlock the door to recovery. If someone with a drug problem comes to us seeking recovery and is willing to try, we gladly share with them how we stay clean.

We develop self-esteem as we help others find a new way of life. When we honestly evaluate what we have, we can learn to appreciate it. We begin to feel worthwhile being members of N.A. We can carry the gifts of recovery with us everywhere. The Twelve Steps of Narcotics Anonymous are a progressive recovery process established in our daily living. Ongoing recovery is dependent on our relationship with a loving God who cares for us and will do for us what we find impossible to do for ourselves.

During our recovery, each of us comes to our own understanding of the program. If we have difficulties, we trust our groups, our sponsors and our Higher Power to guide us. Thus, recovery, as found in Narcotics Anonymous, comes both from within and without.

We live a day at a time but also from moment to moment. When we stop living in the here and now, our problems become magnified unreasonably. Patience isn't a strong point with us. That's why we need our slogans and our N.A. friends to remind us to live the program just for today.

Tell yourself:

JUST FOR TODAY my thoughts will be on my recovery, living and enjoying life without the use of drugs.

JUST FOR TODAY I will have faith in someone in N.A. who believes in me and wants to help me in my recovery.

JUST FOR TODAY I will have a program. I will try to follow it to the best of my ability.

JUST FOR TODAY through N.A. I will try to get a better perspective on my life.

JUST FOR TODAY I will be unafraid, my thoughts will be on my new associations, people who are not using and who have found a new way of life. So long as I follow that way, I have nothing to fear.

93

Chapter Ten

MORE WILL BE REVEALED

As our recovery progressed, we became increasingly aware of ourselves and the world around us. Our needs and wants, our assets and liabilities, were revealed to us. We came to realize that we had no power to change the outside world; we could only change ourselves. The program of Narcotics Anonymous provides an opportunity for us to ease the pain of living, through spiritual principles.

We are very fortunate to have had this program to come to. Before, very few people recognized that addiction was a disease. Recovery was only a dream.

The responsible, productive, drug-free lives of thousands of members illustrate the effectiveness of our program. Recovery is a reality for us today. Through working the steps we are rebuilding our fractured personalities. Narcotics Anonymous is a healthy environment for growth. As a fellowship, we love and cherish one another, supporting our new way of life together.

As we grow, we come to understand humility as acceptance of both our assets and our liabilities. What we want most is to feel good about ourselves. Today we have real feelings of love, joy, hope, sadness, excitement—not our old drug-induced feelings.

At times we find ourselves caught up in old ideas, even with time on the program. The basics are as important to recovery as they were in the beginning. We need to avoid old thinking patterns, both the old ideas and the tendency towards complacency. We cannot afford to become complacent because our disease is with us twenty-four hours a day. If, while practicing these principles, we allow ourselves to feel superior or inferior, we isolate ourselves. We are headed for trouble if we feel "apart from" other addicts. Separation from the atmosphere of recovery and the spirit of service to others slows our spiritual growth. Complacency keeps us from goodwill, love and compassion.

If we are unwilling to listen to others, we will deny the need for improvement. We learn to become flexible and to admit when others are right and we are wrong. As new things are revealed, we feel renewed. We need to stay open-minded and willing to do that one extra thing; go to that one extra meeting; stay on the phone that one extra minute; and help that newcomer stay clean that one extra day. This extra effort is vital to our recovery.

We come to know ourselves as never before. We experience new sensations, such as finding out what it is to love, to be loved, to know that people care about us, and to have concern and compassion for others. We find ourselves doing things that we never thought we would be doing, and enjoying them. We make mistakes and we accept and learn from them. We experience failure and we learn how to succeed. Often we have to face some type of crisis during our recovery, such as death of a loved one, financial difficulties or divorce. These are realities of life and they don't go away just because we get clean. Some of us, even after years of recovery, found ourselves jobless, homeless or penniless. We entertained the thought that staying clean was not "paying off" and the old thinking stirred up self-pity, resentment and anger. No matter how painful life's tragedies can be for us, one thing is clear: "We must not use, no matter what!"

This is a program of total abstinence, however, there are times, such as in cases of health problems involving surgery and/or extreme physical injury, when medication may be valid. This does not constitute a license

96

to use. There is no safe use of drugs for us. Our bodies don't know the difference between drugs prescribed by a physician for pain and drugs "prescribed by ourselves" to get high. As addicts our skill at self-deception will be at a peak in such a situation. Often our minds will even manufacture additional pain as an excuse to use. Turning it over to our Higher Power and getting the support of our sponsor and other members can help prevent us from being our own worst enemies. Being alone during such times would give our disease too much leeway to take over. Honest sharing can dispel our fears of relapse. Serious illness or surgery can present particular problems for us.

Physicians should have specific knowledge of our addiction. Remember that we—not our doctor—are ultimately responsible for the risk we expose ourselves to. To minimize the danger there are a few specific options that we may consider. These are using local anesthesia, avoiding our drug of choice, if any, stopping while we are still hurting, and spending extra days in the hospital in case withdrawal occurs.

Whatever pain we experience will pass. Through prayer, meditation and sharing we keep our minds off our discomfort and have the strength to keep our priorities in order. It is imperative to keep N.A. members close by at all times, if possible. It is amazing how our minds will go back so quickly to our old ways and old thinking. You'd be surprised how much pain we can handle without medication. In this program of total abstinence, however, we need feel no guilt after having taken a minimum amount of medication prescribed by an informed professional for extreme physical pain.

We grow through pain in recovery and often find that such a crisis is a gift, an opportunity to experience growth by living clean. Before, we were unable to even conceive of the thought that problems bring gifts. This may be finding strength within ourselves that we never knew before or regaining the feeling of self-respect we had lost.

Spiritual growth, love and compassion are but idle potentials until shared with a fellow addict. By giving unconditional love in the fellowship, we become more loving, and in the sharing of spiritual growth we become more spiritual.

By carrying this message to another addict, we are well reminded of where we come from. Having had an opportunity to remember old feelings and behaviors, we are able to see our own personal and spiritual growth. In the process of answering the questions of another, we become more clear in our thinking. Newer members are a constant source of hope, ever reminding us that the program works. We have the opportunity to live the knowledge acquired by staying clean, when we work with them.

We have learned to value others' respect for us. We are pleased when people can now depend on us. For the first time in our lives we may be asked to serve in positions of responsibility in community organizations outside of N.A. Our opinions are at times sought and valued by non-addicts in areas other than addiction and recovery. We can enjoy our families in a new way and may become a credit to them instead of an embarrassment or a burden. They can be proud of us today. Our individual interests broaden possibly to include social or even political issues. Hobbies and recreation give us new pleasure. It gives us good feelings to know that aside from our value to others as recovering addicts we are also of value as human beings.

The reinforcement received by sponsorship is limitless. We spent years taking from others' in every conceivable way. Words cannot describe the sense of spiritual awareness that we receive when we have given something, no matter how small, to another person.

We are each other's eyes and ears; when we do something wrong our fellow addicts help us to help ourselves by showing us what we cannot see. We sometimes find ourselves caught up in old ideas. We need to constantly review our feelings and thinking, if we are to stay enthusiastic and grow spiritually. This enthusiasm will aid our ongoing recovery.

Today we have the freedom of choice. As we work the program to the best of our ability, the obsession with self is removed. Much of our loneliness and fear are replaced by the love and security of the fellowship. Helping a suffering addict is one of the greatest experiences life has to offer. We are willing to help. We have had similar experiences and understand fellow addicts as no one else can. We offer hope for we know that a better way of life is now real for us, and we give love because it was so freely given. New frontiers are open to us as we learn how to love.

Love can be the flow of life energy from one person to another. By caring, sharing, and praying for others, we become a part of them, and through empathy, allow them to become part of us. As we do this, we undergo a vital spiritual experience and are changed.

On a practical level, changes occur because what's appropriate to one phase of recovery may not be for another. We constantly let go of what has served its purpose, and let God guide us through the current phase with what works here and now.

As we become more God-reliant and gain self-respect, we realize that we don't need to feel superior or inferior to anyone; our real value is in being ourselves. Our egos, once so large and dominant, now take a back seat because we are in harmony with a loving God. We find that we lead richer, happier and much fuller lives when we lose self-will.

We become able to make wise and loving decisions, based on principles and ideals that have real value in our lives. Shaping our thoughts with the spiritual ideals that we are moving toward, we are freed to become who we want to be. What we had feared, we can now overcome through our dependence on a loving God. Faith has replaced our fear and given us freedom from ourselves.

In recovery, we also strive for gratitude. We feel grateful for ongoing God-consciousness. Whenever we confront a difficulty that we do not think we can handle, we ask God to do for us what we cannot do for ourselves.

A spiritual awakening is an ongoing process. We experience a wider view of reality as we grow spiritually. An opening of our minds to new spiritual and physical experiences is the key to better awareness. As we grow spiritually we become attuned to our feelings and our purpose in life.

By loving ourselves, we become able to truly love others. This is a spiritual awakening that comes as a result of living this program. We find ourselves daring to care and love.

Higher mental and emotional functions, such as conscience and the ability to love, were sharply affected by our use of drugs. Living skills were reduced to the animal level. Our spirit was broken. The capacity to feel human was lost. This seems extreme, but many of us have been in this state.

In time, through recovery, our dreams come true. We don't mean that we necessarily become rich or famous. However, by realizing the will of our Higher Power, dreams do come true in our recovery.

One of the continuing miracles of recovery is becoming a productive, responsible member of society. We need to tread carefully into areas that expose us to ego-inflating experience, prestige and manipulation that may be difficult for us to deal with. We have found that the way to remain a productive, responsible member of society is to put our recovery first. N.A. can survive without us but we cannot survive without N.A.

Living just for today, we have no way of knowing what will happen to us. We are often amazed at how things work out for us. Recovering in the here and now, the future becomes an exciting journey. If we had written our list of expectations when we came to the program, we would have been cheating ourselves. Hopeless living problems became joyously changed. Our disease has been arrested and now anything is possible.

We become increasingly open-minded which opens the door for new ideas, in all areas of our lives. Through active listening, we hear things that work for us. This ability is a gift and grows as we grow spiritually. Life takes on a new meaning when we open ourselves to this gift. In order to receive, we must be willing to give.

Narcotics Anonymous offers only one promise and that is freedom from active addiction, the solution that eluded us for so long. We will be freed from our self-made prisons.

In recovery, our ideas of fun change. We are now free to enjoy the simple things in life, like fellowship and living in harmony with nature. We now have become free to develop a new understanding of life. As we look back, we are grateful for our new life. It is so unlike the events that brought us here.

While using, we thought that we had fun and that non-users were deprived of it. Spirituality enables us to live to the fullest, feeling grateful for who we are and what we have done in life. Since the beginning of our recovery, we have found that joy doesn't come from material things, but from within ourselves. We find that when we lose self-obsession, we are able to understand what it means to be happy, joyous, and free. Indescribable joy comes from sharing from the heart; we no longer need to lie to gain acceptance.

Narcotics Anonymous offers addicts a program of recovery which is more than just a life without drugs. Not only is this way of life better than the hell we lived, it is better than any life we had ever known.

We have found a way out, and we see it work for others. Each day more will be revealed.

101

"My gratitude speaks . . .
When I care and
When I share with others
the N.A. way."

BOOK TWO

PERSONAL STORIES

Chapter Eleven

A GIFT CALLED LIFE

I had always said I would never use drugs. Looking back, everything I said I wouldn't do, I ended up doing. The first time I used drugs, I started with pot. I didn't like it, but I got used to it. If I didn't use it, I wouldn't have felt "cool."

I had a good job at the time; it was "the place" to work when you left high school. I was expelled from school in the tenth grade for starting a riot. For me, just landing that job was fortunate. I was hanging out at the pool hall before work. Around 3 or 4 o'clook, I started to feel tired and someone said, "Try some of this. It will help you stay awake at work tonight." I didn't even ask what it was; I just opened my mouth. Within twenty minutes I felt like a new person; I could talk to people I was normally afraid of; I felt better than them. I started to take about ten diet pills a day. My logic was, "If just two made me feel so good, why not try ten!" It worked! But after six months, I started to miss work. I lost fifty pounds, my hair started to fall out, and my teeth started to hurt.

One day at the pool hall, a close friend said, "Hey, try some of this, you shoot it in your arm." Once again I said, "I'll never do that," but about one hour later, I tried it. From that day on, I was in love with it. I never cheated on it. If it said jump, I would jump. I even quit my job because something like this was too good to miss. I always wanted to forget my problems and with heroin, I could. It always fixed me up. It cost a lot of money, so I did it only when I had the money.

When I started selling heroin, I got ripped off a few times. I can remember saying, "Boy, are those guys in bad shape when they rip off their friends."

Well, six months later, I started ripping them off. I always wanted people to come to me for answers. I like that power. So when I got my income tax return check, I bought some heroin, sold all of it, but saved one shot for me. It sold fast; I made a "quick buck" and got a "free high." I felt like a king and I had control. Everyone came to me for heroin because I dropped the price. When all the other people had shot their supply, that left me the only one holding. Then I raised the price, and started using more than I was selling. I didn't want to do that, but I had no choice. I didn't know that at the time, because I thought I was handling it "OK." I lived in Lancaster, Pennsylvania at the time.

One day, the man I got my drugs from asked if I would be willing to take a chance and go to Puerto Rico with him to purchase some heroin. My answer was, "Sure, why not!" We could have gotten busted getting on the plane to come back home. I had brought some with me and wrapped it in foil. When we went through airline screening procedures, they didn't check me. I got away that time; I was lucky. We came back and my luck ran out. I got busted for a series of crimes consisting of six felonies. This was my first time in jail, and I was afraid of all the things that I heard from the streets. A lot of it was true and some of it wasn't. That didn't make me any less afraid. I stayed for one week and was bailed out. Two months later, I got busted for possession of one ounce of heroin and went back to jail. Again, I stayed for one week and was bailed out. Only two weeks later, I got busted again for breaking into someone's house in broad daylight. I had started to rip off everyone in order to supply my habit, my family, my friends, and strangers. I knew I was going to jail this time, so I just gave up. My sentence was two separate terms, each 11½-23 months in jail. I spent 13 months in jail and got out on early parole.

When I got out, I had made a promise to myself to limit my heroin use to the weekends. I didn't know anything about addiction. Little did I know that it was the very *first* fix that started me. Everyone I knew either went to jail for 5-10 years, overdosed on drugs, or was an addict themselves. Consequently, I was led right back to the streets. In only two weeks, I was worse than I was before. Lenny, the only friend I had, and his sister gave me $1,000.00 to pay off my parole officer in order to move to Florida. In my heart that's what I wanted to do, but my addiction was too great. I got the money and said to myself, "Buy some drugs, sell them, and have spending money when you get to Florida." I went to New York with the money, bought the heroin, but put it all in my arm. Now what was I going to tell them? The excuse-making and story-telling was over. I was addicted! I came back to Pennsylvania and for the first time in my addiction I felt guilt. Lenny came to see me and didn't want to hear any more stories or excuses. He said, "You need help when you rip me off, your friend. You're in trouble." I knew he was right.

I accepted his invitation to stay with him and his wife until I got help. I felt like hell in my guts. I called my parole officer and told him I wanted to go away somewhere for help. He sent me to a treatment center in North Central Pennsylvania. I had heard a lot of bad things about this place but I didn't care. My back was against the wall and I was tired of living the way I was living. Even though I didn't really want to stop using heroin, I went to the center. I stayed there for sixty days.

Looking back, this was the best thing that ever happened to me. Before I got there, I believed once an addict, always an addict. I'd never be able to stop. They showed me a new way of life, a way to cope with being an addict. I decided to move to the area. There were four N.A. meetings each week and I went to all of them. I also got a sponsor and went to a lot of discussion meetings. It helped me to a degree, but the only time I felt strong was at a meeting or after one. Before the meetings, I was always thinking about getting high. This feeling lasted for about six months. Then some good things started to happen to me. They asked me to speak at a meeting. I felt part of the meeting that night. It made me feel good about what I was doing. I started to go to prison N.A. meetings and helped start new N.A. meetings.

Then I fell in love; looking back, I was in heat. This new life and everything in it was a new ball game. Now I not only had to deal with me, but with someone else, too. I was clean for one year and still not ready for all of these new things that were expected of me. I tried as hard as I could, and so did she. We moved to Western Pennsylvania. Unfortunately, there was no N.A. within 300 miles. So I went to the other 12 Step Programs for that year. They were all older than I, not that that should matter, but I felt alone. Well, I came home from work one day and my wife said, "Get out! I don't love you anymore!" I felt like someone had put a knife into my heart and turned it around a few times. With no possible reconciliation in sight, I leaned on a few people to get me through this adjustment. My sponsor suggested working the 12 Steps, and when your knees knock, kneel. Needless to say, I spent a lot of time on my knees. I also relied on N.A. literature because there were no N.A. meetings around. I asked God to come into my life and take some of the pain. He did. My life became a lot better and easier to bear after that.

Then God used me with the aid of other people in starting our first N.A. meeting in our area. At that time in our tri-state area, there was not one N.A. meeting in West Virginia, Ohio, or Western Pennsylvania. I did the best I could, as we all did. We now have approximately seventy-five meetings in a one-hundred mile radius. We have a hot line, an Area Service Committee, and a Regional Service Committee. I attended the World Service Conference two years ago. When I came back from there, I did some public information in radio, television, and newspaper.

A while later, 1 started to date the disc jockey from the radio station we broadcasted from. We had a lot of fun together. We went to the first East Coast Convention, where she was the disc jockey. We started to make plans for our marriage. As most normal relationships go, we had a fight on the phone one night. But a real shock came the next day when her mother called to tell me she had been killed in a car accident last night. I felt like killing myself. I knew there was pain coming, pain I didn't want to feel. I didn't want to turn to drugs either, because I knew that was not the answer. I called my friend and just started crying. He came over to my house and gave me a big hug and said, "Just tell me you didn't get high." Somehow I knew everything would be alright and I guess out of relief I started to laugh. I continued to rely on N.A. even more. I went to more meetings, talked about it and before I knew it the pain was easing and I was handling it without using drugs. I asked God to come into my heart and I thanked Him for putting her briefly into my life. Now I know that everything I have is only borrowed from God.

I met someone very special after that and got married. She is also in N.A. I am working on my seventh clean year. My life is a lot better today than it has ever been. I am happy and I feel good about myself. I still go to five meetings a week. It helps to be in contact with people who have the same problem as I have, addiction. All of my friends are through N.A. N.A. saved my life! N.A. is my life!

Chapter Twelve

IF I CAN DO IT, SO CAN YOU

My first introduction to drugs was at the age of fifteen. A friend gave me some speed and I fell in love. As I approached high school, I had the distinct impression that I could jump right over the building. I never forgot that surge of power which I associated with speed and I sought to recapture it for many years.

I think I was predisposed to addiction. Deep inside, I had feelings of inadequacy and inferiority. In my twisted thinking, it seemed logical that if I could stay up twenty-four hours a day, I could catch up with everyone and be as good as "them." It took a lot of pain and many years of abuse before I realized that no matter how much speed I did, I could never feel that I was OK.

The next eight years of my life were a nightmare of compulsive achievements coupled with large quantities of speed and other drugs. I graduated from high school at the age of sixteen, on the Dean's list. That was followed by two different Bachelor's degrees, both with honors. Yet, I still felt that it wasn't enough. I was caught in a deadly cycle. I knew that I couldn't go on to graduate school without speed, and I knew the speed was killing me.

111

In the process of my using, I tried many other drugs, Foolishly, I would boast of all the different drugs I had used. But, I made a distinction between "party drugs," such as hallucinogenics, alcohol, cocaine and marijuana, and "serious drugs" such as heroin and speed. I used speed because I thought I had a real need for it. I didn't know how to function without it. I figured there was something wrong with me—that I wasn't as efficient as other people and I had to constantly prove myself. I flaunted my degrees and my achievements in order to win acceptance. Today I know that those gnawing feelings of inferiority are a part of my addiction.

Drugs were my God and I prostrated myself before them. I lied to myself and to others, used people, conned them and stole from them. Deep down, I loathed myself for these actions, but I didn't know how to identify or express my feelings. My habit had progressed to the level where I would stay up for a week at a time. During these runs, I would become so irrational that I could not even carry on a conversation. I hallucinated visually and aurally, became extremely forgetful and, needless to say, irritable and grouchy. Then I would level off, and no matter how much speed I took, I couldn't get any higher. My body would ache for sleep, but my mind would race, and I was caught at a halfway point where I could neither stay up nor sleep. It was at these times when the inordinate paranoia and depression would set in. Sometimes I would try taking barbituates to put me to sleep, but I regularly became ill and vomited them up.

Many people, including my family, tried to convince me to give up drugs. But I was impatient with them, insisting that they just didn't understand. I justified my using, saying that I never used drugs "just for a good time," but only when I needed them—which became all of the time. I developed a passion for drugs. I would steal pills from people's medicine cabinets and look them up in a Physician's Desk Reference to see what they were for. Inevitably, I would develop the exact symptoms that that particular pill alleviated. There were no lengths to which I would not go to rationalize my using.

As with anyone who abuses mind-altering chemicals, my life was chaotic and unmanageable. I was well aware of it, but I never dreamed it had anything to do with my addiction. I blamed other people, neighborhoods, jobs and cities for the problems I was having. I tried the geographic cure six times, driving across the country, alone each time. Running scared, I always ran to the same place, Minneapolis, where I was raised, and San Diego where I went to school. I quit jobs at random and moved frequently. I got arrested, overdosed, and finally suicidal depression set in. But I still wouldn't give up my drugs.

What finally made an impression on me was a series of events which happened in rapid succession. My world started falling apart when my brother killed himself. Three months later, I experienced a sudden and severe hearing loss. The coup de grace was my boyfriend of three years breaking up with me. Devastated, I felt totally alone and abandoned. I couldn't communicate with anyone, and again, I felt that no one understood. Instinctively, I realized that the speed was the cause of my hearing loss. Terrified of losing my remaining hearing, I resolved never to use speed again. Not understanding my addictive personality, I thought if I abstained from speed, everything would be fine. But everything only got worse because I then began abusing alcohol, marijuana and food. Because I had no program or knowledge of my condition—only fear and resolution—the time came when I used again. This time, things were looking up for me. I had purchased a hearing aid and gone through therapy. I really felt like I had conquered my problems. I had no mental defense whatsoever. When it was offered, I indulged, without thinking twice about it. After I was high, I remembered—I had quit using drugs! Once again, I resolved never to use narcotics again. This time, I allowed myself "organic" drugs, like psylocybin, marijuana and mescalin. Surely they wouldn't harm like the speed had.

Ignoring my drug problem completely, I became concerned with my increasing weight. I got involved in another twelve step program, but experienced no success. For a year, I continued insanely abusing drugs, alcohol and food, but I kept going back to meetings. The members kept questioning me about my drug usage and suggested I try N.A. Finally, I agreed to go, only so they would stop bothering me about it.

I went to the N.A. meetings stoned and didn't remember anything I heard. I am not sure why I kept going back. Perhaps the love and acceptance in those rooms was what drew me. I continued this way for five months, calling myself clean because I was not using speed. But after a few months, I started sharing with other addicts that I was still using marijuana. To my surprise, they did not make any kind of judgment, but merely shared their own experience and how they had discovered they couldn't recover unless they abstained from all drugs. But I was overly sensitive and distrustful, I argued adamantly that marijuana wasn't a drug, that it was no worse than cigarettes. They only smiled and asked me to keep coming back. It took those five months of going to meetings, using, and watching them, for me to finally get some hope. Before, I hadn't believed that it was possible to give up drugs entirely, so I maintained I didn't want to (just in case I failed). But after five months, I began to believe it really was possible. I saw the same people week after week and they were still clean. I knew from the way they talked that they were true addicts just like me, and I began to feel that I belonged. Best of all, I began to feel hopeful. I saw a way out of the vicious circle my drugs had gotten me into.

The miraculous day of my last high came shortly after New Years' day. It was cold and raining in San Diego, and I was fed up with everyone. The holidays had been a let-down. I didn't get the gifts or attention I wanted, and a man that I had been dating rejected me. I proceeded to use all of my favorites, drugs, alcohol and food, straight into oblivion. Hours later, it stopped raining. I woke up and went out into the back yard. I wasn't wearing my hearing aids. As I stood looking down on a beautiful canyon, I began to pray. I didn't know to whom or what I was talking, but I was asking. I wanted what those people in N.A. had, "hope." I felt desperate, alone and helpless. When I finished my prayer, I stood quietly alone for a few minutes. Very soon I heard the sweet chimes of the phone ringing. It has never sounded so good as it did that day; I heard the phone ring fifty feet or more away without my hearing aids! I burst into joyful tears at just being able to hear it and ran all the way to answer it. The person on the other end was an N.A. member that I knew well. He asked me if I was going to a meeting that night. I hadn't even considered a meeting that night and I told him how I had gotten high again that day. His reaction was totally unexpected, he was concerned! It had never mattered to anyone before whether I got high or not. And, I must point out, that I was not romantically involved with this man. He merely expressed the concern of the N.A. fellowship. When I went to the meeting that night, and shared what had happened, many people gave me their phone numbers. They made me promise to call before I used again. Miracle that it is, I haven't used since.

Like the addicts who had shared with me, I found that growth began once I abstained from all drugs. I was successful in the other twelve step program, once I got clean. Those addicts encouraged me and assured me through all the ups and downs of my early recovery. They entreated me to get a sponsor, and I did. This woman patiently led me through the steps. My Higher Power, at first, was the N.A. fellowship. It represented goodness and caring, and I trusted those recovering addicts. But eventually, the time came when I was alone, in the middle of the day, with no meeting, and I wanted to use. I saw that I needed a Higher Power that would be with me twenty-four hours a day, just as my addiction is with me twenty-four hours a day. I began to pray "reveal yourself to me." I didn't know who I was talking to, but I did it for two weeks. What happened was that I began to see evidence of God in the people around me and even in my own life. So many things happened that were too "coincidental," there just had to be a God! It took some time to be able for me to trust my new Friend enough to work the Third Step. I had to get rid of all my old fears and ideas of the God I had grown up with.

Eventually, I made a decision to turn my will and my life over to the care of God as I understand Him. I went on with the steps and I began to change. My self-seeking, dishonesty and other character defects were revealed to me and they cause me pain. I no longer want to live the way I used to. I asked my God to remove my defects of character. But instead of magically disappearing, as I expected, He has been showing me where and when I'm doing them, and how to change. I saw that in order to get over my fear of people, I had to go to those I feared the most and make amends for my past behavior. When I stop being dishonest, I can stop hiding and I'm no longer afraid of being found out. I can look people in the eye with some self-respect because I've done my best to set matters right. I don't live the old way today.

All of my character defects haven't been removed. I'm not always serene and happy. I'm not cured or perfect yet. Every day I see areas where I need to grow. But I know today, that as I continue in the Fellowship of N.A., working the steps, listening to my sponsor and my Higher Power, I will continue to grow emotionally and spiritually. I pray on a daily basis, asking my Higher Power to help me stay clean one more day. I ask Him to run my life, and to give me the power to carry out His will.

I like the person I'm becoming as a result of working the steps. I've learned that as an addict, my natural disposition is to be high. In order for me to abstain from drugs, I've got to change. The Twelve Steps of Narcotics Anonymous are the only things that have ever changed me for the better. I can't possibly express in words the gratitude I feel for my recovery in N.A. For the first time, my life is precious to me! The fellowship is very dear to me also, and I share the gift of recovery through service. I have had several jobs in the service structure of N.A. and I find them rewarding as well as helpful. Service helps me to stay clean. There have been many times when I have wanted to mope over my own problems, and I have received a phone call from another member needing something. Inevitably, in trying to help them, I forgot about myself and my "horrible" problems and stayed clean another day.

My story is not unique. Hundreds of addicts have told their stories and I see how we are similar in some ways. If I can recover in the N.A. fellowship, so can you! If you are an addict, why not give yourself a chance and try N.A.? It costs nothing to join, and at least for me, I didn't have much left to lose.

Chapter Thirteen

AN INDIAN WITHOUT A TRIBE

Loneliness is something I've lived with for years. From the time I was a child, people always let me know I was different. This was fun for a while. In later years, my feeling of being different was one of the things that brought me to the Program of Narcotics Anonymous.

I grew up in a Texas town. I was one of those kids from the "other side of the tracks." I was the middle child, with a brother eight years older. I always wanted to be like him, so I would tag along with him and his friends. They used to get me loaded. I always got high to a point of not remembering what had happened the night before. This phase lasted about four years. My brother got busted, and that ended that.

I came down with hepatitis, and ended up in the hospital. This was the first of many institutions to come. The doctor told me to quit using drugs. He was the first to tell me I had a drug problem. I knew he was right. I thought that everyone had a place in life, and mine was to be a drug addict. I had accepted this fully. I didn't think anyone could change it. Not only after my bout with hepatitis, I returned to fixing drugs. I became addicted to heroin. I was fourteen years old. Heroin was the answer to all my problems. It made me feel like I could finally fit in. No longer did I feel different. All are equal in addiction.

I was kicked out of my house and I swore never to return. For the next three years I ran the streets, traveling all over the country, looking for that place where things would be different. I got busted for possession, so I joined the Army to beat the case.

This was going to solve my problems. I was shipped to Vietnam, where I really got further down in my addiction. Not long after I arrived there, I was arrested again. This time they sent me to a hospital in Germany for drug abusers. I really liked it there. There were plenty of drugs available, and they were really cheap. Mistakenly, I thought the hospital had cured me. Soon after I got out of the hospital, I was discharged from the Military for failure to rehabilitate. I was sent home with a drug habit.

The drugs on the streets weren't strong enough for me, so I ended up on a methadone program. This is what I thought "cleaning up" was.

Not long after I got home I was arrested again. This time I went to prison. That was in the latter part of 1974. I became institutionalized very quickly.

I was released from prison in 1977, right before Thanksgiving. I remember how frightened I was of all people. A part of me wanted to be back in prison. I got high to cover up those feelings. Before I knew it, there I was again, addicted.

I had a job and was working steady, but here I was, in the place I had become so familiar with, drug dependent. This was the beginning of the end, the start of my recovery. I was in a state of hopeless desperation; I just wanted to lay down and die.

I started looking for a methadone program, but none were available. My boss asked me the next day what was wrong with me. Before I knew it, I was telling him the truth. I said I was a drug addict. He asked me if I wanted help. I told him "yes."

This was the first of many spiritual awakenings. I went to a hospital in Louisiana, and from there to a halfway house. This is where I found Narcotics Anonymous. N.A. was the tribe I never had. I found the same type of people I had run with on the streets. There was something different about them. They had a peace I wanted.

The first six months of my recovery were hard. I couldn't talk without

118

making everything rhyme. I had no control over this, so I stayed frustrated. My head would jerk at the oddest times. My arms would fly up without my permission. Through all these problems, the people of the fellowship kept telling me to come back. I did.

I was told to get a sponsor, attend a lot of meetings, get phone numbers and get involved. I tried to do all these things. I was introduced to the steps and traditions. I got involved early in my clean time. I picked up ash trays, made coffee, and did everything I was asked to do. I gained some self-respect from these actions. Before, I had thought I was worthless. The people in the meetings loved me and guided me back to reality. Through working the steps and gaining a working knowledge of the traditions, recovery became exciting. My old patterns of behavior started to leave me. I didn't react to things in the same ways I had in the past.

I first got involved in Service work during my second month in N.A. This involvement has formed the backbone of my Program. It gave me a feeling that I had something to give.

I have had the good fortune to be involved with a lot of people all over the country who are doing the same thing I am; staying clean. I found that this Program works like my addiction did; it gives me all I need to keep from getting sick. When I was using, sometimes I would get "a little extra." Now, the same is true in the Program. I get that "little extra" with every spiritual experience, and my service work brings me one spiritual experience after another. This is what keeps me coming back. I go to meetings daily, and talk to someone who is doing the same thing I am; caring and sharing the N.A. way. This is what allows me to take a back seat and let my Higher Power take over the wheel.

I'll always be grateful to N.A. for taking me from the depths of my addiction and giving me life; one that is full of love and true concern for others. These are feelings I never thought could be possible for me. As long as I take it easy, and make a commitment with my Higher Power to do the best I can, I know I will be taken care of today. I've come to believe in miracles, for I am one.

Chapter Fourteen

IN SEARCH OF A FRIEND

I "turned on" with marijuana four years ago. I was thirty-five years old and had a very responsible job as office manager for a small firm. I was a "workaholic" and spent long hours and weekends at my job. I was always tired and without a social life other than sporadic one-night stands which never developed into any deeper relationships. I felt martyred and overworked.

I'd avoided street drugs even though my family had used them sporadically because they were illegal and I was a law-abiding WASP. I had had a few long-term encounters with prescription drugs — downers, pain killers, and weight loss pills in the past — but I never had a "problem" with them, because they were legal.

In 1977, the possession of marijuana was considered a misdemeanor in Oregon and many of my friends were getting high. I began spending weekends playing pinball for hours to relax with a friend who smoked pot regularly. We'd sit in the car while he got loaded, then play pinball till he came down. We'd return to the car and he'd smoke another joint. After a few months of weekends, I began encouraging him to smoke more often, because it made my pinball stroke better. After several months of my contact highs, I finally smoked my first joint and loved it. Within six weeks, I was buying $75 to $100 worth of marijuana a week. At first, I only smoked after work, to relax. I needed something "special" because I worked such long hours. I smoked every night, then from Friday night till the wee hours Sunday night. Soon I found being loaded helped my attitude driving in freeway traffic. I felt so mellow! So I began smoking on the way to work in the morning.

My lifestyle had suddenly changed. Everything seemed to be moving faster than I could handle it. I became very emotional and felt a sense of panic because I couldn't assimilate all the vivid new perceptions pot was showing me. I needed time to sit back and sort everything out.

Within ten months of my first joint, I'd quit my job, sold all my furniture, and was living out of my car. I lived on unemployment benefits for a while until they ran out, then I took a waitress job. I was unable to cope with any job that required concentration. I moved in with my sister and her children. Quite often there wasn't enough money to pay the rent, but I always had pot. I began feeling a daily despair and depression. I needed to get loaded to face each day.

A little over two years ago, some friends took me to another 12 Step Program to deal with my weight problem. During this long depression, I'd gained almost a hundred pounds. I began attending these meetings regularly, always loaded. I hated the meetings, but had nowhere else to go. Quite often I'd fall asleep there and wake up as the meeting ended and people were leaving.

I went to a marathon of this other Twelve Step Program last summer, and spent most of the time alone in the woods, getting loaded. However, I did ask a sponsor to read my Fourth Step inventory so I could complete Step Five. After reading my pages and pages of rambling "inventory," (I'd always been loaded when I wrote), she very gently suggested that I might want to "take a look" at my pot smoking sometime.

The marijuana didn't seem to be getting me high anymore, so about a month later I tried to quit—and I couldn't. I would try to go just one day without using, but would find myself pacing the floor unable to focus my concentration on anything else but pot. I thought I was going to go insane. I couldn't get high, but it hurt too much to not smoke dope.

I began looking for another connection who could supply something that would work for me.

One night at a meeting of this other Twelve Step Program, I'd listened to several people sharing their "experience, strength, and hope." I stood up when it was my turn and began to cry. I couldn't look those people in the eye. I felt like a hypocrite. The "rigorous honesty" of the program had me. I told them that I was loaded and had been at every meeting and function I'd attended. I felt like a thief. Several people put their arms around me and said "keep coming back!" I found a piece of paper in my hand with the phone number of Narcotics Anonymous and the names of several people who had been clean for a long time.

I went to my first N.A. meeting the next night, terrified. I knew I wasn't a "junkie" but I was hurting so badly I thought I might hear something that could help me not want to smoke any more dope.

A tall, blonde woman welcomed me and gave me a cup of coffee. I was so nervous and uncomfortable. I'd smoked a joint before leaving for a meeting, but it had not "gotten me off," and my jaws ached from clenching my teeth. She sat next to me and told me she'd stopped shooting heroin three years ago. She showed me ulcer scars on her legs, then introduced me to another woman who had a "problem" with marijuana and would be celebrating her first year clean in two weeks.

I cried all through the meeting. I felt such a sense of grief and loss, because pot had become my lover and husband, mother and father and best friend. And it wouldn't work anymore. After the meeting, these two women took me out for coffee, gave me their phone numbers and told me to call them. They suggested I attend ninety meetings in my first ninety days. I couldn't imagine how I could find the time to do that, but after the first three weeks of attending only one or two meetings a week and not smoking dope between meetings, I found the time! It was too uncomfortable when I was alone without dope. In the meetings, I heard things that kept me clean and hoping for peace till the next meeting.

I soon got a sponsor because I couldn't do it alone. I needed someone who could answer questions and reassure me that I could live without using drugs of any kind. That was a giant step for me—to reach out to someone and admit I needed support. And learning to trust another human being was a second giant step. I talk to her several times a week and, more importantly, I *listen* to her, I respect her, because she's been where I've been, and she's clean today. She helps me to work the steps of the Program and she cares about my life.

Through N.A., I've come to understand that I was an addict long before I ever used drugs. And I will be an addict as long as I live. But if I stay clean today from all mind-altering chemicals, I have a chance for a life of quality. Before N.A. found me, I felt something crucial to my survival missing in my life. As though at birth, every child had been issued a book of instructions on how to live—except me. My life was spent in quiet desperation, trying to figure out on my own how to do it. Today, through N.A. and my Higher Power, I've got my instructions: the Twelve Steps and the Program.

Chapter Fifteen

I WAS UNIQUE

I had nowhere to turn, I felt no one could help me, as my situation was so much different from that of anyone else's. I thought I was doomed to continue in an insane drive toward self-destruction that had already sapped me of any determination to fight. I thought I was too unique — that is, until I found the fellowship of Narcotics Anonymous. Since that day my life has taken on a new meaning and a new direction.

I came from a white middle-class background where success was almost assumed. I excelled academically and went on to medical school in California and in Scotland. I looked with smug disdain on my school-mates who were experimenting with drugs. I felt I was too good and too smart for that. I thought that a drug addict was a weak-willed, spineless creature who must have no purpose in life or sense of worth. I would not, or could not fall into that trap, as I was an achiever, winning at the game of life, and felt to have such great potential.

Sometime after having started my internship at a prestigious West Coast hospital I had my first experience with narcotics. Call it curiosity (I thought), but perhaps I was looking for "something better." I was amazed at the way patients in severe pain would relax when a small amount of morphine was injected into their veins. That was for me! Over the next few months several personal tragedies led to my world crumbling about me, and experimentation quickly led to abuse and then addiction with all the bewildering helplessness and self-condemnation that only the drug addict knows.

Shortly after having started my residency training in neurosurgery, I sought help from a psychiatrist, as the delusion that I could control my narcotic use finally evaporated. I was hospitalized in a mental institution for a few days until I felt better, and then convinced my psychiatrist that I was well enough to return to my training program. He was either naive, gullible, or ignorant (of drug addiction) enough to let me go merrily on my way. I lasted a few months before relapsing. With no changes made in my thinking or behavior, relapse followed relapse, and I established a pattern which I would maintain for almost ten years. I continued to try psychiatrists and mental institutions (five hospitalizations), but after each I would relapse again.

After having performed over one hundred surgical procedures while loaded, I was asked to leave my residency. Another hospitalization followed and I returned to my pattern of relapse. Besides institutionalization, over the years I have tried job changes, geographical relocation, self-help books, methadone programs, only using on weekends, switching to pills, marriage, health spas, diets, exercise, and religion. None of it worked other than temporarily. I was told I was incorrigible and there was no hope for me based upon my track record.

After about five years of heavy using, I started to develop a physical allergy to my drug of choice; insidiously at first, but progressively, each time I used, a small amount of tissue would die around the injection site. This soon led to open sores and draining wounds. I found I could prevent the process by using cortisone initially, but after several more years it returned in spite of the cortisone. In the meantime, I developed all the attendant side effects of the cortisone, e.g., obesity, acne, ulcers and propensity toward infection (as my immune mechanism was knocked out). By the time I reached my last hospitalization, I had a large open wound in the left forearm with exposed infected bone. I had destroyed several tendons so that I could not raise my wrist and the scar tissue prevented me from extending my forearm. On admission, I was very heavy and my hands and feet were swollen and full of fluid. I must have been a sight to behold as I was a physical wreck. Worse yet, I was totally demoralized and suffering from a spiritual bankruptcy of which I was unaware. The denial and self-deception were so great that I hated to see what a pitiful creature I had become.

I entered a chemical abuse treatment facility in San Diego and there, for the first time, was confronted by physicians who were addicts themselves. They asked me first if I wanted help, and then if I was willing to go to any lengths to recover. They explained I might have to lose all my worldly possessions, my practice, my profession, my wife and family, even my arm. At first I balked. I figured there was nothing wrong with me that a little rest and relaxation could not set right. But instead, I made a pact with them: that I would listen and take orders without questioning. I had always been independent and this was certainly a change for me. This was my first introduction to the "tough love" which has helped me so much in N.A.

During that month in the hospital, a great change came over me. I was forced to go to outside N.A. meetings. At first I was rebellious. These people were not like me; they were common street people, junkies, dope fiends, pill heads, and coke freaks. How could I relate to them? They had not come from where I had. They had not experienced what I had experienced. They had not achieved what I had achieved. Yet when I listened, I heard my story, again and again. These people had experienced the same feelings, the sense of loss, doom and degradation which I knew. They too had been helpless, hopeless, and beaten down by the same hideous monster as I had. Yet they could laugh about their past and speak about the future in positive terms. There seemed such a balance of seriousness and levity with an overpowering sense of serenity, that I ached for what they had.

I heard about honesty, tolerance, acceptance, joy, freedom, courage, willingness, love and humility. But the greatest thing I heard about was God. I had had no problem with the concept of God as I had called myself a believer. I just could not understand why He had let me down. I had been praying to God as a child asks Santa Claus for gifts,

127

yet I still held on to my self-will. Without it, I reasoned, I would have no control over my life, and could not survive. It was pointed out to me that perhaps that was the whole problem. I was told that perhaps I should seek God's will first and then conform my will to His. Today, I pray only for His will for me and the power to carry it out on a daily basis and all is well. I have found that His gifts are without number when I consistently turn my will and my life over to His care.

I have now found a new home in the fellowship of Narcotics Anonymous. My life again has meaning. I have found that I have but one calling in life and that is to carry the message to the addict who still suffers. I am so grateful to God and N.A. that I may do this today.

I have found that you people are just like me—I am no longer better than nor less than—I feel a real love and camaraderie in the fellowship of N.A. My great spiritual awakening has been that I am an ordinary addict—I am *not* unique. There are still those who refuse to join us and take the path we have chosen because they too feel they are unique. They may die. But may God bless them too.

Chapter Sixteen

I FOUND A HOME

From the time I was a little girl I can remember feeling like I didn't quite belong. I thought I must be an alien from another planet. It seemed I always said and did the wrong things at the wrong time. I felt like there was a big empty hole inside of me, and I spent the next twenty years trying to fill it.

I always wanted desperately to fit in somewhere. I always seemed to feel better being one of the guys, so I usually just stayed around men. I didn't really understand or trust girls.

I had a very low self-image, I realize now I hated myself. I wished I could be somebody, anybody, other than me. I felt like a loser and, looking back on it now, that's probably why everybody treated me like one. I was a victim by choice, but I didn't know it.

The first drug I ever used was vodka, after which I blacked out, and then passed out. The first time I smoked marijuana was the same way. I had heard marijuana didn't do much, so I smoked four joints in a row just to make sure. It worked!

It didn't take long for me to find harder drugs and start using them. I was afraid of a lot of things, but trying out new drugs wasn't one of them.

More and more I now started to depend heavily on drugs to make me feel better, or at least different. I guess I wanted to get loaded and stay that way forever.

The longer I got loaded, the more it seemed people were getting in my way. After awhile it seemed everybody was against me. I decided people were my problem and I didn't want anything to do with them.

What I thought I needed to get free of them was money, so I went to work. I was fifteen and was determined to make enough money so I wouldn't need anybody ever; I could just get loaded and stay that way with no one to hassle me.

During the time I was getting loaded, I tried a lot of different life styles hoping to fit in somewhere. I went to San Francisco to become an intellectual, sipping expresso and reading poetry. I've tried to be a hippie, an earth mama, a river rat and a desert bunny. I spent a while driving around in Cadillacs with lawyers and stockbrokers. But, wherever I went or whomever I was with, I was loaded, and I was still me. Nothing seemed to fit and I always ended up alone.

I drank, dropped, snorted, smoked, and sniffed my way through the next seven years until something terrifying began to happen. I could take more and more and more drugs, but I would pass out before I ever got that good feeling. I guess the feelings I had always run away from could not be pushed down any longer. They were eating me alive. I tried and tried to use more to get that good feeling back, but all I got was more and more afraid. I didn't know what was happening to me. I couldn't turn my head off. I became more and more afraid of people until I was just living like a hermit.

I felt a lot of humiliation and degradation during my addiction. I did a lot of things loaded I am grateful I don't have to do today.

In the last few years, before I got to Narcotics Anonymous, I really believed I was going insane. I was intent on self-destruction. I tried suicide many times.

In desperation, I went to a psychiatrist. Usually they can be of little help to addicts, but this man, thank God, knew about this Program. He said, "I can't help you, you're an addict."

I was shocked. I had always thought drugs were the answer, not the problem. Didn't everybody take drugs? Drugs were my life. I didn't know how to give them up.

He told me about a hospital where I could get help. I could no longer work or care for myself. I knew I was crazy. I was physically, emotionally, and spiritually empty, and I was very, very scared.

At my first Narcotics Anonymous meeting, I knew I had come home. I had finally found people who were just like myself. I was still scared of everyone, but somehow I knew this was my last chance at life. If I couldn't make it here, it would be the end for me.

Three times I got 89 days clean, only to use again. My disease was more powerful than I had ever imagined. What scared me is that now I really wanted to stop, but found I could not.

Finally, I realized I was still trying to do it alone. I could not stay clean without these people. They had something I desperately wanted. I had heard that if I put as much into the Program as I did into using I could make it.

I got closer to the Program and got a sponsor and called her every day. I went to meetings every night, started trying to work the steps, and just hung on.

Through the Grace of God I have not taken a fix, pill or drink for five years.

Desperation drove me to Narcotics Anonymous, and desperation is what has kept me coming back. I am grateful for the bottom I finally hit because that has given me the willingness to work the steps, go to meetings, and just "LIVE ONE DAY AT A TIME."

I used to wonder "What am I going to do if I don't get loaded?" Today it seems like there aren't enough hours in the day. I have real friends today, including girl friends, and they are very special to me.

The program is my life today. All the pain I felt in using led me only to more pain, but every ounce of pain I experience in the program, staying clean, brings me more growth, and more peace. I have found that the only way that empty place inside me can be filled is through the steps of this program.

The things I have learned since coming here would fill this book. I never knew how to live, and the Program is teaching me for the first time. I am finally facing the old enemy, me. I am learning to accept myself, and even to like myself, a day at a time. I know today I need the people in Narcotics Anonymous, the ones who were here before me, and those who have come in after me.

I don't feel I can ever fully repay what this program has given me, because it gave me my life. Thank you N.A. for being there!

Chapter Seventeen

IF YOU WANT WHAT WE HAVE

My name is Bill, and I'm a junkie and a juicer. For many years of my life I felt the world had dealt me a cruel hand which left me with many inadequate feelings. Fear ate a hole in me that I was never able to fill up with drugs and alcohol.

I was born in Alabama in 1933. My father's job required constant moving which always produced new schools and faces. I was small and sickly and the insecurities and inadequacies around people increased. I fought these feelings verbally and with my fists. Punishment in some fashion followed me everywhere.

My father died when I was seven and I remember the hate I felt because he had left an only child to fend for himself. A grandmother, aunt and mother spoiled me rotten. Every time the church door was open, I was there. At the age of ten, everyone in the family thought baptism was in order. I didn't feel any different when I got up than when I knelt down. Control was the name of the game. I tried to control everyone in our little family and outside, including the nun who caught me stealing cold drinks in a convent where I was taking music.

Another form of punishment I felt was rejection. My mother married a man who later proved to be an addict. We moved to another city and the war within me intensified. Continuous fighting at home created more fear and insecurities. When I was away, I hated my home and resented the people in it. Drawing upon different concepts, I began another way of living. It did not matter to me what lengths I had to go in order to gain love and approval from everyone. Up went the false front; more dishonesty and deceptions. I was to spend many years of my life trying to be something that I was not.

Relief came at the ripe old age of sixteen in the form of alcohol at a dance. Immediately my fear of girls was gone. My two left feet disappeared, and I knew exactly when and where to lay my new found wisdom of people. The effect left, and I was back at war with me.

I believed rules were made to be broken. Society's laws were not for me. They hampered my way of living, and I began to deal with reality the only way I knew, and that was using the drug alcohol. This is the only drug I was aware of in the late forties, and I used it to ease the pain. At this time, this was the best way to cope with them. Anyone could punch my buttons if I thought it was needed for their approval of me.

After a small skirmish with school officials and city authorities, private school was necessary to finish high school. Two years of college proved even further that this world and everything in it was full of crap.

I cared for no one at this stage of the game. However, I met a young lady who met all of my requirements. She was from an old family, very regal in appearance and possessed all of the social graces. We ran off and got married and I entered into a new relationship that I was not mature enough to handle.

I fancied myself in the future as the old southern gentleman, broad brim hat, bow string tie, overlooking his vast domain with a mint julep in one hand and a gold cane in the other. Material things were the basis for happiness in my life at this time. I looked either up to people or down, depending on their seeming net worth. After attaining a lot of these things, happiness and peace of mind did not come. My salary as purchasing agent at a large hospital was not enough. Stealing to support my materialistic ambitions was necessary. The salesmen soon found my vulnerable spot, wine, women and song. They began to supply my demand.

Drinking and partying every night soon made a physical wreck out of me. In the latter part of 1954, I was introduced to a little goodie called codeine by a salesman to draw a clean breath. Something was cruising in me every moment of every day.

I was 21 years old and a full blown addict. Routine encounters of addicts and alcoholics treated at the hospital convinced me that I was unique. I would never become like they were.

The standards and expectations I set for myself and others were too high to be met. Negative thinking and escapism became my total personality. Greediness compelled me to study drugs and experiment. This may have saved my life while I was using. I feared certain combinations in trying to get off.

The sixties came along and I decided I needed a change. I left the hospital for what I thought were greener pastures and began to travel. Life was still hell. That old nest of negativism followed me everywhere I went. Jobs came and went, then they came no more. The jails and hospital stays were more frequent and longer.

In 1973 I came into a mental ward chained like an animal. My psychiatrists, who I constantly conned over the years, knew of my alcohol problem, but not of my other addictions. It was suggested that I try a Twelve Step Program. My family was willing to try anything, so off I went for all the wrong reasons. People there were kind and helpful to me, so I began to use them as I had others all my life. They had never seen me clean and dry, so how were they to know if I was using. I was very careful not to talk about too much of anything lest they become suspicious. Deception and denial were the name of the games that I played and they almost killed me. At this time I had gotten off the hard stuff on to downers, uppers and mood elevators. People there seemed happy and sober and I wondered what they were using. I do not believe there was a fragment of honesty in me at the time. Willingness to change never crossed my mind. Gambling, women and continuing to use were my bag. For over three years I lived in hopelessness and despair going back to using, and going back to the Program.

After hearing the Higher Power concept and about a spiritual way of life, I knew drugs were not for me. I had at one time a God graciously given to me by my environment, whom I did not understand. I knew his God did not want anything to do with something like me.

There were times when I tried to relate, but there seemed to be something missing. I sincerely think that even though the feelings seemed the same there seemed a lack of deeper understanding that I needed. God bless them, they tried. There were no recovered addicts in the area and no N.A. I looked for people with other drug dependencies and finally found one lady in the group. She had spent ten years in and out without any success.

Things did get a little better. There were no arrests and no stays in the hospitals for a period of two years. Then in the fall of 1975 everything went to pieces. Back to the hospital I went. Exchanging the alcohol for pills, I was back in the old paradox again. Then a series of events began that changed my life. There was talk of committing me to the state institution. My family no longer wanted me like I was. Two Program members came one afternoon to see me and they both told me the same thing; that I wasn't crazy, to come back, don't use, and ask for help.

My sponsor, who had fired herself several times from my case, picked me up and took me to a meeting. The girl who rode with us spoke that night; she talked about God of her understanding. Sitting next to my wife that night I began to see where I had missed the boat. I went back to that dark room and thanked God for those people, because somehow I knew they cared. Even though they did not understand many things about me, they gave me time out of their lives and asked for nothing back. I remember the Eleventh Step in the Program and I thought maybe, just maybe if I asked for knowledge of His will for me and the power to carry it out, He might help. I got a little brave, knowing I wasn't honest, I added "P.S., Please help me get honest." It would have been great to say that I left that hospital and never have used again, but it didn't happen that way. It was almost like all the other confinements I had experienced. I came out of that hospital with exactly what I went in with: me!

Thanksgiving, Christmas, and New Years passed just like a wink, blink and a nod, and I was still praying. Everything got worse. My family kicked me out the day after New Years and I knew it was hopeless, but I was still asking for honesty and on or around the fifth of January, I began to ease off the pills I was using. It wasn't any fun, but I know today that all the suffering was necessary. Praying and tapering off had become my obsessions. I felt that this was my last chance.

I took my last pill, shot, etc., in March. By God's grace I was clean! People began to tell me, look what you have done, and I began to believe them. I got to looking so good to me I just invited me out for a drink. What a rude awakening. I came off that drunk cold turkey, no pills, nothing, for the first time in over 21 years. For five days I shook and I mean shook, and on the fifth day I wanted no more. I sat down in my little V.W., bowed my head and told God, "if this was all in life for me, I wanted life no longer. Death would be far more merciful. It doesn't make any difference any longer." I felt a peace come into me that I had never felt before. I don't know how long this lasted and it doesn't matter. It happened and that is the important part. Since then, I have experienced the same feeling from time to time. It was like being brought forward from darkness to light. God doesn't let me stay in the sunlight too long, but he will help me if I choose to stay in the twilight. I walked away from that car a free man. I did not realize this for a long time. Since that day I have not had a desire to use.

A God of my understanding had sent me enough honesty to get started down the right path. I went back to the Program and again I made another mistake. I kept my mouth shut with the intention of letting the winners teach me how to become clean. Today I know for me I walked a different path through addictions and I had to walk a different path through this Program. I had to learn about me. For almost two years in the program I saw people come and go with addictions other than alcohol. One night in Birmingham, I was sharing with a group and also talking about drugs when a man approached me with tears in his eyes. He told me of his son and daughter somewhere hooked on drugs. He said, surely God must have some program for people like them. All the way back home that night I talked to a girl using drugs; a schoolmate of my wife's. The telephone gave us the answer through some new friends from Georgia and Tennessee in Narcotics Anonymous. A visit to share in Chattanooga proved to be a blessing. Several people came up from

Atlanta, and one guy from Marietta who kept telling people that he loved them. I was 44 years of age at the time and that was the first time a man had ever told me he loved me. For some unexplainable reason, I also felt this love. A couple of months later we went to Atlanta and found a repetition of our first trip. I wanted so much to give and feel as these people did. At the close of the dance that night, I overheard something that went like this, "If you want what we have, you have got to take the steps."

I came back to Alabama and began to take the steps. I learned about me and found God of my understanding. Trust God; Clean House; Help Others; explains it as simply as I can. I spent many years looking for something around the corner, or someone coming down the street who would give me happiness and peace of mind. Today through the steps and the people in N.A., I have found a solution. I have to stay honest with me, stay open minded enough to change and be willing to accept God's love for me through the members of N.A.

I am very grateful to our brothers and sisters in Georgia for their tolerance and support during our first year or so in the Program in Alabama. They more or less sponsored me in those early days. Just knowing they were there was very comforting. Many times I called my friend in Marietta, despondent over the way things were going. He always seemed to have the answer. Keep the doors open and God will do the rest.

N.A. groups now have sprung up in several cities and now those people are sponsoring me through their growth in N.A. and God's grace. I finally got it all together, but without God's help I forget where I put it.

There is one thing I feel I can give to every addict to use. I love each and every one of you, and most important, God loves you too! This I found in the wonderful Program of N.A., through God's grace and you people. Come join us; it works!!!

Chapter Eighteen

I QUALIFY

My name is Iris. I'm a drug addict. In the beginning of my clean time, I didn't think N.A. was the place for me. Then again, the stories from the other fellowship didn't relate either. But I sure wasn't as bad as these "dope fiends" that I found myself in the middle of. Since that time—almost three years ago—my ideas have most certainly changed.

I'm the oldest of four. I'm the only one in my immediate family who has any such problem. I figure I started out as a pretty happy kid. We didn't have much money but we were close. Recently, someone said, "a drug addict is nothing but an experienced escape artist." I can relate. My career of running or escaping started after a crisis at age eleven. I went through a lot of pain and humiliation. At first I ran physically—later mentally. I escaped reality through books, TV, sleep, etc. I was very much a loner—but only because I felt no one wanted to be around me. I figured I wasn't pretty enough, wasn't smart enough, wasn't rich or popular enough, and I wasn't funny or witty enough. Everybody was better than I was. At home, I became the black sheep, causing embarrassment and shame. Once I tried to commit suicide thinking the world would be better off without me.

I started drinking and smoking pot heavily the summer after I graduated. I started college for two years to be a secretary because that's what a girl is "supposed" to be. In college, I couldn't handle the pressure. I went to a doctor complaining of headaches and was introduced to barbiturates. I started off taking as prescribed. By the end of that first week I felt "GOOD." I felt so happy and carefree. I even liked Iris! The day was nice and fresh, and I even bounced when I walked. I remember looking at the bottle of pills thinking, "I'm going to hold on to these." And I did—faithfully for the next three years.

To put it simply, I thought pills were the answer to my problem—then the answer became the problem. There was no real "fun" involved. From the beginning, I was using pills to cope. I remember somewhere along the line someone saying. "You're going to get addicted to those things." As long as they made me feel this good—I didn't care. Then I found out what addiction was really about.

After only six months of taking barbituates daily, I remember going through my first withdrawal experience when I couldn't get around to anything. After that week, I thought I'd be starting over again. Little did I know. By this time I had stopped drinking.

I was a bit of a loner to start with. Life was turning bad again. I had a car accident that I never dealt with. I started building a bigger wall around myself and I "needed" something to calm me down enough to drive. I "needed" a little help to get me through work. I "needed" a little something for the courage to talk to people and even my family. Time became nothing but a gray haze where nothing seemed to matter. For me, therapy was a joke. I graduated college on the Dean's list but couldn't sell myself, so I ended up with two part time jobs. One was a Christmas job selling. There I learned to put on a show so that no customer would leave without a smile on their face. I felt that "the show" was all there was to my personality. In the other job, I was a clerk typist. Quickly, I came to believe the girls there hated me. At a Christmas party I decided, out of fear, to stop the pills and limit the drinks. .By the end of the third drink, the party seemed to stop and all I could think of was another drink. Back at the office, things got so bad that one day I came in with ear plugs and told everyone I had an inner ear infection in both ears.

140

If you wanted to talk to me, you had to tap me on the shoulder. That was one of the last bricks in my wall; blocking out the world.

At home, I slept 10 to 12 hours a day. I tried to "control" and even stop drugs but I couldn't. I wondered what happened to the flower children and drug addicts of the 60's — were they all dead? And what was going to happen to me? Depression was a normal state of mind. There was no conversation between me and my family. My only enjoyment in life was watching TV. I remember rocking back and forth in bed thinking, "no one knows loneliness like I do." I felt like a walking corpse. The only emotion I had was hate and that was directed at myself. Later, I found out everyone was waiting for me to commit suicide — they didn't know what to do. The only thing I remember of my family at that time was my dad hated me and in that gray haze, my mom was a warm soft light that was out there somewhere. She always seemed to love me no matter what I did. I didn't understand.

When the time came that my Higher Power took control of the situation (against my will), a series of events happened that got me to break down and turn to my mom for help. I said, "Mom, I think I have a problem with drugs." She said, "Well, we're going to the doctor's today. Maybe he can give you something to help." We were so ignorant, but it felt so good to share. . .and cry.

Things then started to move real quick. First detox. I loved it. My own room, TV, telephone, and all the hot water I wanted. My own private world. I didn't have to deal with anyone. I only went to a rehab so that I wouldn't have to return home so quick. I started to get into a romance until someone asked me, "What do you have to offer him?" I didn't have much to offer at that time and I knew it. I did learn about drug addiction and was given some tools to work with. Again, I only went to the halfway-house because I didn't want to go home and back to my old way of life. At the halfway-house, I learned how to live clean and to use the tools.

The main tool, the basis of my clean time, was meetings. I attended my first N.A. meeting in the rehab. The only thing I remember about that meeting was this one guy who looked so good that if he spoke to me, I'd melt. Later, I was told — doesn't matter why you come in the beginning—just come. So I came. And I strutted, and I smiled, and I did what I could for a cookie, a compliment, a look, or a stroke. My ego needed anything it could get. At that time—I still didn't really know what being clean was all about—but I kept coming back. Eventually, I started coming for me. I realized I'm a drug addict in many ways. I may not have taken a great variety of drugs. I may not have done the things other "drug fiends" have done, I may not have gone as far down the road—but only because I didn't have the opportunity. I am a drug addict, not only because of the drugs, but because of the defects as well. Because of the lying, manipulating, conniving, self-will, thieving, and escaping—I qualify.

I also found out that drugs were only a symptom of a disease. With meetings and the help of the people in those meetings and my Higher Power—I started to grow. I got rid of the fear and the guilt. My confidence was built up. I learned how to handle pressure and responsibility. I learned to reach out one hand "for" help and the other hand "to" help. I learned how to make friends and I learned respect for myself. I could go on and on. The main thing is, I'm growing by using the tools of the Program. Thank God for the N.A. Program. I'm alive. I'm free, and I have a lot to offer—today.

Chapter Nineteen

WHY ME? WHY NOT ME?

My God what am I doing here! Why am I in so much trouble? What am I going to do? Nothing had gone right for me in such a long time. Was I going crazy? Was there hope for me in this horrible existence I called life? The only words I could describe my life with at this time are fearful, desperate, aimless, and hopeless.

As I thought of my past with remorse and disgust, I tried to think of anything I had done or accomplished which was positive in any way. I had three beautiful children, a wife, two cars, a new house, and a good job. However, I could not think of a single thing in my life to be grateful for. I felt as though I was a complete failure, with nothing left to live for.

For the past fourteen years, I had been drinking heavily, and had experienced numerous consequences due to drinking, but I thought that was part of the game of being a responsible adult. I never liked responsibility, and made a point to avoid it whenever possible.

I was introduced to narcotics completely by accident. The accident was due to my drinking at 7:00 a.m. while driving. I suffered a broken neck in a head-on collision, and was taken to the hospital. I learned to enjoy the life of being waited on and having no responsibility. This was exactly what I thought I had been looking for; soap operas and narcotics. I recall the hospital staff telling me I was an excellent patient. With all this encouragement, I devised many lies and cons to ensure a lengthy stay at their wonderful institution. Little did I know that I was setting a pattern of thinking that was to last many years, and that would be a very destructive force to my family and lifestyle.

After being released from the hospital, I returned to alcohol. I thought I missed all the benefits of having a good time, so I went after all the gusto I could handle; the countless days and nights I spent praying to the porcelain altar, the smashed fingers in car doors, the fights with my wife and family. All this, just to escape responsibility. As I continued to become more insecure with my actions and attitudes, I went even deeper into the bottle. I felt as though there was something horrible always ready to happen to me.

I was seemingly satisfied with my alcohol use, and only occasionally thought of drugs. I still thought about the wonderful treatment I had received at the hospital, and occasionally fantasized myself back there being a wonderful patient. For a period of six years, I had been unable to laugh and enjoy living. I was just a miserable human shell. My attitudes were negative, and I had started to suffer physically, acting out my fantasies, and looking for sympathy.

Recalling the thought of my treatment in the hospitals, I was impelled to seek medical help for my ailments. I had developed stomach ulcers, due to what I thought was a bad diet and a very demanding job. I had begun to have problems with my knees, because I seemed to fall down a lot. After playing a good con on the doctor, I was finally hospitalized for tests. This was the beginning of the end. I had been able to convince the doctors that I was suffering from incurable and painful diseases. When I was released from the hospital, I was given scripts for various kinds of narcotics and downers to help me eliminate my suffering. I continued drinking alcohol while taking my drugs. I became such an excellent patient, that I was hospitalized twenty-three times in four years. During this time, I had surgery after surgery — even to the point of having my stomach removed. All just to insure my drug supply.

I was becoming a physical, mental, and spiritual mess. The constant conflict inside of myself was more than I could deal with. With an ever increasing amount of narcotics, I was able to function as a human being. I would even convince my children to watch their dad use a needle with his medicine, so that they would not fear the needle when it was their turn to get medicine.

In the fall of 1979, I had an accident at work, where my hand was caught in a machine. As it happened, I looked at the machine operator and told him, "It's a good thing I'm on drugs, or I'd be very mad." Nothing that was happening to me made any difference, as long as I was taking my medicine. I had no idea that I might have a problem with drugs. Many times, I thought I may be taking too many, but I never thought I would have any problem quitting whenever the pain was gone.

I was getting drugs from the drugstore, (writing my own scripts), at an alarming rate. It was quite a job to record and keep track of all the drugstores I'd used every day. There were times when I'd wish I would get caught, just so I could end the existence I was experiencing. Three days after my discharge from the hospital from my accident at work, my wish came true. In desperation, I tried to pass a bad script, which I had written with my hand in a cast. I can't describe the fear I felt when the druggist made her phone call. Before I knew what was happening, I was in serious trouble.

I considered running, suicide, insanity, anything to help me get out of this jam I was in. I recall the thoughts I had as I was talking to the police. They were the same thoughts I'd had many times before. Perhaps I could act very innocent and naive; after all, this was my first offense. I made a plea to see my doctor. The police would see I was terrified, and hurting as any drug addict hurts when he can't get drugs. I was told to see the doctor and get help. I instantly thought that I was going to get over on the law, if they saw I was serious about getting help.

Through the doctor and other friends, I was sent to a drug rehabilitation center back in my home state. This was going to be my ticket out of trouble. I just had to comply with their program, and that's all the law would need to drop charges against me.

I went into rehab, knowing that I took too many drugs. While I was doing my time, I was asked questions like: "Do you think you're an addict? Do you think you may have a problem with alcohol? How do

145

you deal with anger?'' I answered these questions with: "possibly; no; I've never been angry a day in my life." I knew I was in trouble when they diagnosed me as a pathological liar.

I had many problems facing me when I got out of rehab. The law didn't go away, my wife was very bitter about the fact that I could do anything like that at all, my job was on the line because of my inability to function at work, and I didn't have very much money to pay the bills I had incurred.

Many things were happening to me, and I didn't know what to do. The rehab gave me the tools and knowledge of my drug addiction, but I needed something to give me the tools I needed for my inability to cope with the things happening to me in my life.

One of the things I was told to do in the rehab was to go to N.A. meetings. Ninety meetings in ninety days. I didn't know what to expect, but I would try them anyway. What did I have to lose? The court also gave me their version of an after-care plan. It was attend a meeting every day for three hundred sixty-five days. It was easy to comply with their plan. If I didn't, I was to go to jail for seven to ten years.

I was resigned to the fact that I was going to be going to meetings for a while, so I "may as well make the best of them." I did the things that were suggested to me. Now, I was going to be clean and serene. WRONG. Thank God I stayed clean, but in the last two years, serenity has been interrupted on many occasions.

After one year clean, my wife just couldn't understand why I was still going to meetings every day, and leaving her and the children alone so much. When I told her that I now planned to attend meetings of Narcotics Anonymous, even after my sentence was fulfilled, she just went absolutely off center, making sure I knew she didn't like that at all. I had picked a sponsor by now, and I was constantly crying to him with my problems. He told me to say the Serenity Prayer. I couldn't believe he would tell me something so idiotic. How could that help my situation? I was being very negative in all situations in my life. I was told to work the Steps of Recovery of N.A. One thing I had not done was to come to believe that a Power greater than myself could restore me to sanity. I had known all along that I was powerless over my addiction, and that my life was unmanageable, but I just didn't have the faith I needed to be restored.

The next few months were very tough for me. I got divorced. When I was able to look at the entire scope of my relationship with my wife, I found that we were married for all the wrong reasons. I had never known what true love or true caring was all about. I was totally selfish in every relationship I had ever been in.

I was hurt. My ego had been crushed. I was humiliated. I have come to believe that humiliation is nothing more than being humbled against my own will. With this major trauma in my life, I found a Power greater than myself. I found through the fellowship of N.A. that I could either be very miserable with my situation, or I could accept it and carry on. All these words still didn't stop the hurt. What finally did stop the hurt and pain I was feeling was the suggestion I took to get active in the Fellowship of N.A. It started with picking up ash trays; now I am able to serve the people who saved my life in various ways.

One thing that was given to me from the beginning was "Keep coming back—it works." Thank God for N.A.

Since that time, I have tried to be a little more caring and loving when I deal with people. The first relationship I had with another addict made me see even more how much of my pride, ego, self-centeredness, and lack of faith I still have. The program of N.A. is a new way of life for me, and it is taking me a long time to learn how to live. You see, I'm as close to death as the person coming off the street, clean one day. All I have to do is take any form of drug, and I'm dead.

Today, I am experiencing a freedom I have never had. This freedom is the idea that no matter what happens to me today, God and I can handle it, if I don't use drugs. Sometimes I still want to be a little crazy, (especially where women are concerned), but it is getting better.

WHY ME?   BECAUSE I'M AN ADDICT, AND GOD HAS BEEN VERY, VERY GOOD TO ME.

WHY NOT ME?   BECAUSE THE LARGEST ROOM IN THE WORLD IS THE ROOM FOR IMPROVEMENT.

Chapter Twenty

JAILS, INSTITUTIONS AND RECOVERY

I first came to Narcotics Anonymous in a state prison. It was my third term in prison over a seven year period, with only a few months at any one time in the streets.

In this prison, one night, I heard of a meeting going on about something to do with drugs. Well, I could relate to this, so I decided to check it out. Besides, it would get me away from the cell for awhile.

I can remember how confused I was leaving the first meeting. Back in my cell, I dwelled on all those years in and out of jails and all the things I'd been through just to get loaded. Most of all, I began thinking of how tired I was of living this kind of life. This group called Narcotics Anonymous (N.A.) seemed then to be a little too much for me. I told myself that I wasn't a hardcore dope fiend, but just a guy who liked to get loaded every day and a thief who could not stay out of jail. Although in those first meetings I did not see N.A. as a solution to my craziness, I did hear some things I could relate to, so I kept going back. I heard the people in N.A. say they didn't take drugs anymore, not even grass. I listened. Sure I wanted to stop all the insane situations in my life, but I didn't think I had to give up drugs altogether to do it. I thought all I needed was to learn how to handle it better.

Some of the N.A. members who came into the prison to share at these meetings had been inmates themselves, and said they attributed the change in their lives to the support of Narcotics Anonymous; one addict sharing and helping another addict. I enjoyed hearing these people tell how it was, and how it is today, and soon felt a real kinship in the pain we had all been through. I began respecting these people in N.A. who talked about how they found a way to live without drugs, alcohol and jails.

I continued to get stoned in the institution whenever and whatever way I could while still attending Narcotics Anonymous meetings regularly. The members told me to keep coming back no matter what, so I did. Besides, it sure beat talking that talk in the yard.

Soon, I was to be transferred for pre-release to a much looser security prison. I had been there before and gotten busted for smoking grass, for which I was sent to a more maximum prison. Now, as I was packing my property for this transfer, I remembered a lot of trouble I had gotten into at this institution, for the sake of getting loaded. The "Man" knew me there, and I was pretty nervous now, thinking about being eye-balled from the time I stepped off that bus. I was already thinking hard about getting loaded when I could, and scared stiff inside knowing what would happen if I got caught again.

So, I smoked a joint that morning before the long bus ride. I didn't know it then, but this was to be my last. Back in the beginning when I was attending these N.A. meetings, I would wonder why it wasn't working for me like it did for others. I was tired of this drug and institutional life, but at that point, I guess I wasn't tired enough, because I was still using when going to the meetings. I had a decision to make on that bus ride which was paid for by the Department of Corrections. The decision I made that day was mostly out of fear, and some things I heard in those first N.A. meetings.

I remember being in that bus, moving down the highway with chains wrapped around my waist and shackles on my feet; uncomfortably looking up at a resentful guard behind a cage with that shotgun. Staring out the window as the miles of freedom passed me by, I wondered why I couldn't be a part of that world. Getting loaded did not feel right anymore, yet, thinking about not taking anything sure felt strange. What a relief, when sometime later, I learned that this was easier doing it just one day at a time.

Upon arrival at this other prison, I was met by an inmate, who was an N.A. member who I knew from meetings we had both attended at another prison. It really made the difference to see his face when I drove up, because again, I knew I had the support that would help me make it. I continued in the fellowship at this prison, and became active in the service part of the Program in the institution.

So, during these last six months I had to do on my sentence, I would wake up in the morning and say, "Just for today, I won't take anything to get high on," and I hung with N.A. people in the institution to keep myself away from temptation. There were plenty of opportunities, so it wasn't easy, but I now had the support of the N.A. fellowship. Once, I was let out to attend an outside meeting, which made me want the Fellowship on the outside even more. I started going to the meetings clean for the first time, and something happened. The Program began to work.

Today, I know what makes N.A. work. One really starts understanding why it can work only when totally abstaining from all mind-altering chemicals.

I also was beginning to understand what caring means; and by helping each other, we can make it. I felt that the only one who really understood me was another addict. And the only one who could help was a clean addict.

I was so proud to stand before the group in prison and announce that I had 90 days clean. Feeling proud sure was not what it was about before. It was such a relief, not having to hustle drugs out on the yard, and do the crazy things I did to get high. I had never done time like this and it sure felt great.

I made another decision through the advice the N.A. members gave me, which was the second most important decision I had ever made in my life. This was, to have someone from the Narcotics Anonymous Program at the gate to pick me up when I was released. A person I knew understood what I needed my first day out, because I sure didn't, at this point.

When I go back into the prisons today, to carry the message of Narcotics Anonymous, the message I suggest is to have a member at that gate when you get out. I heard so many say, "Oh, I'll check it out, but I've gotta do this first, or be here first." Don't kid yourself; you might die first, if you are an addict like me.

That first day out was SO RIGHTEOUS. I was taken to a home where N.A. members were expecting me. This one member gave me a new address book with N.A. phone numbers in it, and said, "Give me your old address book, you don't need those old numbers of your connections anymore." Another member took me to his closet, and gave me some clothes. I went to a bunch of meetings that day, and sure received the love and care I needed, which seemed to make up for all the attention I missed over the years, being locked up.

Recently, one of the many benefits, for me, was being able to stand before the Judge of the Superior Court and receive my Certificate of Rehabilitation. I never thought I would be standing in front of any Judge for this reason. I am so grateful, today, to say that I have been able to go beyond the fellowship for the support I need. I'm speaking about God. I mean a God I can understand and talk to when I need a Higher Strength, the God I found in Narcotics Anonymous.

So, if you are in a cell reading this, my message goes to you. If you are wondering whether drugs or booze, or both, are screwing up your life, find out where a N.A. meeting is in your facility and check it out. You might be saving your own life, and learning A BETTER WAY. If one addict can make it, so can another. We help each other in Narcotics Anonymous.

Chapter Twenty-One

FEARFUL MOTHER

.

I thought an addict was a person who was using hard drugs, was on the street or was in a jail. My pattern was different; I got my drugs from a doctor or friends. I knew something was wrong yet I tried to do right, in working, in marriage and in raising my children. I really tried hard. I would be doing well and then I'd fail. It went on like this and each time it seemed like forever; it seemed like nothing would ever change. Wanting to be a good mother. Wanting to be a good wife. Wanting to be involved in society yet never feeling a part of it.

I went through years of telling my children "I'm sorry but this time it will be different." I went from one doctor to another asking for help. I went to counseling feeling everything will be alright now, but the inside was still saying "What is wrong?" I was changing jobs, changing doctors, changing drugs, trying different books, religions and hair colors. I moved from one area to another, changed friends and moved furniture. I went on vacations and also remained hidden in my home. So many things through the years. Constantly feeling, I'm wrong. I'm different, I'm a failure.

When I had my first child I liked it when they knocked me out; I liked the feeling of the drugs they gave me. It was a feeling that whatever is going on around me, I don't know and I don't care, really. Through the years the tranquilizers gave me the feeling that nothing is really that important. Toward the end, things became so mixed up I was not sure what was and what was not important. I was shaking inside and out. Drugs and alcohol (another form of drug) would not help. I was still trying, but very little. I had quit work and was trying to go back but I couldn't. I was trying to communicate with my family but I couldn't. I would be on the couch afraid of everything. I was 103 lbs. and had sores on my lips and in my nose. I had diabetes and shook so that I had a hard time putting a spoon to my mouth. I felt I was out to kill myself and people around me were out to hurt me. Physically and mentally I had a breakdown. I had just become a grandmother and I could not even communicate with a small child. I was almost a vegetable. I wanted to be a part of living but did not know how. Part of me said I'd be better off dead and part of me said there has to be a better way of living.

When I started on the program of N.A. there were a lot of people who suggested just everyday things for me to do. Things like: eat, take a bath, get dressed, go for a walk, go to meetings. They told me, "Don't be afraid, we have all gone through this." I went to a lot of meetings through the years. One thing has stuck with me, one thing they said from the beginning, "Betty, you can stop running and you can be whatever you want to be and do whatever you want to do."

Since being on the program I have listened and watched many people and have seen them go through many ups and downs. I have used the teachings I felt were best for me. My work area has had to change and I have been going to school. I have had to relearn all the way back to the grammar school level. It has been slow for me but very rewarding.

I also decided that I need to know me better before I can have a meaningful relationship with a man. I am learning to communicate with my daughters. I am trying many things which I wanted to do for years. I am able to remember many things that I had pushed out of my mind. I have found that Betty is not that big pile of nothing but is someone and something that I never really stopped to look at or listen to. April 1st will be my fifth N.A. birthday.* How's that for April Fools day!

*Written in 1976.

I have been asked to update my story. This April 1st will be my 10th year birthday.* I feel like, where have I been and have I really grown? I know that I have gotten married. I would like to say I love my husband very dearly, and at times this is hard for me to say. Expressing a deep feeling for any person has been very hard for me. I have felt like it would be taken away, or that he would hurt me or laugh. That has happened at times but I have still loved him and it has not been that big and crushing a deal. I am learning not to put him on a pedestal and myself also. If I am expecting too much of him that means I had better look a little closer at myself. There are times we can talk, and there are times it takes time before we can talk. How boring if we both thought alike and everything went smoothly or we fought constantly. I still get feelings of running away from home. Maybe going back to the Islands or Michigan. I have been living in the same place for almost four years. I think that is a record for me. I am still moving furniture around. I love it and would like to put everything on rollers — it would be a lot easier. I still do not understand men. Every once in awhile, I tell my husband I am a woman and I need to be taken to a movie or somewhere. I am learning to verbalize my needs to another person. I also go to the show alone once in awhile.

I graduated from high school two years ago. Would love to graduate from college — maybe some time in the future. Everyone needs something to look forward to. My daughter, son-in-law and granddaughter gave me a violin for Christmas. When I was in grammar school I took lessons for a very short time. The school stopped giving lessons and took back their violin and I never forgot that. I started out this year slowly taking lessons and became obsessed. I was going to two teachers and studying out of three different books. I found myself looking at one of my books and saying, "where am I?" So now I am back to one teacher and one book.

I had a breast operated on and they removed part of it. I will not say this was a whiz because it wasn't. But I was luckier than some. I had the program and the people to walk through it with. I cannot say my life has been like tiptoeing through the tulips because that is not reality. I can say that my life now is getting better to where I am more open to look and

*Written in 1981.

155

walk in reality. With the world in such a turmoil I feel I have been blessed to be where I am at. I look at how N.A. has grown. We are in Germany, Australia, England, Scotland, Italy, Brazil, etc., etc. Maybe some day we will reach the countries that are so hard to reach.

I have been told there are not many women with a lot of time on the program. I am surprised when I hear this. I just assume there are and maybe they have moved to other cities and states. Maybe even to some of these countries that are so damn hard to reach. When a woman wants something bad enough, look out — she can move heaven and hell. One of the first things told to me was, "No one else in this world knows what you want, but you. If you want to survive in this world you had better do what is right for you because no one else is going to do it." I sure get bumps and bruises and I suck my thumb once in awhile, but I sure get stronger each time. I have a dog named Baba Wawa and she was very tiny when my daughter gave her to me. My daughter said, "Mom, here is a little dog and she will never grow very large." Well, she has grown very big and she surprises me every once in awhile. Last night she tried to fight a big dog right through a chain link fence. Now I thought she was still a puppy but she can stand her own and I guess it's like me. I have grown more than I realized and unlike Bawa Wawa, I have been known to climb the fence and go after whatever I have to. I have also been known to knock those fences down. I feel like there is more to say but who can put all of ten years down on paper. I would rather spend my time living it than writing it.

I have been active in N.A. answering phones, typing, working in different areas of N.A. I go to meetings and talk and still feel funny and awkward. Sometimes I am a kid, all hyper; and other times it goes so smoothly, I can't remember what happened or what I have said but I feel good. What I am trying to say is, thank Heaven nothing is as bad as it used to be and there is so much more of what there should be in my life.

Chapter Twenty-Two

I FOUND THE ONLY
N.A. MEETING IN THE WORLD

My name is Bob B. from Los Angeles. Getting to the subject of people, places and things, my story is not much different from the executive — just the opposite end of the stick.

I grew up on the wrong side of the tracks, poor, deprived, during the depression, in a broken home. The words of love were never spoken in my household. There were a lot of kids in my house.

Most of the things I remember about my life are in retrospect. While they were happening, I didn't know anything about it. I just remember going through life feeling different, feeling deprived. I never felt quite comfortable wherever I was, with whatever I had at any given time. I grew up in a fantasy world. Things on the other side of the fence always looked better. My grass was never green enough. My head was always out to lunch. I learned all the short cuts in order to make it through school.

I always had a dream of leaving home. It was not the place to be. My great fantasy was that there was going to be something good out there somewhere.

I started using drugs fairly late in life. Eighteen years old, I say "late" in comparison with the age they are doing it today.

My mother ruled her house with a big stick. That was her method. The constant way I gained attention was getting my butt whipped on a daily basis. I found another way of getting attention was to get sick. When I got "sick," I got the things I felt were necessary; love and attention.

I blamed my mother because she didn't make better choices in her life so that I could have been happy growing up.

I went into the Military because it was a place to run to. I stayed in the Military for a long time because they afforded me the same opportunities I had at home; three hots and a cot, and no responsibility. I can say I was a responsible person because I had rank and did this or that, but it was only because they gave me advance directions of what to do and when to do it, and how much.

This was one of my first bouts as far as drugs were concerned. My first drug at the time was alcohol. I found there were two personalities; when under the influence of alcohol and, later, other narcotics, there was a personality change.

I found out later, however, that this personality change went back even farther, I was two people before I even started using. I had learned how to steal early; I had learned how to lie early; I had learned how to cheat early. I used these processes "successfully." I was addicted to stealing long before I was addicted to drugs; because it made me feel good. If I had some of your "goodies" to spread around, I felt good. I had a thing about stealing. I couldn't go into a place unless I took something.

Talk about being naive, I knew nothing about drugs. Drugs were something that was talked about in the 30's and 40's. It is not that drugs have changed, they just didn't talk about them. They didn't talk about sex, or drugs, or religion; at least as far as discussing or explaining them. It just wasn't one of those things that was talked about.

I first experienced my drug of choice, heroin, in the Far East. I heard about opium and tried that. I found you could cook up heroin and put it in a spike. There was a great variety of drugs in other countries that you could get by just walking into a drug store and asking for them. So I stayed out of the country for nine years. That way, I wasn't confronted with the attitudes and restrictions in the United States.

I knew nothing about the progression of my disease. I knew nothing about addiction. I ran around in the "ignorance of addiction" for a lot of years—not knowing. Just not knowing.

No one explained to me that when you use drugs over a year's time you can get hooked. No one told me about withdrawal from drugs. The only thing anyone told me was, "Don't get sick," and the way to do that was to keep on using.

One of the problems I found in the Military was that they give you orders, ship you out, and they don't send your connection with you. You get sick. You try to back that up the next time by trying to get a big enough supply, and your month's supply lasts a week, or two or three days.

I knew nothing about progression of the disease nor the consequences of my actions. The progression of my disease caught up with me, as far as the Military was concerned, when I started transporting and smuggling. Also, when you use drugs to the extent that you can't be there for duty, they frown on it. The next thing they do is take you away and lock you up. Then the Military did a cruel thing, they put me out on the streets.

I was ill-equipped to take care of myself. I had gone from mama to another mother. They had taken care of me, then I found myself on the street with no one to take care of me. I knew nothing of paying rent, working or being responsible. So I had to give that responsibility to whomever I could give it to. I ran through a lot of "mothers." I had to learn how to hustle on the street. You have to realize the Military has a lot of equipment that can be sold, and I used to sell it, because I liked to steal. You see, I had to learn other processes, like running through stores winging steaks and cigarettes under my arm, jumping from second story windows, and running from policemen. . . .

I think there is a certain excitement that goes along with drug addiction. It was a lot like childhood games of cops and robbers. I found out they have more policemen than drug addicts, it seemed. They were standing around watching you. I could never understand how they could go into a crowd of people and pick me out, and say, "Let's get in the car, let's go." Nine times out of ten they had me dirty.

During the process of finding mothers, one mother found me. I thought I should hem this one up and get papers on her, then she couldn't run away.

I chose correctly by choosing someone who wasn't using. I knew about the ones that were using. They were never there when I got locked up. They never had bail money. They could never visit because they were too busy taking care of their own habits.

So I found one of those unsuspecting ones. She was in school, working, had a place to stay. She had one shortcoming: she didn't know she needed someone to take care of. I was a prime candidate. I wanted to be taken care of. She was going to help me get my act together. She proposed to me in jail, and I said, "Yes, I do. Just go down and pay the bail."

For the next three years I ran her crazy trying to keep up with me. Then she went out and found the *Only* Narcotics Anonymous *Meeting in the World.* How she did that, I don't know. At that time, there was only one meeting in the whole world, and she went out and found it, and I sent her off to the meeting. I had her go check it out.

You have to realize that in those days, drug addicts were very unpopular. To just intimate that two drug addicts were going to congregate anywhere would constitute a police stakeout. That's the way they treated drug addicts at the time. There was very little understanding about addiction. I was very leery about anything to do about helping drug addicts. I knew what they did with drug addicts; they locked them up. Period! There was no Program to go to, except Ft. Worth and Lexington.

I always had a sad story to justify my using. One day after one of those six month trips to go get a loaf of bread at the corner grocery, I came home and my bags were sitting by the door. She had told me fifty times or a thousand times, "You got to go." This time was different. There was something in her voice this time. So I took my bags and went to the only place there was to go; the streets.

I had become accustomed to living in the streets. I knew how to live in the back of old cars, old laundry rooms, any old empty building, your house or my house. Of course, I never had "my house." I couldn't pay the rent. I never knew how to pay rent. If I had $3.00 in my pocket that

$3.00 was going for drugs before a place to stay. It was that simple. I think I paid rent one time while I was using drugs and living on the streets, that was just to move in. It was called "catch me if you can" from then on. It usually didn't make any difference, because I was a ward of the state much of the time anyway. I just ran in the streets until they locked me up. Then I had a place to stay. I could rest up and get my health back in order to go back out and do it again.

I came to Narcotics Anonymous nearly 21 years ago.* But I didn't come for me. I came just to keep her mouth shut. I went to meetings loaded.

I didn't have a driver's license. I was unemployable. I had no place to stay. I was the wrong color. I had no money. I didn't have a car. I didn't have no old lady, or I needed a new one. I took them all these problems and they would tell me, "Keep coming back." And they said, "Work the Steps." I used to read the steps and thought that was working them. I found out years later that even though I read the steps, I didn't know what I had read. I did not understand what I read.

They told me in many places that I was an addict. I had been labeled, "addict." From the Military to the jails right on down the line, I had been labeled. I accepted that, but I didn't understand it. I had to go out and do some more experimenting, before I got back to the Program.

One of the things I had to learn to do was to understand what the Program was all about. I had to become willing to find out what the Program was about. Only after standing at the "Gates of Death" did I want to understand. I think "Death" is the "Counsel Permanent." I had O.D.'d a number of times, but that was kind of like the place where I always wanted to be. It was just before going over the brink and everything seemed okay. Coming out of it, I could say, "Wow, give me some more." That's insanity!

The final case for me was that I was about to be shot off a fence, and not by my own doing. That, I didn't like. Playing cops and robbers is dangerous, "out there." They have guns, and I don't like being used for target practice. There were more and more cases of policemen sticking guns in my mouth and upside my head, and telling me to lay upside a wall.

*Written in 1981.

161

My last day of use of narcotics, drugs of any type, I had just fixed and two policemen got me spread-eagled on a chainlink fence I was trying to get over. I became immediately sober and clean. Everything became very clear, and I didn't want to die that way. Something clicked on in my mind, "it doesn't have to be this way."

After that last "rest and recuperation," I found out I could work these Steps. The sum total of my life has changed, as a direct result. I got involved in *working* the Steps, trying to understand what they were talking about; to *really understand* what they were talking about. I found there is a certain amount of action that goes with every Step. I had to get into action about how the Steps applied to *me*. I always thought the Steps applied to you, not me.

It got down to talking about God and spirituality — I had canned God a long time ago, then I put that in church, and I didn't have anything to do with church. I found out that God and spirituality have nothing to do with church.

I have to learn to get involved. It has been one hell of an adventure. My life has changed to such an extent that it is almost unbelievable that I was ever there. However, I know from where I came. I have constant reminders. I need that constant reminder of newcomers and talking with others.

This Program has become a part of me. It has become a part of life and living for me. I understand more clearly the things that are happening in my life today. I no longer fight the process.

I came to meetings of Narcotics Anonymous in order to take care of the responsibilities that have been given to me. Today, I care; I am addicted to the love and caring and sharing that goes on in N.A. I look forward to more of these things in my life.

My problem is addiction; it has nothing to do with drugs being the means of not coping with life, it has something to do with that within, that compulsion and that obsession. I now have the tools to do something about it; the Twelve Steps of Recovery.

Chapter Twenty-Three

ALIEN

$\mathbf{F}$rom a very early age I had intense feelings and beliefs that I WAS DIFFERENT! While other girls my age were trying on Mom's clothes and playing with Barbie Dolls, I was playing football with the guys, smoking pot, and pondering the mysteries of the universe.

I started using somewhere close to the age of 12. My parents were concerned about the drug problem in our neighborhood, so I was enrolled in a semi-private school in Ft. Lauderdale, Florida. All this did was introduce me to a more sophisticated drug usage. There are many years of my life that I have no memory of, and some I wish I could forget. Sometimes, periods have come back to me in recovery, but many have not. I have been a skeptic from a very early age. I questioned everything. Everything BUT using. I used to completely block out any feelings and perceptions that I had towards life. I never was very fond of living, although I wanted to be, and this became evident as the years rolled past and my self-destructive behavior magnified itself.

At one time in my life, I decided that sports was the avenue of personal freedom and acceptance that I desired. And so the addict within me attacked the sports world with vigor and determination. I also felt that if

I could succeed at something, and be the best at it, I would surely get somebody's attention. I succeeded in society's eyes and in my peers eyes. I made the papers, was on the All-State team twice, an All-American nomination, team captain . . . I had plaques, trophies, and titles. Regardless of my success in sports, I was feeling empty and the success didn't really matter to me. In fact, it turned out to be more of a hassle than it was worth. I was beginning to hear an endless monologue of, "You have so much potential, why are you messing up your life?" Regardless of the intense physical training I put myself through, I simply could never stop using. In fact, I thought that using drugs enhanced my ability in sports and they also became a reward to myself after a hard workout. I did not attend my senior year in high school. Most of my friends had either quit, been kicked out, or already graduated.

Being born and raised in the Miami-Ft. Lauderdale area, at age 15 I had had enough of geographic stability. My heartbeat was travel, and I diligently pursued this road. I spent one winter in a tent in the High Sierras of California. It was at this time I was introduced to the drug of all drugs, peyote. The next few years were spent in a desperate attempt to match that particular experience. Still, the main question I addressed to myself was: who am I and where in this universe do I fit? I alienated myself from my family. I did not think that I belonged with them any more than I belonged in this "screwed up society." My main outlet was writing and I retreated farther and farther into the world of isolation.

I did, through the years, try and make things work for myself. I became a Christian, was Baptized, chanted to Krishna, became a Christian again, stared at Maharishi Yogi, went to Bible College, got kicked out, went back, and got kicked out again. I went to school for training as an Emergency Medical Technician, started nursing school and still felt unfulfilled and like this world just was not doing its job to fulfill my every need. I still never felt like I fit into the plan of the universe, and my disease of addiction progressed. Thinking back, I think it was why I used as well as how much I used that gave me problems.

I went from California to Florida to get clean, and when that didn't work, I went to North Carolina, and then to Connecticut and on and on. When I became uncomfortable somewhere, I moved elsewhere. The same went for my employment situation. When I didn't like my job, or I was getting close to being caught at ripping an establishment off, I would simply get another job. Geography was not adequate armor to fight the war that was taking place in my mind, body, and spirit. I spent a summer on the Amazon of Brazil. That did not cure my addiction. Even in the Andes of Peru my addiction progressed. I learned that Custom Officials loved to see Bibles in your luggage, and they also loved to hear that your item of business in a particular country was Church or Missionary affiliated.

A few months before I found the Program I was working in retail and found a wonderful supplier for my habit, my manager. Now all I had to do was to make it to work. In fact, all of a sudden, work was not all that bad. I began to work 14 hour days. It was my perpetual and ultimate connection, and life became more blurry every day. I found myself doing things with myself for drugs that for years I had never rationalized. But I did anything I had to do to stay high. Using became so much of my routine that, at one point, it was accepted behavior to cut lines of cocaine on the restaurant table. I became oblivious to the fact that what I was doing was illegal. I never could figure out why it seemed like people were always staring at me! I remember thinking, "God grant me the power to change the people, places, and things that do not agree with my way of thinking." I could never figure out why this world would not devote itself to making me happy.

Today I realize this is insane thinking, and insane thinking helped qualify me for the Program of Narcotics Anonymous. Insane thinking is one of the obvious characteristics of the disease I suffer from; that of drug addiction. I had an "ideal" of the world as I thought it should be. I often visualized myself as existing on a moonbeam in a utopian state for eternity. I have always been a baby in an adult body. I want what I want when I want it.

Finally, in Atlanta, Georgia, I found a Program of Narcotics Anonymous. Psychiatry was not helping. Prescribed medication did nothing but make me want more. When I was doing amphetamines, the doctor would put me on tranquilizers to calm me down, and when I was doing downs, I was put on antidepressants to "help stabilize my mood swings

165

and depression." At one point, I remember being told, "Just face it, you will never be able to live without being on some kind of medication.

Depression eventually became my normal state of mind, and spirit. Suicide remained my dominating thought. My favorite pastimes were hanging over an interstate overpass, or seeing how close I could get to moving trains. My social life was non-existent, and my zest for life was so low I even lost the energy it took to get more drugs. My bottom had arrived and somehow I was still alive. My therapist at this point was a lady who understood the disease of addiction. She refused to continue seeing me if I would not attend a Narcotics Anonymous meeting.

I went to a few meetings and told her that there was no way the Program could work for me. When she wouldn't buy that excuse, I told her I thought the people were using because there was no way in my mind that people could look and sound so happy, and have so much freedom, without being loaded. I remember sitting in a survivors meeting one night and asking the guy next to me, "Are these people for real or are they all loaded?" He looked at me rather emphatically, and replied, "They are for real."

Then there was the Higher Power concept. For me, having had two years of Bible College and a lot of theology in my head, I confused Spirituality with Religion. This was one of my biggest obstacles in developing conscious contact with a Power greater than myself. Again, my struggle became evident when finally at a meeting where a Higher Power was the topic, I told them, "I don't believe in a Power greater than myself, and I am sick of hearing this topic discussed." After about two minutes of silence a guy across the room stood up, walked over to me, and whispered in my ear, "I know where you're coming from, and I want to tell you that this group of people is a Power greater than you." So, that was the foundation of my Higher Power concept. Today I choose to call my Higher Power God, yet there are many times today when the group is used. God, as I understand him today is a gentle, loving, and understanding Spirit. I believe today that my Higher Power kept me alive long enough to find the fellowship of Narcotics Anonymous. I am grateful to be alive. The day I surrendered to the fact that I was powerless over my addiction, enormous weight was removed from me.

The weight of addiction said, "You can handle it" but I knew I couldn't. One of the hardest things I have encountered is change. I have had to change my playgrounds and my playmates. For me, that was one of the easier areas of change. It was at day one, and remains so today, essential for on-going recovery. What has been hardest is changing attitudes, ideas, patterns, and reactions. When I encounter people today who don't agree with me, I need to try and respond to them in a spirit of love. This is quite a change from ignoring them as I did in the past.

As a result of working my Program, going to meetings, changing my attitudes, and relying on my Higher Power instead of people, even my face is changing. When I first came into the Program, one of my fellow addicts nicknamed me "ROCKY," due to my stern facial expression. I showed no emotion, would not smile, (even if I was laughing on the inside) and refused to talk. There were also many times when I simply could not talk, and do nothing but make a meeting and listen. Many times I would shuffle into a meeting, sit in my corner, and hope no one would see me. I sometimes held on to the fantasy that I was a type of Casper the Ghost. The reality was that people really did see me. They tried to talk to me, and they tried to hug me, regardless of my stone face expression. Eventually, love broke through and I began to respond to the people that God was using as instruments of His love, and grace.

What matters is that the Program I have found gives me the tools to live clean, regardless of pain, whether it be emotional, spiritual, or physical. It is OK to hurt and feel pain today. It is not OK to use. In fact, it is growth to feel anything at all. Apathy was my middle name for years. It feels wonderful to care. It is recovery for me to be able to laugh, cry, or simply share some word of encouragement. It wasn't but a year ago that the death of a friend would not have brought a tear. Today I can cry over a man disabled in a wheelchair.

I have had to face a bizarre situation or two in recovery. I am learning that there is no problem too small to bring to a meeting. One night I brought the problem of eating a chocolate eclair to a meeting because I was afraid of using over it and I noticed my thinking changing. The outcome of it was that in the future I would make sure my favorite bakeries do not saturate their eclairs with alcohol. I do not have to use no

167

matter what.

Sometimes I find that when things start going good, I deliberately try to destroy it. My absolute limit for any relationship used to be 5 months. It became habitual to dump someone before they dumped me! Sometimes I find old thought patterns creeping up, and I find myself being obnoxious and trying to get people mad at me. It sometimes shatters my ego when someone catches my tricks and tells me they won't work. Today I can look in the mirror and laugh at myself. I won't say that I have a good self image today, but it's better than it used to be. When I was using, I mastered the art of fight or flee. I would either run from a situation or fight it out, but never face it. Most of the time, it was me I was running from. The words serenity and surrender were foreign to my vocabulary. I am learning that I usually have as much serenity as I have surrendered.

For half of my life I have been careening wildly through the sea of chaos and destruction. The Program of Narcotics Anonymous has shown me serenity and direction. I am growing to realize my experience can benefit those who still suffer. The freedom I have always sought after, I have found in the STEPS of the Program. The loneliness that has been with me for years is alleviated by other recovering addicts in the Fellowship. Today I am not responsible for having a disease, but I am responsible for my own recovery. Today, I can study, keep an apartment, and I can even emotionally commit myself to another human being. Many people are in my life today. When I found the program I was alone. My purpose for being on this planet has been resolved in my mind and spirit. Today I know I must carry the message of recovery. Today I am grateful. I belong in the universe.

Chapter Twenty-Four

A LITTLE GIRL GROWS UP

I was born the youngest, to a family of eight, on Christmas Eve. I heard all of my life how my coming into this world was a special occasion, and as a result, I too thought it was a celebration, and continued to for the next 26 years. My parents were close to 40 when I came, so naturally I felt like a grandchild. Every day to me was supposed to be special. I demanded and got all the attention I needed and wanted. My conception of myself at this time was that I was to be taken care of the rest of my life, and that all I had to do was be pretty and smile and the rest would be a piece of cake. I put the responsibility of my existence on everyone but me and if I wasn't happy, they weren't doing their job. Of course when things went my way, I took all the credit. To me, no one knew how to make me happy. I was constantly filled with frustration and anxiety because nothing I did seemed to get me to that place called "Happiness."

I was brought up in a religious atmosphere, but I never seemed to be able to grasp what it all meant. I couldn't understand how God could love me one minute but the next strike me down to hell. This understanding of mine sent me to rebel against all that I was taught to be "sinful." I was determined to prove that if I danced, smoked, cut my hair, or wore pants, I would not go to hell. I began to do all these "sins" in Jr. High and ended up pregnant at 15. I did not want to get married and be a housewife. My first reaction was to have my baby and raise it myself, but that didn't go off very well, so I got married and had my child at 16. You see, again I didn't want to take the responsibility of my actions, so I went into the marriage bitter but determined to make it work.

My husband and I were two kids playing house. We began going out to clubs, drinking and living it up. My thinking at this time was that I had found it, this was the life! Right before our third wedding anniversary, my husband was shot and killed at one of those "live-it-up" night clubs. Well, needless to say, I really had a good excuse now. I now had another reason to "cop-out" on this big bad world. I honestly felt that mean God up in the clouds was really paying me back for all the sins I had committed. I hated Him! I'd lay awake many a night in agony wondering if God and my husband could see and hear the pain of loneliness I felt. I never got an answer.

After my husband's death, his best friend and I began spending time together crying and laughing at memories of the past. Not too long after this I was introduced to "Acid". My first trip was spent on the floor with me crying and wishing my old man hadn't died on me. The bad trip didn't seem to bother me because somewhere in my mind I knew I had found something new — a new world. Maybe "happiness." I was constantly in search for relief from the pain and about this time another man came along, except he was different because he had cash. This man saw a scared little girl in agony and wanted to buy the hurt away. Well, I tell you, it didn't take me very long at all to grab on to that and hold on till I used him completely up. With the access to so much cash, it was just a matter of time before I was burnt out on the pills I was taking; the high just wasn't the same. Again, I began a search for escape from myself and I found it; the needle!

My first shot was ecstasy. The feeling that ran through my body and veins, when I got off, was one of contentment and exhiliration. I had never dreamed anything could feel so good. During this time of discovering the new highs I was trying to keep two men happy. My sugar daddy was constantly forking out cash and I was forking out lies. My old man and I really thought we were something having all that cash to buy all the dope we needed or wanted. But there was something wrong that I couldn't quite grasp, and that was that I was slowly running out of whatever it took for me to lead a double life. For about a year I shot dope for fun. My feelings were, if it feels good, do it! It wasn't very long before the needle had taken full control of me—no more was I in command. This dependency led me to be very careless and the next thing I knew I was busted twice in a period of a few months. I'll never forget the feeling I had as I was being photographed and fingerprinted. All I wanted to do was go back and fix drugs. My mind and body were so screwed up I wasn't even aware that I had a daughter at home waiting for me.

Someone told me that if I went to a hospital and kicked that I could probably beat the case. So that's exactly what I went for. I knew I had been doing too much dope, but I thought I just needed rest. I ended up having my friends bring me dope through windows, and in the meantime proceeded to drive my family crazy. My husband was sentenced and I got 2 years probation. Well, that really did it! Again God had taken away my reason for living. Before my husband left I made promises that I would be faithful, save money that my sugar daddy gave me, and only shoot dope occasionally. I was only able to keep one, and that was "to be faithful."

I literally stayed in my bedroom and bathroom for two years waiting for the day my husband would come home and make me happy again. But there was a problem. The needle slowly became my friend, lover and my reason for living. I lost that glimpse of self-respect I had left. I spent hours in the bathroom fixing and crying because a syringe owned me now. There was nothing I could do. As a result of shooting dope, I began to "miss," a lot and those "misses" turned into infected sores from my head to my toes. I spent a lot of time telling my daughter and parents that those sores on me were just boils. I didn't realize how sick I had become. I lost everything. I was a zombie with no feelings for anyone or anything except my rush. I remember thinking that when my husband came home I could quit and everything would be alright. It wasn't.

I tried staying clean for awhile, working in a furniture store my father had started for us, but nothing worked. Before long I was at it again and by this time I was out completely. There were no veins left, so I had to go in about an inch and a half to find one and I nearly lost my veins for good. All this time I was trying to be a mother, wife, and girlfriend. I'd dress myself up for a day, put on my mask and perform my duties, but it never did work. I had no motivation to help myself.

During the worst time of my addiction my thoughts were never suicidal. I just wanted to sleep till it all went away. My old ideas told me it was a "sin" to take my own life. I couldn't really see that I was slowly doing just that. As deep as I now was into my habit, it wasn't long before I was selling everything. I had run out of lies to tell my money man, so, next went my house, cars and jewelry, but I didn't care, I had to have my dope.

There were people reaching out to me with all they had, but all I could do was shoot more dope. When someone tried to get close to this scared little girl, I didn't have any idea how. I didn't have the strength to get out of it at all. It wasn't long till I got busted again. This time it was different. It was the end for me. I had never been one to assist cops in anything but now the running was over; I knew it. I told them exactly what I had done and I didn't really care what the consequences were, I just wanted out. I was picked up at a drugstore and taken to jail. I was so messed up that nothing mattered — nothing.

I was unable to walk, both my legs were bent from infection so that I couldn't straighten them out. I was carried by the nurses before the judge to have my bond set. As foggy headed as I was I'll never forget the voices of disgust and pity as I was carried into the courtroom. Something inside my sick mind and heart told me it was all over finally! I suddenly realized how close I was to death or even prison.

Without my knowledge, my father had found a lawyer to get me out. The nurses informed me that I was on my way to a hospital, police escort and all. Before I left the jail my lawyer arrived. He came in, introduced himself, and then proceeded to tell me the most frightening words I'd ever heard, "It's time for you to grow up!" He told me the only reason he was taking my case was because he hated to see a grown man cry and my father had sat in his office and cried like a baby, pleading with him to please help his little girl this last time. He informed me there would be no more calling my parents, brothers, sisters or sugar daddy for help. I was to stand on my own two feet for once and take the responsibility for my actions. I had never been so scared in my life. The things he told me scared me more than anything; even my arrest and losing my daughter weren't as scary as having to grow up. I didn't know where to begin. I had no idea of how to grow up and no idea of what he really meant, except that it had to be done somehow.

When I arrived at the hospital, I was informed that there would be no phone calls in and no phone calls out. I couldn't even talk to my parents. I didn't like it too much but I knew I had better listen for the first time in my life. My lawyer was the only visitor I had for the first few days and he really helped me laugh at myself. I was laying in the bed one day feeling sorry for myself and counting my scars. I had 22. He looked at me real serious and said, "I know what we'll do, we'll paint you green and play dot to dot!" I had never in my serious, condemning mind found that I could ever laugh at myself in such a forgiving way. Before, if I laughed at me, I was judging me for being such a failure at life. Now there seemed to be some relief and hope; nothing was THAT BAD anymore.

My next trip was to a treatment center. I was determined to make it work this time. I spent a lot of that time preparing myself to go to prison because there just didn't seem to be a way out of it. My lawyer told me there would have to be a miracle somewhere, because I had really gone my limit. I knew this, people just didn't get out of three narcotic arrests (including fraud), without ratting and without going to jail. The song "Why Me Lord" came into my head while I was there and stayed. Every time I laid down to go to sleep it was there. I had begun to know what gratitude was. My prayers were limited to just, "help me." I didn't know what I was really praying to, but I had to pray anyway. I couldn't carry the burden alone anymore. The people around me were telling me I had to believe in something bigger and greater than me or I would die. I could look in their eyes and see that they must be telling the truth, because something was there and I wanted it.

For the first time I was told I could have my own God, who would love and understand me. I could have a God that no one else had if I chose. Wow, what a relief this was to me. I no longer had certain rules and regulations to belong somewhere. My God and I could make up our own. Now I was beginning to know what faith was and I had taken the first three steps in my life. My heart told me now that whatever happened in my life would be God's will and that my worries could be taken away if I just prayed and believed. It all seemed so simple to do, but my will just wasn't ready to give up. I kept telling myself, "You've made a decision, stick with it for once and see what happens." The words in the Third Step, "Made a decision" scared me because I didn't know what "decision" meant. I had never decided on anything; I had just reacted.

To the best of my ability, I stayed with the Third Step throughout my time at the treatment center. My next trip was to a halfway house in Birmingham. My counselor recommended that I go, so I could get some time behind me and see what it was really like to be clean for more than 30 days. When she told me the name of the place, I had second thoughts. I thought there were be a bunch of sisters in robes greeting me. I couldn't conceive living with 18 women under one roof for too long, but I knew I had to go. To my surprise, I was greeted by several lovely women who were not nuns, but alcoholics. I knew I had come to a place of love, acceptance and understanding beyond my comprehension. They told me everything was going to be alright, and I believed them with all my heart.

My stay there began with mixed emotions. I often wanted to leave, get my little girl and take off somewhere to get away from all the pain of reality. I also read a great deal about the Fourth Step and knew it was time to take a Fourth Step in my life. I spent numerous hours writing about what had happened in my life, the pain I had felt, and the pain I had caused. I wrote about everything! There was a great deal of pain and embarrassment involved, but also an overwhelming feeling of relief. I was finally able to get out all the pain that had been with me all my life. To look at me on a piece of paper and realize how irresponsible I really was, just verified the fact to me that there would be no more running. The old me was finally beginning to die. I began to see that I really didn't deserve all the punishment I had bestowed upon myself, and that maybe I was worthy of that thing called "happiness."

I spent several months on the 4th and when it came time to do the 5th

Step there was no planning. It was just time to do it. The only way I could have held on to all that garbage would have been for me to start rationalizing my actions again. I could not stand the thought of losing the honesty. To my astonishment, the woman I did my fifth with didn't laugh, snicker or frown at all. She only had compassion when I cried and laughed when I laughed. Hallelujah! Someone finally knew the crazy thoughts I had and the crazy things I'd done.

I now felt completely forgiven and was truly ready to have God remove the old me and my sick ways. But I soon found out that the key word to Step Six was "ready," and that it would have to be done when God was ready, not when "I" decided. Step Seven came with the Sixth because, as a result of Step Five, I now had some idea of what my defects and shortcomings were. I needed someone desperately to take it all away. I now had started to understand willingness.

Steps Eight and Nine hit me when I came into the Program. I was ready to have everyone accept my apologies instantly, when I wanted them to. I was so relieved that God had forgiven me and thought everyone else had too. But again, it was only to find that I had to wait for God's time, not mine!

I work Step Ten daily, searching for where and if I have wronged another human being by allowing my defects to overcome God's love. As a result of the Twelve Steps, I'm not able to hold on to old ways of deceiving myself, for as long a time as before. God allows me short periods of time for rationalization; He knows I'll die if I keep it.

Step Eleven is my way of getting out of myself. My time for prayer can be anytime/anywhere, because I now have a friend who listens whenever I pray. Meditation was hard at first for I couldn't hear anything God was saying. As I work the Program, I find that Step Eleven is when I work Ten, my listening to God to tell me when I've wronged another.

Step Twelve is my reason for being alive today. Being able to share what Narcotics Anonymous has done for me has allowed me to be alive. I now have an identity. I know who and what I am. Maybe somewhere, someone can relate to the pain my addiction caused me. If this is so, I've achieved my purpose for being alive and happy today!

The Program of Narcotics Anonymous gave me an identity. I can now hold my head high and tell anyone "Hi, my name is——; I'm an addict." Before I came to the program and was asked, "Who are you?" I wouldn't answer because I had no idea what it really meant. I love the newly found me. I love getting to know me and getting to know other people who are like me. I now can feel emotions that were buried deep within me for many years.

The Program has given me everything non-material. To me, "happiness" (I used to think) was what and how much I could buy. How little I knew of true "happiness". I'm beginning to accept pain as growth. I know pain is essential. Through pain God can break down many false personalities little by little, in His own time.

There is so much hope for me today. The program was a challenge I needed desperately and was given to me as a gift. Each day I want more of what it has to offer. I want so much to learn, and have a long way to go to reach the understanding I'm searching for. That's okay; I'm at least searching.

To put into words what God and the program of Narcotics Anonymous have done for me has been difficult, there aren't words to express God's love. I hope that my story can reach someone, somewhere; but if it doesn't that's okay because it has reached me.

Thank you God. Thank you Narcotics Anonymous for giving me, me.

Chapter Twenty-Five

IT'S OKAY TO BE CLEAN

On one of my first drunks, at 13, I made a fool of myself, got very sick, had trouble with my parents, and was kicked off the basketball team. In one night, I made plenty of reasons not to drink again, a preview of coming attractions. Two important reasons outweigh all the pain and trouble and kept me using for years. First, was the attention I got at school. I was a celebrity for a short time. The other guys who drank welcomed me into their group and I felt the acceptance I craved. Second, and just as important, I liked the way the alcohol made me feel. I first smoked pot at 14, and by the time I finished high school I was smoking several times a week and getting drunk most every weekend.

I had experimented with drinking hard liquor, eating acid, mescaline, speed, mushrooms, and smoking different kinds of hash and pot. Being from a small town in Washington State, most drugs were hard to get, but there was always pot. The pot was easier for me to get than beer. I could buy the pot right at school, but I had to find someone of legal age to buy alcohol. I always partied with the same group of friends throughout my using. We shared our common interests in drinking and drugging and I was afraid of meeting new people. I was always looking for happiness, fun, those good times. Whatever I did, the plans included drinking and smoking.

I graduated high school at 17 and moved to a nearby, larger town with my school buddies. At last, I was free of my parents' control, and had a place to party. For the next 2½ years I had my chance to live my life the way I wanted to. Doing things MY way. I got arrested for drunk driving at age 18 and spent the night in jail. I didn't consider then that I had a drinking or drug problem. I had a police problem, I just needed to let my friends drive.

The best way to describe the last couple of years of my drug use is boring. I worked in a factory to pay my bills and to buy my pot and beer. Most of my spare time was spent sitting around the house with the T.V. on and the stereo turned up. I smoked every day and got drunk every weekend. Sometimes my friends and I would get in the car and drive out in the country to the same places we had gone when we had first started using.

In the beginning I had some fun times when I used. In the end, it was a habit, the old fun just wasn't there very often. I always stayed around the people who partied the way that I did. I didn't think that there was anything wrong with smoking a joint by myself before grocery shopping. I told myself that it would help me enjoy the experience. Or course it was perfectly alright to go to a drinking party and keep a case of beer in the car in case the keg goes dry for 15 minutes. Or sitting in one spot after eating acid, watching the numbers change on the digital clock. Didn't everyone?

At 20 I got arrested for drunk driving again and spent 3 days in jail. As I sobered up I realized that every time I got in trouble with the law I had been drinking. Of course, nobody had gotten a drunk driving ticket for smoking pot. Maybe some acid or speed once in a while. To get out of spending 6 months in jail and paying a big fine, I agreed to go to an alcoholism treatment center.

I learned a lot there. Mainly that it is alright not to get high, that there are a lot of people who want to stay clean. I loved to sit and listen to the other patients talk about their experiences. "If I was as bad as these people, I would want to quit too," I thought. I learned that many of them started out just like me and ended up going through years of pain. I decided that I had gone down far enough and wanted to live clean. I also decided to treat pot and other drugs the same as alcohol. Getting high is getting high no matter what I use to get there. I started to like myself. I opened up to people and let them get to know me and they still liked me.

I got out of treatment with 30 days clean, but I hadn't truly accepted Step One. In two days I smoked some pot. The sensations were familiar, but all the knowledge about addiction kept racing through my head. I realized that those counselors were right, I am an addict. I am powerless over that first smoke or drink. That was the last time I got high.

Within a week I had moved out on my own, away from the old friends that I had depended on. I started going to meetings regularly and hanging around afterwards, meeting and talking to other members. I couldn't relate to the type or amount of drugs or behavior of most of the people. If I kept an open mind and listened for similarities instead of differences, I saw that we all share some common feelings and a desire to stop using. I first got involved by helping set up and clean up the meeting room. Later, I drove to the treatment centers and picked up patients to go to the meetings.

As time goes on, the Third Step becomes more real and important. It wasn't too hard for me to believe that there is a Higher Power working in my life. I just thought back to the car wrecks and blackouts when I could have gotten hurt or killed and wasn't. The things that I used to call luck or coincidence, I just call God's work. I use the word God because it's easy to spell. This God must really love me. He let me go through enough pain in using that I might learn a lesson from it, and have experience to share with others. He has guided me to this new, full rewarding life at a young age. If He has been this good to me so far, I figure I can trust Him to take care of me each new day. I repeat Step Three in the morning and say thanks at night.

When I was using, I would sit around talking and fantasizing about the things that I'd do some day. Now I do them. Travel, meeting new people, and being trusted with respectable positions. Hiking, biking, skiing, dancing and even dating. I have got friends all over the United

States now, and I feel closer to some of them than I ever did to my drinking buddies.

It has been over 3 years since that relapse and I have had quite an adventure so far. I am not always happy or comfortable. I have had to reach out when I am scared or lonely. I have had to watch people I like go back to their old ways. I have trouble with resentment, jealousy, and fear, among others. I have found the Tenth Step very helpful there. Yet, I can't compare a few uncomfortable hours to the years of hangovers, remorse and blackouts.

God is sure good to me. He has given me health, the N.A. principles and fellowship. When that old thinking comes back that "I'm not that bad," I just remember "how bad does it have to be before I want to get better?"

TODAY I LIVE—Thank You!

Chapter Twenty-Six

NOWHERE TO TURN

My name is George and I am an addict and a member of Narcotics Anonymous. Today I am able to live clean and sober because of the fellowship of N.A. I am now thirty years old and began using about twelve years ago.

As I was growing up I remember the feeling I had of wanting to belong or be a part of other groups of people. I was a loner and did not know how to do this. Fear and inferiority feelings were a part of me since childhood. I was unable to participate in sports and other activities because of these feelings that I could not do it. I had a fear of people, especially in groups, so I lived in a fantasy world where I was somebody. I had few close friends as a child and tried to control and isolate the friends I did have. I wanted to keep them to myself for fear that others would only take them away.

I was an only child and my father died at my age of three. I was raised by my mother and grandparents. I was very sensitive and did not want others to see this so I tried to hide it.

I didn't like myself and always tried to be somebody other than the person I really was.

At an early age, I would escape the reality of the here and now by fantasizing about the future. I thought somehow if I could change me or find the right situation that I could be happy someday. My need to control and dominate people only drove them away and I felt rejected. As I got older, I began to rebel at the society that I was blaming for my inability to be happy. At the same time on a deeper level I blamed myself. I started to get into trouble at home and at school for attention. Inside I was hurting and was very confused, but solutions were not at my disposal and I felt as though I must do whatever it took to be accepted by any crowd. I chose other kids who were getting into trouble and breaking all the rules. But even in that crowd, I felt different.

Somehow, I made it through high school and went on to college to please my family. I was not ready for the responsibility of college and I wasn't motivated to learn. I felt out of place there and did poorly. At the end of my first semester I left school and got a job. I thought that hard work and low pay was what I needed to prove my manhood. This got old quick.

I would develop problems with people wherever I went and would run from one situation to another, blaming others for the problems that would arise.

I began to identify with the peace and love movement that was catching on around the country. I thought the musicians of this era really had the answer and part of that answer was to escape to enlightenment with drugs. I felt that I could be accepted by the long hairs because they talked of unconditional love and other spiritual principles.

I started smoking pot and then came that first acid trip, then speed and barbituates. My first experience with each drug was wonderful to me and I wanted to keep doing it. I especially liked the speed and acid in those days and smoked pot to keep that stoned outlook on life. I thought the drugs went along with the philosophies we all talked about and that it was all spiritual and mystical. One by one, I tried all of the drugs that I said I'd never do.

My relationships with women were few and none were successful. This drove me deeper into escaping with drugs. I felt fear and excitement with this new destructive way of life. Sometimes I had doubts and second thoughts about drugs, but when I was high, I felt reassured and confident. I left the world behind to those moments until I came down confused and afraid. Fear of death became an obsession with me when I wasn't high. The effects of the speed and acid helped nurture the fear.

I went back to school and continued to use more and more. At one point I cut my hair and started to drink a lot. I thought a change of lifestyle was the answer, but I still managed to find reasons to take pills to study and any other excuse I could find.

I felt that life was empty and meaningless. I became more and more isolated at school and my consumption of speed increased until I was using it daily and my health began to deteriorate. I became paranoid and fearful of people which made it harder to function.

I would hang out with users on the weekends back in my hometown. It seemed that their solution to the dilemma of using was to use more until you reached the point of not caring at all. I finally quit trying to control my using and deciding to quit fighting it. If I was going to be a dope fiend and self-destructive, I was going to do a good job of it. It seemed that it was becoming more and more accepted that dopers were losers and we might as well stay loaded completely. Take as much dope as you can constantly became my new philosophy for survival. The speed runs left me burnt out. I had sores in my mouth. My skin was turning yellow and much of the time I couldn't go out at night because I couldn't focus my vision and I would hallucinate.

I came home from school in the summer of 1971 totally wasted; it was then I was introduced to heroin. Shooting morphine and heroin was becoming more and more a part of the local dope culture and I had a few friends who were well into it. I tried it and thought it was good for me because I could relax and eat and sleep.

I learned to use a needle and by mid-summer I was shooting dope two or three times a day.

Jails, doing time, violence were the new topics of conversation; no more peace and love. Now it was coming, ripping people off and doing whatever was necessary to get narcotics. I did not like any of this new talk, but the dope made it more and more acceptable. Finally, I got involved in breaking in houses and forging checks. I stole from my family, lied, sold my musical instruments for money to get drugs.

At the end of the summer I was arrested for check forgery and put in jail where I went into withdrawal. It was a nightmare to realize how far down I had fallen and was going to have to answer to the law for my actions. My mother bailed me out and the local drug council sent me to a psychologist for therapy which did no good because I was still using. So my lawyer suggested that I go to Lexington to the federal drug hospital. I stayed long enough to detox and came home with the idea that I would go to school and everything would be okay. I also thought one shot wouldn't hurt anything.

Back into active using again. I sought help again at the local drug council because I knew they were sending people to a doctor who was writing scripts for methadone and bartituates for addicts. So my addiction took a new direction. I began to get my supply legally from doctors. Things were going well, so I thought, for about a year until the doctor said he could not give me any more methadone. I got panicky and bought some speed on the street and while I was in withdrawal from the methadone I started speeding. After a few days, I got crazy and started shooting a shotgun off in my back yard at imaginary foes. I ended up in jail for two miserable weeks of insanity and withdrawals.

The court sent me to the state hospital where they put me on two Quaaludes a night, for all the dope fiends on the unit were requesting them for insomnia and bringing in other drugs from visits.

After thirty days, I was released and I went straight for the doctor's office with another drug to add to my requests. I continued to pop pills and drink codeine cough syrup and booze.

I started dating a girl who used and my dependence on her was a means to get more drugs. Her dependence on me was emotional. I feel that she kept me alive through those times when my using was so insane that I would have died without someone to keep me from harming myself more than I did.

I had become a garbage can for drugs. Street drugs, prescription drugs, paragoric, cough syrup with codeine, whatever I could get. I had been put on probation for the check forgeries and I kept getting arrested on drunk driving or brandishing weapons. Needless to say, I was always in trouble with the probation officer and they would lock me up for a while and then send me off to another rehabilitation program or hospital.

In 1974, I was sent to a long-term therapeutic community after spending about four months in county jail. I was very sick emotionally when I got there and stayed withdrawn for the first couple of months. I went through many intense changes in the time that I was there, most of them were positive. I learned to function with other people and started to become responsible again. They gave me a place to belong and something to believe in. What they couldn't give me was a way to live without drugs outside of the confines of the therapeutic community. I finally graduated their program in 1977 and as a graduate and also an employee, I was allowed to drink.

I decided that I wanted to return to West Virginia because the lifestyle of New York was not for me. Really, I wanted to get away from them so I could try to use successfully. I got a job in my old hometown and started to see my old girlfriend who was still using and it wasn't long until I just let go and started shooting speed, and eating codeine pills and methaqualone. I hit the depths of despair because the dope had me again after all that time away from it and nothing changed.

After all that therapy, I still couldn't control my dope; it controlled me. I felt hopeless and worthless like a total failure. I couldn't go back to the rehab house because I felt like such a bad person, like a traitor.

I lost my job and continued to use getting most of my drugs legally from doctors. One doctor had become a friend of mine and felt sorry for me in my dilemma and I used his compassion as a means to con him out of more and more drugs. I was using amphetamines, sedatives and various synthetic opiates all at the same time.

I was miserable, my highs were like lows. I couldn't live with drugs but it was worse without them. I just tried to stay numb or seek oblivion.

No longer could I blame my using on others like before, although I tried, but I really knew the truth. I was off of probation so that was no longer a threat, but still I was a prisoner to my addiction.

Between my sprees of using I started to try church. I began to feel as though God was my only hope, but I wasn't sure if God really existed.

Maybe I felt as though God might just be a philosophical idea to comfort man and make sense out of life, but I needed something real. I could not work and I hit another bottom and found myself alone and sick. It seemed as though being alone and sick were a way of life for me. It was at this point I was ready to ask for help in a sincere way.

I didn't believe in coincidence any more and it was a miracle that I stumbled upon a phone number of a N.A. member in the Atlanta, Georgia area. I spilled my guts to him over the phone and asked him what he thought. He said it sounded as though I needed to learn how to live without drugs. That was so simple but it said it all.

With God's help I caught a bus to Atlanta. In withdrawal and praying and some crying, I made the journey. I feel that the willingness and courage to make such a move came from a power greater than myself. God as I understand him has worked many miracles in my life in the past two years of my recovery.

In those first meetings I heard people share honestly. They sat and talked with me and they understood. They really cared because they were like me. They had been there. There was no condemnation or lectures. They gave me hope by their example. It really was possible to get a new way of life filled with happiness and usefulness to other people.

I didn't have to be alone ever again. I could use my past to help others and pass this new way of life on to others who were in despair and misery. It was okay to let people know when I hurt. I didn't have to pretend to be cool and have all the answers or hide my true feelings.

They loved me back to health, people were patient when I needed to talk, they listened and shared what had worked for them. I was a part of their lives.

They taught me that the steps were the foundation of recovery. The Program has freed me from my prison and shown me how to be myself and live life on its own terms. I owe my life to Narcotics Anonymous. God works through the people in this fellowship and it works if you want it. Surrender has been the key for me.

If I work this program, my life gets better. Today I have friendship, love a family of brothers and sisters from all over the world from all walks of life. We are united in a way that was once impossible for the addict. We have been delivered from a living and dying hell to happiness, peace, joy and a fulfillment that escaped our wildest dreams in the past. It has been freely given to me out of love. The Program is simply sharing, working the Twelve Steps, attending meetings and practicing the principles of the Program.

First and foremost, I must remember that I suffer from a disease called addiction and that using is insanity and death, so I cannot take that first fix, pill or drink. Drugs in any form are poison to me and will kill me emotionally, spiritually, mentally and physically.

God has revealed his love for me through the fellowship of N.A. I am grateful to be able to write my story and share it with whomever may read it. I pray that it may be of some help and bring hope to someone like me who once had no hope. May God be with you in the spirit of this fellowship. I pray that this new way of life will bring all the joy and love it has brought me.

God Bless.

Chapter Twenty-Seven

RECOVERY IS
MY RESPONSIBILITY

My name is Jo. . . I am an addict. Like most addicts that I have met, I did not begin my addiction with the intention of making myself sick, physically and morally. As I had done all my life, I was seeking escape from the stresses and demands of living. In later life, I called this "having fun." Any pressure was too much to bear; and as my illness progressed, I retreated into a world of isolation and chemicals.

During my childhood, I found escape in pretending games. I was not like I thought my friends were, so I sought the changes that were necessary for me to be acceptable. I tried new clothes, different hair styles, even different sets of friends. I wanted to be liked. It never occurred to me that I must change inside. As I became older, my opportunities to alter my external environment expanded. I could change residences, find new jobs, get married or get divorced. I did all of these. No extreme was too far reaching.

My introduction to chemicals came in the middle 1960's during my teen years. Along with my friends, I partied on weekends, drinking alcohol at every opportunity or occasion. While everyone seemed to be enjoying the party, I was hiding in the ice chest. Later in life, I became the perfect hostess, fixing everyone's drink from the kitchen or bar. It was always "everyone else" and then there was me, with no connection. I drank more than I served, I am sure.

My senior year of high school found me experimenting with amphetamines. My consumption of alcohol had begun to affect my grades, as were the late night hours. I believed that by taking uppers, I could improve my study habits. I continued to believe this even as my grades plummeted. Graduation prevented my failing at school or my dropping out all together. I came to the graduation ceremony drunk, much to the chagrin and disgust of my family. I had become argumentative with everyone. I couldn't even stand myself.

During the next fourteen years, my life decayed tragically. I tried changing everything but myself. After I was married, I joined a church, which strongly suggested that its members refrain from drinking. I so wanted to be accepted, I did not drink for a year. I was at war with myself. I felt as I had as a child, that I was different. Try as I would, want as I would, I was not, could not, be like those good people at church. They did not understand me any better than I they. That I had decided to refrain from any drinking or drugs had nothing to do with my inability to handle them. Even abstaining from chemicals, I did not "fit." It was not a new hurt. I began drinking again, feeling guilty as I had never dreamed that I was capable of. Because I was a housewife and had no outside income, I padded the grocery bill in order to pay the liquor store and doctors and pharmacists. I felt myself clever indeed; and also I believed that I "fit" at last.

The delivery of my first child was a learning day for me. After I was admitted into the labor and delivery area of the hospital, I was given a shot for the relief of pain and anxiety. I was never to forget; and I suffered pain and/or anxiety for another twelve years. There was always a drug for a symptom; and I learned quickly how to manipulate one to acquire the other. My life became one of appointments to doctors' offices, lies to them and to myself, prescriptions and trips to the hospital. I had many surgeries that could have been and should have been avoided. Tragically enough, I often believed that I was sick.

A few weeks after the birth of my second son in 1970, I suffered a total collapse. I was given tranquilizers; and later hospitalized, where I received shock treatment for God only knows what purpose. The first hospital stay set me on a road of psychiatrists, mental health centers, and sure, certain ruin, although my symptoms were clearly drug related, I was treated with the very drugs that were killing me.

I took depressants and became depressed. I took diet pills and mood elevators and became edgy and wouldn't eat. My behavior became manic-depressive when I took both; and I became psychotic when I added the drug alcohol. I had odd notions about life and I hated myself. I loathed my body. In the face of all of these bizarre "symptoms," I was hospitalized innumerable times, where medications (drugs) were administered indiscriminately. Eventually, as I moved into a drug culture, I learned to "play the game." Copping prescription drugs was far easier than hustling, and somehow more respectable.

My personal life was a shambles. I prostituted my mind and body. Nothing mattered. I wanted to die. During these years, my family tried to warn me of my warped state of mind, I still hung on to the belief that they didn't "understand." When I told my doctors of the conflicts at home, I was advised that in fact the family did not understand. I was given a prescription for yet another panacea, and I went on my way. In the end, the only people who had any time for me at all were the mental health professionals. I had an army of paid "friends."

I don't blame doctors, or anyone else, for my addiction, for my addictive personality is and has always been a part of me. Certain individuals in the mental health and medical health profession who should know better did contribute to my addiction and allowed it to continue. I know that recovery is my responsibility, with the help of God. I manipulated the medical profession; and not knowing what else to do, they obliged with prescriptions for symptoms, as they are so trained. I share this tragedy with too many. Ironically, it was a psychologist that guided me into N.A. and another Twelve-Step Program. She had given up on me; and as a last resort, insisted that I attend these meetings. I went and have been clean since May, 1980.

At that first meeting I was hugged and made welcome. I "fit." I cried and found the road to a happy recovery. My world expanded and I began to grow. I had been "looking for myself" inside of myself, and had found myself empty. Coming into the Twelve Steps of N.A., I have found happiness outside of "me." I have made the discovery that I must share so that I might keep anything at all, and that in the giving there is joy and satisfaction. I have learned that to be free, I must surrender; and that surrendering brings comfort. I have learned that it was, as much as drugs and alcohol, my total sense of "self" that was seducing me into death.

The greatest discovery for me this past 20 months is that there is a power in the universe, that I know as God, who loves me. If I am to be a part of this world, I must always be aware of my Creator. If I seek out His will for me and endeavor to carry out his will, my recovery is secure.

The growth that I have enjoyed has not been without pain. I am continually made aware of my own character defects, and as I become willing, I rejoice in letting them go, as I turned my addiction to narcotics over to God. Growing up at age 34 still baffles me, but my tears mean something. I have comfort in my hurts and a solution to my problems, whatever they might be. I have, today, something that will last.

Chapter Twenty-Eight

UNMANAGEABLE

We are the same people cut from the same cut-of-cloth. I am a person who did a lot of time. I started drinking at first. I remember getting drunk at the age of fifteen and falling across the grass and knocking my front tooth out by the sidewalk. So I have never forgotten that I love to do anything that will keep me out of the "here and now."

I am nothing but another person "acting a part of Narcotics Anonymous," nothing but another person trying to live clean and recovering. I know for a fact that the Program works and I know that because I am one of the miracles, just like everyone in these rooms is one of the miracles.

I remember my bottom. It was a typical night for someone without any money, any drugs or any friends. I was lying in a house where the people had gone to jail. They set out to score and they did not ever come back. I was left there. I was watching the house just waiting for someone to come, just waiting to score, so that I would just be able to get well. But God just saw fit for me not to have that happen. As I sat on the bed, and I pushed the cockroaches out of my face (and there were a lot of them) I had a war going on with those bugs. I would turn out the light, my hand would catch a bunch of them and then I would put them down the toilet. And I was thinking, "Is this all there is for me in life?" My arms were swollen from shooting drugs, my lips were red from drinking wine, and I felt like there was no hope. I remember I reached into my pocket and I had a twenty-five cent bus ticket left from the Welfare Office. I packed up a little bag of the little bit of clothes that I had left, and I caught the bus to the V.A. hospital. All the time I was riding my head was telling me, "I just want to go and lay there. Find a domicile or something. Just to lay down and die." But, that was the day of my spiritual awakening. I was at the V.A. with "spit creases" I had placed down the front of my pants, another notch I had put in my belt with an ice pick to hold them up, weighing 160 lbs., looking like a skeleton of my former self, with 30 years of using behind me. While trying to get in on the methadone program, I ran across a person on the program who was to become my sponsor. We had spent time in prison together. He asked me how I was doing. At first I told him, "I'm doing OK." But I knew deep in my heart, I was not doing worth a damn. I remember feeling that of the words just coming out of my mouth, and I said I wanted to go into his recovery house. I wanted to try it "one more time and give it my best shot."

I had thought that I had had a heart-attack and I thought I was dying because I felt just like an empty shell. They took me into this hospital and got me back to health. First, there was my health back in line, then my thinking got a little clearer. I remember when I first started going to meetings after being dry for about ninety days.

I remember seeing people at meetings. It sounds corny, but I wanted what they had. I wanted to be able to say: "My name is Bill and I am an addict. And that I am doing something about my life!" I used to think the people there were conning. That's what my head was saying, but deep in my heart I knew what they were saying was true.

Today, I have learned how to be more of a person. I have learned how to feel a lot better. When I was sitting in the rooms of N.A. meetings, I kept going back—kept doing what people said to do. I did my inventory, took a Fourth Step and a Fifth Step. Then I took a look at my character defects and then I could understand what people had meant and talked about.

I never will forget when the light flipped on and I knew that this was all about living. After that, I went right into the steps to the best of my ability. It started because I knew for a fact that my life was unmanageable, because *I* was! Unmanageable...this was where drugs and alcohol had brought me to, and left me. I knew that if I stayed around this Program, followed directions, and if I prayed, then maybe God would restore me to sanity. I am not wrapped too tight now, but I realize that some are sicker than others. I know for a fact that it works when I ask that my will be removed and I just to the will of God, this is the Third Step.

It's hard—it's hard to work His will inside of my own, but I do it to the best of my ability today. And, then when I took my Fourth Step and wrote out all those little things—those little things that make me think I am less than someone else.

My Fifth Step was one of the hardest for me because I did not want to share with another human being those things that made my character defects so glaring. Yet sharing with another human being and God is another action step. It has taken me 1½ years to really understand what a Sixth Step was because I was clean and recovering and just becoming aware of my character defects. But the willingness that I had learned from my Third Step and the knowledge that I have obtained through my Fourth and Fifth Steps gave me strength to ask God to remove these defects (which I have to do every day). I did my Fifth and Seventh Steps together not really knowing the difference between character defects and shortcomings, which I am not too sure about today. Working the Eigthth Step was not too difficult because of my awareness of the Fourth through Seventh Steps. I remember when I made my first amends. God, how I felt, but when I made my last one, I felt all the weight of the world being lifted off of me. One night I was speaking at an N.A. meeting when I looked over and there was my crime partner's sister. The very girl who I owed my last amends to. God gave me the willingness and the courage and the opportunity to complete my Ninth Step. I knew then that I never had to go back out again because of snitching on someone. You can't go back to the ghetto where you came from. I realized it was all over and I felt good. I am one of those for whom taking a Tenth Step

195

at night was not hard. That fear and that guilt I had inside of me is gone!

Something that was difficult for me was the Eleventh Step. It took a "spiritual lady," and other things I won't get into now, to learn to meditate, and I am grateful for those experiences because after that conscious contact, I review and look over each step each day.

I love the Twelfth Step like I love the Program. Like I love my God and my life today. The Twelfth Step had given me a way to go. I work with others, sharing at meetings, supporting N.A. as a whole, by being active. I am just so, so grateful that God has seen fit to let me live again, and for the people who have been put into my life.

When I started working the steps, I was in my 2nd year going into my 3rd year of being clean and just like the miracle of the Program, I am finishing my 3rd year of being clean and going into my 4th year. Now I have 6 years...SMILE!*

I never would have thought while going into the V.A. hospital one rainy morning that my life would become so rich and so full. I have more friends than I ever thought I would have. I have more things — not only materially, but things like respectability — like love — like willingness to share and care. I can safely say that I have an "attitude of gratitude" to God today. I have gratitude for the rehabilitation center I came out of, my sponsors, for my fiancee who I love and to the Program of N.A. — to which I owe my life. All I can say to the newcomer is that the Program works, the promises are there if you work the Program — give yourself a break. For a person who was a complete 'stomp-down dope-fiend' addict — in jail or out of jail — I just want to thank God for letting me be a survivor.

*Written in 1979.

Chapter Twenty-Nine

HOW DO YOU SPELL RELIEF?

When I first entered the Program of Narcotics Anonymous, I was sixteen years old and full of reservations. After all, I was too young to quit using drugs forever. I thought there was still lots of fun to be had. The only reason I was there was because if I wasn't, I would have been put in prison for two years.

What I failed to remember was that there had been no good times for quite a while. Sure I had a few cheap thrills or maybe a nice rush, but it had been years since I had actually felt good inside. If I looked closely, I could see that I felt miserable. I entered the Program on my knees, so to speak; devoid of all human feelings. I was like the walking dead.

My addiction first started when I was around 11 or 12. I was just cutting school, smoking pot or getting drunk. By the time I was 13 I was shooting heroin, living on skid row, 3,000 miles from home, with a man who didn't even speak the same language as me. When I look back and see this, I can't help but be frightened of how quickly addiction can progress.

My addiction took me to many places that I didn't like. When I was 14, I ended up in a women's maximum security prison for about four months. I lied about my age so that they wouldn't send me back home, they believed me! I look back on this as a prime example of my insanity. As for my spiritual self, well, that was non-existent. I had an "emergency God" I would pray to when I got locked up or in a tight situation. I figured that God had pretty much checked me off the list and I was on my own. My self esteem was nothing to write home about. I had ceased to think of myself as a person, much less someone who could love or be loved. I felt as if I was spent and had a wet brain at 16. During the last six months of using, I shot every chemical I could get my hands on, and still couldn't get enough to find relief. I had never in my life felt so lonely and hopeless. I felt as if I were 65 years old, and had experienced everything of a hard and ugly nature. I had sold myself totally and completely. I had been raped several times, had an abortion, lived with six different men, been beaten, and was now locked up again. None of this, however, was worse than the prison I kept myself in.

In the condition I was in, it was not hard for me to surrender. It was plain for me to see that the people I saw in the meetings were just not suffering as much as I was. This was my first incentive to stay clean. I suppose this was all I stayed around for during my first year.

For that first year in the Program, I was also in therapy. This was a great excuse not to work the Steps. Who needs s sponsor? I had a therapist. Who needs to do a Fourth Step? I go to a group to dump all my feelings. As a result of those rationalizations, I stayed a depressed and unhappy, but clean person. I had yet to find recovery. Then something happened. I started getting involved in service work. This put me in contact with an addict who had experienced recovery. These were the people who talked about a Higher Power, and Turning Over of the Will. They also told me to get a sponsor, and do a Fourth Step. Once again, I could see that these people weren't suffering and I was. So I followed their suggestions.

The first thing I did was to look at myself, and surrender unconditionally. I sincerely believed that a Higher Power could restore my sanity, and that I would stop trying to figure out what God's will is and just accept things for what they were, and to be grateful.

I got a sponsor, took my Fourth Step, and shared my Fifth. It was right about that time that I felt a real and true relief. I call the inner peace "serenity." With such great content, it was easy to continue through the Steps.

I no longer hated myself for my defects, for I had faith that they would be removed by my Higher Power, in His own time. I am no longer afraid of my past. I know who I have wronged. I have squared with these people and I am willing to square with those I cannot find.

I practice the Tenth, Eleventh, and Twelfth Steps on a daily basis, and have experienced a 180° turn around — which I call RECOVERY.

I really feel good today, and I'm grateful to my Higher Power and Narcotics Anonymous for giving me a Recovery that I can enjoy and share with other addicts.

Chapter Thirty

PHYSICIAN-ADDICT

I have a recollection of sitting in my office late one afternoon listening to the story of a heroin addict consulting me about a problem with his gall bladder. He needed hospitalization and surgery and I was informing him about the procedure he was about to undergo. I felt a strong sense of revulsion as he confided to me about his habit and his concern about his need for strong analgesics in the hospital. I told him in my own unknowing way that I thought it would be very helpful if he could at least stop using for a week or two before the operation; I had ingrained images of him in acute withdrawal, writhing around on the floor pleading for his next "fix."

It had been a long day, and after the patient left I thought about his terrible plight and the disgusting thing he was doing to himself. I sat back, reached into my top drawer, pulled out a short acting narcotic and syringe and gave myself free passage into a world of relaxation from the tensions of the day. Like most physicians, I had practically no comprehension of addiction in others and certainly no recognition of it in myself. I was a busy surgeon insidiously developing a disease which cleverly had insinuated itself into my life. Addicts and addiction were foreign to my understanding, and my medical school training had barely even touched upon the subject. I was also the unknowing, indiscriminate supplier of thousands of major and minor tranquilizers and narcotics to patients, many of whom became addicts themselves.

From intermittent bottles of codeine cough syrup in the Air Force to increasingly stronger medications for headache, insomnia, and stress, I developed a slow but progressive desire for something to ease my pains of living. At some point, I crossed that magical line separating me, the addict, from the occasional user. I lied to cover up my habit, and yet my wife always knew and this led to progressive deterioration in our marriage. I would use late in each day and would arrive home in a semistuporous state, eat a quick dinner and fall into bed early in the evening. By morning, I felt rested and ready to face another day. The more I used, the more I felt an impending sense of doom and destruction. Periods of drug induced relaxation were often followed by periods of severe anxiety and depression. My colleagues noticed the change and one recommended that I seek psychiatric help. The pattern of my illness would have been obvious to any physician who knew as little as I did. On one occasion, I was actually caught and confronted by a colleague, whose only comment to me was a cajoling "cut it out before you get into trouble."

I spent long hours spilling my emotions to the psychiatrist and for a while things seemed better. I even used less for a while. But eventually I got back into the regular and progressive pattern of using. The psychiatrist even knew about some of the drugs I was using and allowed himself to be manipulated by my own thoughts on the subject. "I could stop anytime and only take the drugs when I really need them to relax." How often has the addict mouthed those words? Interestingly enough, at no time did the psychiatrist or any of my friends or my wife ever use the word addict. After all, in my social sphere, an addict was a degenerated tattooed person in a leather jacket who probably rode a motorcycle and committed heinous crimes to pay for his heroin habit.

I was a successful surgeon, making a great deal of money, living in a beautiful house and driving a beautiful car. I was supposedly an intelligent man who had completed years of training. Had I been called an addict at that time, I would have laughed it off in a casual, arrogant fashion. Ridiculous! But I was sinking deeper and deeper into a morass of depression and I didn't even know why. I knew that I needed the drugs, but I couldn't comprehend why. When I tried to stop, I could manage for a day, only to be beset by a greater depression and all the physical sequelae of early withdrawal. I would drive to work in the morning, and, promising that I would not use that day, would end up finding some excuse to give myself that ever lessening satisfaction and relief in the form of a pill or syringe. My life, with all its positive "fixtures" to the onlooker from the outside, had become a living hell, only partly aided by drugs, a thirst that could never be assuaged.

My wife would ask, "Why" I was doing this to myself, and I could answer neither her nor myself. I had been in control of myself and my destiny up to this point, or so I thought, and now in the midst of financial and professional success, I was dying a slow death. With millions in assets, I was poverty stricken emotionally and bankrupt spiritually. I was ready to die, but held on for some strange reason because of a persistent though steadily waning love for my family.

As if by some outside force, my life and future was then snatched from a precipice as I was about to fall for the final time. I was confronted by two concerned and worried physician colleagues who saw my condition as one sees the summit tip of the iceberg peeking above the ocean. They knew little of my problem and understood it as I understood it — not at all. But they insisted that I seek out help or they would have to take measures to protect me from myself and to protect patients. I was bereft of any stable judgement, and had lost all my self-esteem and desire to live. I gave up at that moment and called a "hotline" established for physicians. I met with an individual a few hours later who started to listen to my story. After only a few moments, and after seeing my physical and emotional condition, he held up his hand as if to say, "Stop. You're addicted. Do you want to do something about it?" When I answered "yes," he stated that I needed to be detoxified in a hospital. I put up a token resistance, but quickly acquiesced and was taken to a drug rehabilitation center.

Nothing more seemed to matter; my pride was gone. I often reflect on those last moments and how my self-will deteriorated to such a point where I was ready to give in. I don't understand even today what happened to convince me to go into a hospital and that was perhaps my first introduction to what I later grew to understand as a "Higher Power" in some way watching over my life. Until the day I walked into the hospital and this Program, I was an intellectual and staunch atheist, who could not reconcile any force outside myself in my comings and goings. I had always done for myself and by myself and was convinced that man must make his way alone for life. I was in for a rude awakening.

Some come into this Program by attending meetings alone and some are fortunate enough to be hospitalized, medically detoxified and gradually helped into the program of Narcotics Anonymous. I am a stubborn man and somehow I feel that nothing less than the intensive hospital course was needed to turn my head. I entered the facility an arrogant, wealthy physician devoid of humility and looking down upon tragic, deplorable individuals around me. I had the audacity in my first moments in the acute detoxification unit to ask the therapist for her qualifications and what she thought she could do for me. She smiled at my hostility and merely replied, "I'm clean, baby, and you aren't for starters!"

People on the Program often talk about reaching the bottom before being able to take the first step toward recovery. We are surrounded today by people who have entered the group at what appear to be very different levels of personal, economic, and social collapse. But I feel that most have reached their own bottom. Something inside cries out "Enough, enough, I've had enough," and then they are ready to take that first and often most difficult step towards dealing with their disease. So it was with me. With all I had outwardly, I had lost almost everything inwardly. I had reached my bottom as surely as the addict on skid row.

I remember clearly my fourth day in the hospital sitting in a session with a group of male addicts, trying to remain somewhat aloof from the wretched individuals around me. After all, I was a physician, not a bum! And the man who was leading the session, noting my arrogance, suddenly turned and staring icely at me asked, "What do you think about all this, junkie?" Something inside me snapped at that moment and as the tears welled up in my eyes, I sank into the deepest depression I had ever known, only to be followed by a clearer vision of who I am, than I had ever had before; and from that moment on I was able to say without hesitation or qualification, "I'm an addict." That has made all the difference!

I began to change over the next few weeks and I began to attend N.A. meetings regularly. I initially felt that it would be impossible to attend more than one or two meetings a week. It just wouldn't fit in with my busy schedule. I later learned that my priorities were 110 degrees reversed. It was the "everything" else that would have to fit into my meeting schedule. An individual much wiser than I told me that my recovery had to come first: Before everything else in my life; before my wife and children; before my job and my friends, because if I didn't make that commitment, I would lose all those things anyway. So first things first . . . not using is the bottom line and all else follows.

My Program now consists of attending meetings regularly, reading the literature and following the Twelve Steps to the best of my ability. I have learned the meaning of the word "honest" both with others and myself, and I am slowly learning that once foreign word "humility." The Program has not only given me a way of not using drugs, "a day at a time," but has also given me a program of living, also "a day at a time," that had previously been unknown to me. I have learned that in N.A. there is a veracity to such sayings as "I can't, but we can," and "keep coming back" to meetings. Most of all, I am learning to accept myself for what I am.

Recently, I went on a skiing vacation in the mountains and I sought out the Fellowship of addicts at a meeting there. It was heartwarming to be immediately welcomed into a new group so far from home where I again met people from all walks of life united by our common bond. It's a fellowship that I cherish, for these people are helping me to stay drug free and helping me to maintain my intellectual as well as physical recovery.

Recovery is an annealing process from which I am emerging stronger and more able to face the tasks ahead of me. It is sad that we must pass through such Hell before reaching the serenity of peace of mind in recovery. Over the gates of Dante's Inferno is a sign which reads, "Abandon all hope, ye who enter here." They fit well the portals of the addict's personal hell. It has been a slow but progressive passage back through those gates into a world where there is once again hope for those who follow the N.A. program and its Twelve Steps out of the abyss of addiction.

As the years pass, I am sure that the growing awareness and understanding of addiction by the medical profession will parallel a public awareness which will make Narcotics Anonymous and its Program more prescient of the world of the addict.

Chapter Thirty-One

PART OF THE SOLUTION

What it used to be like: living on a farm as a child I felt inferior and was shy around other people. I was full of fear and became angry when things didn't go my way. This behavior continued during my adolescent years.

When I was 21 years old I married and still continued to try and change reality, wanting everyone to agree with me, thinking I was right and reacting with temper tantrums when people disagreed with me.

I became a mother of three children. With my first child I still felt in control, with my second I became overwhelmed, my third I felt desperate. I wanted somebody to take care of me rather than me taking care of others and being responsible as a mother frightened me. Wanting to be perfect made me feel more scared and angry.

One day my husband went to our minister hoping something could be done for me since I was so angry towards him and life in general. The minister didn't feel he could help me, so they found a psychologist in a city 200 miles away for me to drive to and from for weekly appointments. It was at this time a mild tranquilizer was prescribed for me by a doctor who was a friend of the psychologist. The psychologist was kind and tried to be helpful, thinking seeing him and taking medication would help me with my anger. Hopefully, I would start coping with reality better. It wasn't long until the psychologist thought I would be better if I were put on a different tranquilizer; so with the help of the doctor, my prescription was changed.

Still, the results were not being seen in a change of attitude by me, so it was decided that our family should move to the city where my psychologist lived and this would solve our marital problems caused by my anger.

It was very early in my pill popping that I became dependent on them, thinking that I could not exist without their help.

We continued to move as my husband's jobs changed, living in the Midwest and even eventually I remember sitting in a rocking chair and the thought of suicide crossed my mind, yet I told myself my life wasn't that unmanageable. Today I believe that may have been when I crossed from dependency to addiction.

Continuing to use, abuse and overdosing my pills, I ended up in the hospital in the psych-ward. It was at this time the need for a psychiatrist to visit me in the hospital to help me with my problems became apparent. The psychiatrist came in and told me, "You don't like yourself very well, do you?" I said, "You aren't telling me anything I don't know." I left the hospital in a few days, came home with the understanding that I would see the psychiatrist weekly.

I would go to the psychiatrist's office and things didn't seem to get any better, being fearful he would take my prescriptions for my pills away from me because I was not taking them as prescribed.

Changing my prescription from one brand of pills to another brand didn't seem to help. When I didn't have enough tranquilizers to take I would take the anti-depressants. I expected the pills to be a miracle cure for reality.

I went to great lengths to get attention during my addiction. One day I turned on the gas before my husband came home, making sure I turned it off before he came in the door, thinking he would be alarmed and caring what happened to me. He was alarmed and decided with the help of the minister and psychiatrist that I needed to go to the hospital for more help. I knew from past experience that psych-wards didn't seem to help me with my mental problems.

Things calmed down for a while with me changing brands again and seeing the psychiatrist to renew my prescription. In the meantime, I was visiting a social worker telling her when I was on one of the tranquilizers, taking it as prescribed, making the world OK. "I wonder why everybody isn't taking this type of drug." Approximately 6 weeks later, the effects of the pills wore off and I was abusing them.

When the tranquilizers were running low, I'd overdose the anti-depressants and toss and turn in bed feeling terrible but still using, abusing and overdosing them. One night after taking several anti-depressants, I ended up in the hospital on the cardiac ward lying to the nurses which pills I had taken and being told that I, "should feel lucky to be going home so soon." However, I didn't feel lucky or care about living.

I was a pill counter, making sure I had enough for my drug of choice, tranquilizers, left in my cupboard, thinking this was the way to face reality—taking pills each day.

One evening dissolving 50 aspirins in a glass of water, drinking it until my ears rang, then dumping the rest of it out, did cause attention to be focused on me in a negative manner.

Eventually, my husband and I parted and I remarried. Less than a month into my second marriage I became angry, stood at the kitchen sink, pills in my hand, thinking I have no reason to take them, swallowing the handful anyway. After sharing with my husband what I had done, he suggested I call a mutual friend we had in the other fellowship. She shared with me I had a pill problem. It was revealed to me that I had a problem with tranquilizers.

I went to open meetings of the other fellowship and sat back not wanting to level my pride and identify myself as a drug addict at N.A. or the other fellowship.

After not being able to stay away from abusing pills from the medicine chest, and after my friend moved to another city, it became apparent if I wanted to live mind-altering drug free, I had to go to meetings and admit I was a drug addict.

When I started going to N.A. after 5 months of living drug-free, the obsession was lifted from me and a burning desire was given to me to stop using. I would look myself in the mirror and say out loud, "you are a drug addict." and between my first and second year, I was able to admit to my innermost self that all pills were a problem for me and not a select group.

The first half of the first step is the only part of the Twelve Steps I can work perfectly a-day-at-a-time. Today a free gift has been given to me: that I am powerless over all mind-altering drugs.

For years, my pills were a power greater than myself. I took them for the effect they produced. Today, because of the grace of God, I have been restored to sanity. The insanity of the second step is the thinking that precedes the first fix, pill or drink.

My life is made up of daily situations which, if I want to live a life of peace and serenity I turn over to the care of God as I understand him. Being willing to do this has made my life more manageable, for I am letting go of my own self-will run riot. Turning things over to a Higher Power who cares helps me with my faith and trust that there is a divine plan for my life. There is an acceptable place for me in society and the Program. I have taken this step with another human being.

When I wrote my inventory, it was suggested that I write about my anger, my fear and my guilt. I wrote it as an autobiography, starting as far back as I could remember, before I started school as a child up to my time when I came off drugs. I named the names of the people I resented, remembering I was taking my own inventory and not others.

The Fifth Step I took with my first sponsor. With her, I shared the dark side of my life and eventually relief and freedom have come into my life. My understanding is if I share the wrongs I have done then the good spiritual feelings will automatically become a part of my life.

The Sixth Step reminds me to become entirely ready to become honest, open-minded and willing to have my defects of character removed. I listed my defects in the inventory I wrote down, and in time more have been revealed to me a-day-at-a-time.

Through working the Twelve Steps, the obsession and compulsion to use will be removed. Having my shortcomings removed is a goal to strive for the rest of my days. It's been shared that the Sixth and Seventh Steps are often the forgotten steps of the Program. I ask each day today to have my anger removed from my life.

I made a list of the people I had harmed and have made direct amends to those I have, which includes my children. Each day I don't use, I am making amends in kind to my Higher Power, myself and society.

Today, I spot check myself when I'm off the spiritual beam and share my resentments with another human being so it will be cut in half.

Each day, I say "please" in the morning and "thank you" at night. It has been shared that those who sincerely say "please" (and if you don't think of it in the morning, say it when you think of it) won't go back to using. When I heard this, I started making a business each day of saying "Please." I read literature from both fellowships and go to a Step meeting to help me grow spiritually.

My way of living before I was an addict and after I became one didn't work, so I have had to work the Steps and try to practice them in my daily living so I can become useful and whole. Today I'm grateful to be a part of the solution, rather than the problem.

Chapter Thirty-Two

RESENTMENT AT THE WORLD

I had living problems before I ever started using drugs. At an early age, I developed a strong resentment against alcohol. I was hit by a car and the driver was drunk. Later I had resentments towards gays, after I was raped. I had resentments towards my parents after I found out that I was born illegitimate. By the age of 13, I hated almost everyone.

I also started using at that age. My first experience with drugs was smoking pot and drinking alcohol; it relieved me of all my pain. Although I did get sick, that didn't matter. I loved it anyway and I set out to find ways not to get sick. I didn't drink very much after that. I started getting in trouble at home and at school. I was blaming my troubles on authority. I started rebelling at school and I refused to communicate in any way with my father. Things just kept getting worse. If I didn't have pot, I felt very lonely and left out.

At about this time, I lost my ability to think clearly and as a result I got thrown off the football team. I became very resentful over this. I blamed it on one of my teammates because he told the coach I was smoking pot. At about this time my parents decided to move because of my reputation. They thought if I moved away, I would get better. This, of course, didn't work. Wherever I went, my disease went with me.

In the new town, I was introduced to harder drugs and I got into them because they got me further away from reality. I started using acid and speed heavily and I also started dealing. After a short time I was busted dealing in school and I was sent to jail. This was the first of many times to come. I was repeatedly getting busted in school so as soon as I could, I quit.

After that, I hit the streets. I was dealing acid and using it very heavily. The progression of the disease set in. I kept getting locked up. I had no one and I would do anything to get my drugs.

As time went on, I just kept getting more into acid. Everyone told me I was living in a fantasy world and I was. I wouldn't look at reality at all. I had no time for it in my world. My spirituality had changed from Roman Catholic to Satanism. I felt like I had no place in any kind of good world.

I had tried to stop using many times, but it never worked because I couldn't deal with the world. I started to try suicide about this time. I didn't feel I had any reason to live, but I was too afraid of death to kill myself. I felt totally insane after my last suicide attempt. I tried to kill my brother. At that time my mother threw me out. When I was packing to leave, it hit me that I was really sick and I asked to be committed to a mental institution. I saw a psychiatrist and he recommended a drug detox. I wanted help, so I went.

When I was in detox, I was introduced to Narcotics Anonymous and I finally felt like I fit in somewhere. They showed me the Twelve Steps of recovery and told me if I used them I'd get better. Having been beaten enough, I admitted to the First Step and I felt relieved.

The Second Step was hard for me to do at first, but I used the group as the Power greater than myself. To believe in God, I had to pray for faith and shortly the belief came to me. At this time I took a Third Step, which I followed by a Fourth and Fifth Step. At that time I experienced a relief and freedom as I hadn't experienced anytime in life. I used the rest of the Steps to keep my life in order, and a sponsor helped me do the Steps.

Now I go to meetings at least 6 times a week. In meetings, I found I can share with other people involved with recovery. We have a common bond.

A few months ago, I went to my first service conference, which gave me the faith to start new meetings in the area I lived. At the time, we only had one meeting a week and now there are 7 meetings. Being involved in service makes me feel worthwhile.

Chapter Thirty-Three

MID-PACIFIC SERENITY

I am a happy, grateful drug addict, clean by the grace of God and the Twelve Steps of Narcotics Anonymous. Life today is fulfilling, and there is joy in my heart.

It wasn't always this way. I drank and used drugs for twelve years, on a daily basis for ten of them. I was an addict of the hopeless variety. It really seems to me that I was born this way.

I was born and raised in Southern California, in a loving middle class family. Both my sister and I were wanted, loved children and were shown that in every way. As far back as I can remember, I have felt separate from this family, and all of life. Of course, I am talking of an intense fear of life. I cannot remember feeling the simplicity of being a child.

I had the addict's personality growing up, self-will run riot. I always wanted my own way, and if I didn't get it, I sure let everyone know.

Growing up in Southern California, I seemed to get into all the normal things, going to the beach, getting into sports, yet always, the fears and feelings of inadequacy never let me live up to my potential.

I was an average student throughout school, had lots of friends yet I withdrew, dominated by the fear. I guess I was about fifteen when I tried my first drug, alcohol. From the first drink it was oblivion. Finally I had found freedom from fear, or so I had thought. From the beginning, I identified with the rejects, the people who slept on the beach, under the piers.

As I look back over these 12 years, I see how I loved each new drug I tried, alcohol was only the beginning; if it got you loaded, I wanted to try it and I always wanted more. It didn't matter if it was sniffing glue or shooting the best coke or heroin. I wasn't a rich, choosy addict, I just needed to stay high and all my energy was put into that direction.

I quit school in the 12th grade, surfing had become part of my life, so it was off to Hawaii. My parents were very confused concerning their son who didn't do a very good job of hiding his *desperation*. To all who were sane and living life, I appeared very lost and unhappy. You see, it was a very short time after I started using, that the alcohol and drugs quit doing for me what they did in the beginning. The fear had returned, only much worse than before.

This first trip to Hawaii in 1962 was only the beginning of many more to come, trying to run from myself. Hawaii was, and is, a paradise, but I only saw it through the eyes of being loaded. Thanks to the warm weather, it was easy to pursue the only life I knew, the way of life was to wander the streets and sleep in parked cars or other available shelters. At the age of 19, I was back in Hawaii for the 3rd time, a full-blown addict and so lost and confused, I only knew I had to drink and use drugs and there was no other way.

Returning to California at the end of the summer of 1963, I found myself joining the Navy. Being lost, that seemed to be the easiest thing to do, just sign my name, it was easier than looking for a job. I was so burned out already and wanted something different, yet didn't know how to ask for help. The Navy, of course, was not the answer, the drugs continued and after two years I was discharged. The psychiatrist said my mind had become so disordered from the use of marijuana and LSD, plus I had jumped overboard in rage at the Navy.

I had convinced myself that once I got out of the Navy things would be different, no one would be telling me what to do, yet I met a new friend at this point . . . the world of fixing. This was in 1965, and the next six years were the worst years of my life, and yet, as I see it today, they played the part to get me in the Program today.

After getting out of the Navy, I got married. How and why this woman married me is a mystery even today. On our wedding night, I shot some dope and slept on Venice Beach with my dogs. This is the type of behavior a selfish, self-centered addict has, concerned only with himself and getting loaded. The way I was able to stay loaded was by dealing, always being the middle man. The house we lived in was being watched, it was on the Venice canal in Venice, California.

My parents knew all that was going on, so with my wife four months pregnant they helped us get out of there and it was back to Hawaii. We lived on the north shore, it was a more isolated part of Oahu, lots of young people lived there. This was the year 1967 and at this time, LSD was real popular and everyone was into the Spiritual thing; Eastern Religion and gurus. There were two Harvard professors who were taking LSD and saying that you could find God, so I thought all that love, peace and joy sounded good. I wanted out of the feelings that I was having. Fear dominated my life. I had been shooting a lot of speed in California the past year. I decided to clean up my life in Hawaii, so I took psychedelics, smoked hashish and tried to meditate.

Somewhere I had read that when the student was ready, the teacher would appear. Little did I know that the Program of Narcotics Anonymous was about to be introduced to me, and that it would become my teacher.

I was able to stay away from shooting dope that year. My wife and I had a baby girl and were on welfare, living in the country. I seemed to be fitting right into the movement of the time; flower children, the everything is beautiful consciousness. Yet still, inside, everything wasn't beautiful.

There was a four-bedroom house next door to us for rent, and one day this woman appeared and told us that God had told her that she was supposed to live there. She was in her fifties, had long gray hair to her waist and wore a bikini most of the time. She had no money, but said she was led to this house.

This woman seemed to radiate a feeling of love and joy that I had never felt from anyone else before. Immediately upon meeting her, I felt as if I had known her forever. Something in me was drawn to her. Little did I know that she was to become my sponsor, and play such a big part in my life! This was the beginning of a journey that even today amazes me. It is a way of life, a way of learning complete trust in a Higher Power. Through a series of miracles, which I now have come to see as quite normal to my life, this woman ended up in this house with the rent paid every month. Needless to say, this house became a Program house.

A meeting was started at this house, it was called the Beachcombers Spiritual Progress Traveling Group and through the years it has traveled throughout the United States from Hawaii to the East coast and through Europe twice, always attracting the addict who still suffers, offering a way up and out.

I remember my first meeting at this house in 1968. For the first time, I felt as if I really belonged. Not so much because I heard people talk of using drugs as I had, but because they spoke of what was going on inside, for the first time I found out that other people had fears also. Yet with all the hope this meeting brought me, it was only the beginning of a three year period that I would not want to live through again.

I identified from that first meeting and wanted a new way of life. I would stay clean for a short period and then I would use again. First I would just pick up a beer or smoke a joint, but I would always end up shooting dope again. I couldn't understand it then, today I realize that I still had reservations. There was still that thought that I could use.

In the year 1970 I stayed clean for three months, two different times.

The last time was right before Christmas, I smoked two joints and went into convulsions. After that, I took two downs once and that was it. For almost an entire year I didn't know what it was to be clean again. I drank, took pills, and shot cocaine and heroin daily.

Living on the North Shore made it easy to stay out of trouble. There weren't many police in that area. I stayed loaded, my wife left and I knew that I would never stay clean again. One time I ran out of dope and I shot several hundred milligrams of caffeine tablets and went into the shakes for hours. I seemed to be so desperate to die. Although I never woke up in the gutter or on skid row, I woke up on the beach, under a

218

palm tree, with my face in the sand. The feelings were the same, skid row is in the mind.

I really feel that it doesn't matter what or how much we use, where we live or how much money we have, it's what is going on inside that counts. For me, I know I was dying but still couldn't stop. I'd given up on N.A., everyone I knew in the Program had left. My sponsor and a group of clean addicts were in Europe and one of the clean addicts was living on another island and would call every so often to see if I was still alive.

On the morning of October 20, 1971, I woke up with dope in the house and for some reason I walked out to the beach and didn't get loaded the moment I opened my eyes. I remember it was a gray, overcast day and I was feeling hopeless. I just sat on the beach crying, just wanting to die; I couldn't go on. A feeling went through me I had never experienced before in my life. I felt warm and peaceful inside. A voice said, "It's over, you never have to use again." I felt a peace I had never felt before.

I returned to the house, packed some stuff and headed for the airport. I was going to the island of Maui, where my friend who was clean was. My recovery started with miracles. I had no money, yet I WAS LED TO THE RIGHT PLACES AT THE RIGHT TIMES AND I got to Maui. I walked in and told him that I was ready to go to any lengths to stay clean. Staying clean today goes a long way beyond not taking that first fix, pill or drink, it is a way of life, a life that I call an adventure.

I have an outline for living, it is the Twelve Steps of N.A.. I either practice and live these Steps or I die! I really believe that a person who stays clean for any amount of time is staying clean through periods when it seems to make no sense to stay clean. I feel we all have felt like that at one time or another.

I've stayed clean by the grace of God. The Steps have become my life. I've had to take many inventories, the Fourth and Fifth Steps, and I will continue to have to write down what is going on inside me and giving it away.

For me, this is the way it works; keep giving away the old and making room for the new. For me, it never gets real easy to do, usually I have to be backed up against the wall and humiliated and then I share. They say this is a Program of action and that you can't keep it without giving it away; how true it is. In the beginning, I thought I had to say all the right things and save everyone, today I realize I only have what's in my heart to share. Today, I can walk into a meeting and if I am full of the Father's love, then I share it, yet there are times that I walk into a meeting and want to throw the coffee pot through the window, yet I have to stay honest for that's the way I stay clean.

I know today that staying clean and having a relationship with God as I understand Him is the most important thing in my life. When I do that and carry the message to the ones who still suffer, then all else is provided in my life. I really believe that I don't have to prove anything to anybody. I carry the message by letting the newcomer know who I am inside and sharing how I work the Steps one day at a time.

Since getting clean in 1971, life has been anything but boring. I have traveled all over. My sponsor was an able example of following your heart, and that wherever we went, N.A. was alive. Our houses were always open, with a coffee pot going. We started meetings wherever we arrived. Sometimes, we had no money, but we went out to do our primary purpose, and God always showed us the way.

My sponsor died three years ago with eighteen years clean. Most of the group has family now, and we are scattered around the United States, learning different lessons, yet N.A. always comes first. Today, I am married and pursue different things than during the first seven years of my recovery, yet I know that the only way I can have any outside gifts is to put this program and God first. We really have found a way up and out, and so long as we keep giving it away, no matter if it is love and joy or tears and fears, it will be all right.

Today, I live because people are there who care and will listen. I really believe in magic, for my life is full of it. God is loving us now.

Chapter Thirty-Four

THE VICIOUS CIRCLE

I am Gene and I am an addict. In writing this I hope that I can help other addicts like myself, who are trying to overcome their addiction by substituting one thing for another, that was my pattern. I started drinking, whenever possible, at the age of fourteen. With this I added weed so that I could feel at ease and be comfortable with my surroundings in the social activities in high school. At seventeen, I started on heroin and quickly became addicted. After using heroin for one and a half years, I decided to turn myself in to Ft. Worth. When they accepted my application, I got scared and joined the Army after kicking at home. I thought that being away from my environment I would be able to solve my problem. Even here I found myself going AWOL to get more heroin. I was then shipped to Europe and thought that if I just drank, that would be the answer, but again I found nothing but trouble. Upon my release I came back home to the same environment, again I was using heroin and various other sedatives. This lasted for two years. The rat race really began when I tried to clean up—cough syrup, bennies, fixes, etc. By now, I didn't know where one addiction left off and the other started. A year before I came to Narcotics Anonymous I found myself hopelessly addicted to cough syrup, drinking five or six 4 oz. bottles a day. I needed help so I went to a doctor; he prescribed dexedrine and would give me a shot that made me feel good; I found myself going to him practically every day. This continued for about eight months and I was very happy with my new found legal addiction. I was also getting codeine from a different doctor. I now became insanely afraid and began drinking, too; this went on around the clock for a month and I ended up in a mental institution. After being released from the hospital, I thought I was free from narcotics and now I could drink socially. I soon found out I could not. It was then that I sought help through N.A.

Here I learned that my real problem did not lie in the drugs, including alcohol, that I had been using, but in a distorted personality that had developed over the years of my using and even before that.

In N.A. I was able to help myself with the help of the others in the Fellowship. I find I am making progress in facing reality and I'm growing a day at a time. I find new interests now, that mean something, and realize that that was one of the things which I was looking for in drugs. Sometimes I still find it difficult to face things but I'm no longer alone and can always find someone to help me over the rough and confused spots. I have finally found people like myself who understand how I feel. I'm now able to help others to find what I have, if they really want it. I thank God, as I understand Him for this way of life.

Chapter Thirty-Five

I WAS DIFFERENT

My story may differ from others you have heard, in that, I was never arrested or hospitalized. I did, however, reach that point of utter despair which so many of us have experienced. It is not my track record that shows my addiction but rather my feelings and my life. Addiction and dependency were my way of life; the only way of life I knew for many years.

Thinking back, I must have taken one look at life and decided I didn't want any part of it. I came from a "good old-fashioned, upper-middle-class broken home." I can't remember a time when I haven't been strung out. As a small child, I found out I could ease the pain with food, and here my drug addiction began.

I became part of the pill mania of the 1950's. Even at this time I found it hard to take medication as directed. I figured that two pills would do twice as much good as one. I remember hoarding pills, stealing my mother's prescriptions, having a hard time making the pills last until the next refill.

I continued to use in this way throughout my early years. When I was in high school and the drug craze hit, the transition between drugstore dope and street dope was a natural. I had already been using drugs on a daily basis for nearly ten years. These drugs had virtually stopped working. I was plagued with adolescent feelings of inadequacy and inferiority. The only answer I had, was that if I took something I either was, felt or acted better.

The story of my street using is pretty normal. I used anything and everything available every day. It didn't matter what I took so long as I got high. Drugs seemed good to me in those years. I was a crusader; I was an observer; I was afraid; and I was alone. Sometimes I felt all-powerful and sometimes I prayed for the comfort of idiocy (if only I didn't have to think). I remember feeling different—not quite human—and I couldn't stand it. I stayed in my natural state . . . LOADED.

In 1966, I think, I got turned on to heroin. After that, like so many of us, nothing else would do the thing for me. At first I joy-popped occasionally, and then used only on weekends; but a year later I had a habit, and two years later I flunked out of college and started working where my connection worked. I used stuff and dealt, and ran for another year-and-a-half before I got "sick and tired of being sick and tired."

I found myself strung out and no longer able to function as a human being. During this last year of my using, I started looking for help. Nothing worked! Nothing helped!

Somewhere along the line I had gotten the telephone number of a man in N.A. Against my better judgement and without hope, I made what may well be the most important phone call of my life.

No one came to save me, I wasn't instantly cured. The man simply said that if I had a drug problem, I might benefit from the meetings. He gave me the address of a meeting for that night. It was too far to drive, and besides I was kicking. He also gave me the address of another meeting a couple of days later and closer to home. I promised him I'd go and have a look. When the night came, I was deathly afraid. Afraid of exposing myself, afraid of getting busted, and afraid of the dope fiends I would find there. I knew I wasn't like the addict you read about in books or newspapers. Despite these fears I made my first meeting. I dressed in a 3 piece black suit, black tie and 84 hours off a two-and-a-half year run. I didn't want you to know what and who I was. I don't think I fooled anybody, I was screaming for help, and everybody knew it. I really don't remember much of that first meeting, but I must have heard something that brought me back. The first feeling I do remember on this program was the gnawing fear that because I'd never been busted or hospitalized for drugs, I might not qualify and might not be accepted.

I used twice during my first two weeks around the program, and finally gave up. I no longer cared whether or not I qualified, I didn't care if I was accepted, I didn't even care what the people thought of me. I was too tired to care.

I don't remember exactly when, but shortly after I gave up, I began to get some hope that this program might work for me. I started to imitate some of the things the winners were doing. I got caught up in N.A. I felt good, it was great to be clean for the first time in years.

After I'd been around for about 6 months the novelty of being clean wore off, and I fell off that rosy cloud I'd been riding. It got hard. Somehow I survived those first doses of reality. I think the only things I had going for me then were the desire to stay clean, no matter what; faith that things would work out "OK," so long as I didn't use; and people who were willing to help when I asked for help. Since then, it's been an uphill fight, I've had to work to stay clean. I've found it necessary to go to many meetings, to work with newcomers, to participate in N.A., to get involved. I've had to work the Twelve Steps the best I could, and I've had to learn to live.

Today, my life is much simpler. I have a job I like, I'm comfortable in my marriage, I have real friends, and I'm active in N.A. This type of life seems to suit me fine. I used to spend my time looking for the magic; those people, places, and things, which would make my life ideal. I no longer have time for magic. I'm too busy learning how to live. It's a long slow process. Sometimes I think I'm going to go crazy. Sometimes I think "What's the use." Sometimes I back myself into that corner of self-obsession and think there's no way out. Sometimes I think I can't stand life's problems anymore, but then this program provides an answer and the bad times pass. Most of the time life's pretty good. And sometimes life is great, greater than I can ever remember. I learned to like myself and found friendship. I came to know myself a little bit and found understanding. I found a little faith and from it freedom. And I found service and learned that this provides the fulfillment I need for happiness.

Chapter Thirty-Six

POTHEAD!

My mother started calling me a pothead when I was fifteen. Today when I go to a Narcotics Anonymous meeting I call myself an addict.

My first addiction was to food. I remember my mom putting me on a diet when I was five years old and I've been on one ever since. I've always had problems dealing with my feelings and socializing with people. I was born into an alcoholic family and we were not encouraged to express our feelings. I didn't know it was OK to be angry, sad, and depressed. As a child I isolated myself in my room and read. I don't remember going outside to play with my friends. I do remember hurting inside and feeling sorry for myself.

I continued to get sicker inside and when my older sister offered to turn me on to a joint in the seventh grade I accepted. I had told myself I would never smoke marijuana but I thought I was smart enough to handle it. Problems associated with using began happening immediately. I started skipping school, I lost interest in my pastimes, and I was getting in trouble at home. My attitude was rotten. I was belligerent and indifferent. I thought I was cool and getting high was the "in" thing. I began to realize I was having a problem with pot when I bought a bag for my thirteenth birthday and it was all gone before the big day even arrived. My friends told me that was not normal. I tried to quit that summer and I did for three months.

When I started getting high again it was worse. I was smoking more pot and I started taking a few chemicals. I started school again and it was obvious I had a problem. I would go to school high and then skip school to get high again. My grades dropped from A's to C's and D's. Luckily we moved and my parents never saw my grades.

I met a girl who was also in junior high and who liked to party, so we started using together. I managed to maintain through junior high. In high school my addiction started progressing more rapidly. I drank occasionally. I didn't like to drink because I always got sick. I took acid and speed occasionally, but I was dropped out of high school my first year. I went back the second year and I dropped out again.

I got a G.E.D. the spring of my junior year and was sent to the State Hospital that summer. I was suicidal. I thought I should kill myself because of all the things I had done and since I didn't, the world was going to end. I lost it and I didn't think that would ever happen to me—I was too smart. My friends, parents, and doctors told me it was the drugs. I could still handle it and started smoking pot again. In eight months I was worse. I was smoking pot every day and selling it to support my habit. I had tripped a few more times and was taking speed to lose weight. I ended up in the hospital again except this time it was a treatment center.

The first few weeks were a struggle. I still wasn't sure what was real and wasn't. I was afraid. I didn't know what was going to happen to me. I was too scared to go to meetings. I thought everybody belonged to some weird cult. The people gave me phone numbers and told me to call. I didn't go to meetings and I relapsed. I remember feeling like I didn't belong in N.A. because pot was really my problem although I had used other drugs. I read the little white pamphlet "Narcotics Anonymous." It said an addict was someone who "lived to use and used to live" and that "our lives and thinking were centered on getting and using of drugs." That sounded like me. Then it said they didn't care what drug I used and the only requirement for membership was the honest desire to stop using. I thought, well, maybe, just maybe they would let me stay. I started going to a meeting every day or I talked with another addict. The members told me they needed me and I began to feel a "part of!" I attended regularly and tried to support new meetings. I learned about the steps and I tried to work them. I didn't use, I took inventories, I made amends, and I prayed. That's one of the things I'm grateful for is having the freedom to have a God as I understood Him. One day I realized I was being freed from my addiction. The obsession and the compulsion were no longer the dominating force in my life; growing spiritually was.

I got a sponsor and I talked to her. I listened to others who had clean time. I watched others hoping I could learn from their mistakes, like what happens to people who don't go to meetings. I learned about spiritual principles: honesty, openmindedness, willingness, humility, gratitude, forgiveness, and love. I slowly grew to accept myself, to love myself, and to love others. I'm still growing in these areas. I've heard it shared, I am able to love others for I know I am loved. N.A. has given me the love I needed to grow. I worked on being willing and on helping others. I learned about service work. It started with picking up ash trays, giving members rides to meetings, cleaning up after meetings, to being secretary of a group and taking meetings to institutions. I've learned that being of service is a way to show my gratitude to N.A. for saving my life.

I feel real privileged to be clean today. I'm twenty years old now and I've been around the Program for over two and a half years.* Some days are better than others and other days, all I can do is hang on with both hands. I've learned that it's on my bad days that I can grow the most. I just keep on believing that it'll all be right as long as I don't use. I still do the same things I did in the first year of my recovery. I say "please" in the morning, "thank you" at night, go to meetings, read the literature, live the steps, and talk to other addicts.

Thanks to N.A. one of my greatest joys was the day I realized "Just for Today, I never have to use again!"

*Written in 1980.

Chapter Thirty-Seven

I CAN'T DO ANY MORE TIME

I came to the fellowship of Narcotics Anonymous as an addict, out of the California Institution for Women at Corona. I came the first night I got out and it's been here that I've learned how to live, so that it hasn't been necessary for me to drink, or to use pills — barbiturates, amphetamines or tranquilizers — or to use any narcotics in my daily life. It has been here that I've learned a lot about myself, because we are so very much alike. I've always seen another side of myself, whenever problems and suggested solutions have been discussed at our meetings. I have learned from those who are following the program of recovery to the best of their ability, how I can do the same if I am willing to make the effort. Also I have learned from those who have made mistakes. I feel bad when I see that some leave this fellowship to try the old way again, but I know that I don't have to do that if I don't want to. Also it has not been necessary for me to steal or to write any bad checks.

My addiction goes way back. I was drinking alcoholically when I first started at sixteen. I realize today that the reason for that was I was sick to begin with. I had this emotional illness and it was very deep. I don't think that if I hadn't been emotionally ill to begin with, that I would have been carried away with alcohol and drugs. When it became notice-able that I was using alcohol more and more, being in the nursing profession, I tried experimenting with drugs. It grew and grew and became a horrible problem. Although this is certainly a suicidal path in itself, I did, when I was aware and in a lucid moment, realize I was hopelessly addicted. I did not know that there was any answer. There really wasn't at that time. I now think that if it had been possible for me, I would have come at that age, like a lot who are here today. My pattern, however, continued and when I finally reached Camarillo I had lost not only my self-respect but the respect and love of my family, my children, and my husband. I had lost my home and my profession. Somehow or other, I hadn't reached the point where I wanted to try this way of life or to try it all the way. I just had to go on and try in my own way. I tried drugs again and alcohol again and was finally committed to the Institution at Corona for the third time. The last time I went there I just felt that I couldn't do any more time. I didn't immediately connect it with my addiction. I just couldn't do any more time. It wasn't the thought "I can't use drugs," just "I can't do any more time." I just felt completely hopeless and helpless and I didn't have any answers. All of my emotional and spiritual pride had gone. I'm sure that at Corona they doubted my sincerity in ever wanting to do anything about my problem. However, I did want to do something about it, and I know that this program doesn't work until we really do want it for ourselves. It's not for people who need it, but for people who want it. I finally wanted it so badly that I knocked on doors of psychiatrists, psychologists, chaplains and anywhere I could.

I think one of the counselors at Corona, who just naturally loves all people, gave me a lot of encouragement, for I thoroughly took my first three steps. I admitted I was powerless over alcohol and my addictions; that my life was unmanageable. I had tried so many things that I decided a Power greater than myself could restore my sanity. To the best of my ability, I turned my life and my will over to the care of God as I understood Him, and tried in my daily life to understand God. I had read all kinds of metaphysical books. I agreed with them and thought they were great, but I never took any action on them. I never tried any faith in my daily living. It's amazing getting just this far, how I began to get a little honesty and could see myself as I was. I doubted that I could get honest, but I became aware of myself by looking outside myself. I looked at the addicts around me, getting to know them, understand them, and be friendly with them. I would like to give credit where credit is due. I do believe that in my daily attendance at psychotherapy groups in Corona, some very understanding psychologists, helped me become aware of myself so that I might do something about my problem. But when I came out, I thought, "Oh! Can I make it outside?" Many times, institutions took so many years out of my life, that I wondered if I could stay clean and sober and do ordinary things. I doubed whether I could go ahead with normal living, but God has seen fit so see that I have been provided for. In this last year and a half, I've been able to work regularly. I didn't have steady jobs at first, but there was never any long period in between them. Although for a time, I threw out the idea of going back to my profession, which is nursing, I have since reconsidered this and am now in the process of perhaps returning to full-time nursing. With the help of some very understanding people I have met, the future here looks very bright. Despite the fact that when I left Corona everyone throught I was unemployable I now give of myself, as best I can, at my job everyday.

To me this is a spiritual program and the maintenance and growth of a spiritual experience. Without the kind of help and the therapy of one addict talking to and helping another, I know that it wouldn't have been possible for me. The obsession to use drugs or to drink has been completely removed from me during this period. I know that it's only by the grace of God. I now give my attention to my daily problems. It's amazing, having a pattern of fear, anxiety, resentments and self-pity, how much of this too has been removed. No longer do these sway my life. I ask for help every morning and I count my blessings every night. I'm really grateful that I don't have to go through the sickness that accompanies the taking of drugs of any kind, including alcohol. I think one of the biggest things that helped me was that this is a program of complete abstinence. I got over the idea that I had a dual problem. I don't have a problem with drugs or alcohol. I have a living problem, and that is all I need to think about today. I felt that my family and friends had let me down, but I have had a lot of help from my sponsor. I don't know what I would have done had it not been for the doors that she opened with her letters. She shared her experience, strength and hope with me, and it was very beneficial. She continues to be my very good friend. Here in N.A. I have found a family, friends, and a way of life. My own family has also been restored to me through working these steps, though not by directly working on the problem. A lot of wonderful things have happened to me. I can't conceive of anything ever happening that would make me want to forget this way of life.

Chapter Thirty-Eight

FAT ADDICT

I am an addict. I used at least fifty different types of drugs on an ongoing basis for a period of eighteen years.

I didn't know it when I started using, but I used drugs for only one reason; because I didn't like the way I felt. I wanted to feel better. I spent eighteen years trying to feel different. I couldn't face the everyday realities of life. Being a fat kid, fat all my life, I felt rejected.

I was born in Arizona in 1935, and I moved to California in the early 1940's. My family moved around from state to state and my father was married several times. He was what you would call a periodic alcoholic; either he was in a state of self-righteousness or a state of complete degradation. This is one of the many reasons we moved so often.

As I moved from school to school, I related various experiences that I had and I would talk about my various step-mothers. For some reason, I was thought to be a liar. It seemed the only company that accepted me, no matter where I went, was the so-called lower level people and I never felt I was a lower level person. It made me feel like I had some self-worth by being able to look down on them.

My family life was confused and painful but a lot of sound moral values were passed on to me in my upbringing.

I always made an attempt to stay employed. As a matter of fact, on most occasions, I managed to be self-employed in some type of business. I was even able to maintain some civic status by belonging to fraternal organizations.

I was 5'5" tall, and weighed 282 pounds. I ate compulsively to try and handle my feelings and emotions and to make me feel better. As a matter of fact, this was how I originally got into using heavy drugs. I wanted to lose weight so desperately that I became willing to use heroin. I thought I would be smart enough not to get hooked and that I could use and lose my appetite, feel good and outsmart the game. I ended up in penitentiaries and jails and bounced around the country. This was the beginning of the end; not only was I a compulsive overeater and remained fat, but I was also addicted to the drugs I was using.

Somebody told me about the Fellowship of Narcotics Anonymous when I was in a complete stage of degradation and desperation. Seemingly having no place to go, I walked into this fellowship feeling as low as a person can feel; like there was no way out. I was completely and totally morally bankrupt. I knew nothing about spiritual values. I knew nothing about living. Life ultimately was nothing but pain on a daily living basis. All I knew was to put something in me—food, drugs, alcohol—or to abuse sex to feel good, which just didn't do it for me anymore. I just couldn't get enough of anything.

When I came to this program, I found something that I had never experienced before—total acceptance for who and what I was. I was invited to keep coming back to a fellowship that told me there were no fees or dues. They said that I had already paid my dues, via my past life, and that if I kept coming back, I would find total freedom and a new way of life.

Today, many years later, I find that I am free from drug addiction, compulsive overeating, and I have status in the community. I have a nice home, family, executive position and most of all I have a personal relationship with my God, which has made all these things possible. I am able to feel good, to feel joyful, blissful and to feel serenity, even when things are not as good as they might be.

There is no question about it. I owe my lfe to the Narcotics Anonymous Fellowship and God. I can only extend my hope that if you, too, are suffering, as I once was, that you will practice the principles of Narcotics Anonymous and find freedom from pain and a meaningful, prosperous life.

Chapter Thirty-Nine

EARLY SERVICES

I started using and drinking when I was about ten years old. My stepfather and I would go down to his boat and drink beer and smoke pot. Then, he would force me to engage in homosexual acts with him. I was always very scared that he would beat me up. By age eleven, my drinking had gotten worse and he did start beating me. I finally went to my mother. She told me that we needed him to support us, for me to just do whatever he said, and don't make waves.

By age twelve, I couldn't take it at home any more. I stole $100.00 from my mom and left home. After being gone for three nights, a man came up to me and asked if I wanted to earn some money. I agreed because I was almost broke by this time. I went to his house to take a shower. After I got dressed and came out, he asked if I took drugs. I said, "I like everything." We snorted some cocaine and he started taking off my pants. The next day, he took me to his friend's house. On the way there he said, "you are going to get good money and all the drugs you want."

When we arrived, movie cameras were set up and I began my career in "porno" films. There were also two men in the bathroom fixing heroin, and this was my first experience with heroin. By this time, I had no feelings of self-worth and I did not care whom I hurt or what I did to hurt anyone else.

By the time I was 14½, I had my first overdose of heroin. When I got out of intensive care, it was hard for my "sugar daddy" to find me a recovery house. He finally got me into an adult program because he knew some people. At this program, I went to my first N.A. meeting. I was scared, lonely and didn't want anything to do with anyone. At my second meeting, I threw a chair at the leader. I kept coming back for 90 days, and I had to celebrate. I went out and got a fix. I thought it would be easy to get 90 days again. But after I went back out, I couldn't even get one day.

I decided that I couldn't clean up where I was, so I relocated 3,000 miles away. Things got worse. I had to turn tricks to support my habit. One night, I blacked out in a club, got violent and was taken to a mental hospital. The doctors kept me so severely sedated that I wandered around in a shuffle. Because I was only 15, the doctors called my father whom I hadn't seen for two years. He came and got me. When we got into town, he dropped me off and said, "Call me sometime." At that point, I thought I might want to stop using. For the first time I can rember, I cried. I just sat at the airport and cried. I got right back into tricking and using, but I was so tired of lying, hustling, stealing and using that I went to a meeting.

I had just fixed before the meeting, but because I wanted to be accepted, I got up and said that I had six months clean. Then I went outside because I knew I was dying and I didn't know how to scream for help. My stepfather was at the meeting and I didn't even remember what he looked like. He followed me outside and said, "We have to get you in a recovery house." Then he looked me straight in the eye and said, "I love you." For the first time in my life I knew he cared. He then found a recovery house that would accept me.

Before I got to the recovery house, however, I overdosed on barbiturates in a telephone booth while telling someone how to get where I was so they could take me to the house. I stayed in the recovery house for 30 days.

I go to a meeting every day now, and usually make eight or ten a week. Every morning when I get up, I look at myself in the mirror and say, "I'm okay for today. God, just for today, keep me clean."

I'm almost four months clean, and I hurt most of the time. But today, I know that without this program, I will die. At this point in my recovery, I am actively involved in N.A. service. It keeps me busy and shows me a spiritual part of the program I never knew was there. I am slowly learning to trust my fellow members and know that I never have to be alone again. Today, I know there is hope.

Chapter Forty

I FELT HOPELESS

No one in my family ever used drugs, except as prescribed by a doctor. In fact, no one in my family even drank, and I was taught that drunks and addicts could not solve their own personal and emotional problems and were moral degenerates. That's what I thought.

In high school, I started to use drugs, because they helped me feel good about myself. I was so self-conscious and embarrassed about my looks that sometimes I just felt subhuman. I started to get high and became an overachiever to compensate for these feelings.

College was a bore, until I discovered pot. I became a "hippie," met a girl who liked to party and we were married. After school, I started using speed while traveling in my work. Soon, the constant traveling and using caused my first wife to divorce me. This gave me a good excuse to go wild. I wanted to try every drug I could. A combination of narcotic stimulants and hallucinogens became my favorite.

I started to lose the small business I had built up and felt guilty about what I had become—a business and social failure. I had to use something every day to obliterate my feelings of self-hatred, shame and guilt. I decided to get rich and go "big time," dealing between Chicago and New York.

In order to finance the trip east, I set up my fifteen-year-old lover selling acid to her schoolmates. I began buying wholesale in the midwest and reselling to students at a major eastern university. Dealing drugs while traveling for business gave meaning to the words "fear" and "paranoia."

I fell in love with a woman and thought I could change for her. I thought everything would be okay. She helped me control my use and I set out to impress her. My business revived for awhile, but then I began to use heavily again; things got worse. My second wife left me. My business failed.

I felt hopeless. I needed to use to feel okay. I tried to stay high and began drinking heavily and daily again. I just did not want to feel anything. I didn't like me. I just wanted to escape from myself. I overdosed on synthetic narcotics and woke up in the hospital. While still in the hospital, I began to feel better and publicly declared my intention to stop using. I was going to enter the mental outpatient clinic, solve all the problems that I thought caused me to use "hard drugs" and never have to use again. Of course, I continued to smoke pot and drink beer; after all, everyone I knew did.

My business gradually fell back together and I had money in my pocket again. That was my downfall—I could now afford that most glamorous, "non-addictive" substance—cocaine.

How wonderful was my new chemical lover. She made me feel so, so good, again and again. I began to lie, steal and over-charge my clients to get the money for my new habit. I went to several doctors, feigning symptoms appropriate to get prescriptions for large quantities of sleeping pills and sedative hypnotics. I used some of the prescribed drugs, but mostly sold them to get coke. Often, I used too much coke and was always in fear of a heart attack, but I could shoot some downs to knock me out. Eventually, I overdosed this way.

Again, I wound up in the hospital. Once again, I started to feel better after a few days clean in the hospital. I resolved to stop using again and agreed to get help from a psychiatrist. I tried. I told him how bad I was, how I felt about myself, and sometimes how good I felt when clean. I stayed away from my old friends for awhile. The psychiatrist seemed to want to help me. He suggested I take some mood-balancing pills, so I bought some and tried them.

The mood levelers didn't make me feel any better, so I traded them in for some cocaine. I felt better for a little while, but it soon got worse. I began to fantasize a lot about my suicide. Something inside wanted me to live, so I talked to my doctor and he put me in a mental hospital for evaluation. I was detoxed, sent to a rehab center and attended my first N.A. meeting. Now I knew there was a way to stop.

Recovery became a real possibility. It took nine months of regular attendance at meetings before I surrendered and came to believe that I, too, could recover. The problems that I felt had caused me to use began to melt away. The fellowship and a newly discovered Higher Power have helped me stay clean. My attitudes toward other people and my feelings about myself have begun to change. I understand today that I suffer from a disease, not a moral deficiency.

Honesty is beginning to chip away at my guilt. Slowly but surely all my old excuses are losing validity. My life before N.A. earned me a jail term that I never received. I qualified for extended psychiatric care. My physical survival baffled the hospital staff and my family doctor. I believe that I'm alive and free today so that I can help someone else like me find the amazing truth: Narcotics Anonymous works!

My recovery today is firmly based in the Twelve Steps and expressed through service. The steps provide a spiritual resolution to all my problems. Active service work helps insure that there will always be a place for me to go when I need to share. When I am desperate and frightened, I need to share with other addicts who are seeking recovery.

It was suggested to me that I start an N.A. meeting in my area. I was frightened and didn't think I had enough clean time. My friends told me that I could be miserable as long as I wanted to be. With the help of God and other addicts, that meeting began and continues to thrive.

I want to keep what has been given to me, so I actively share through loving service to N.A. wherever and however I am asked. The spirit of this fellowship is in me today. I have come to know unconditional love.

Chapter Forty-One

I KEPT COMING BACK

It was a warm summer night in New York. I was seven years of age. It was late in the evening, but the room was still full of life. My brother and his friends were having a party at our house. I remember the night well. I had a crush on my brother's girlfriend. She was seven years older than I was. I had stolen one of my mother's rings, and I offered it to her. It seemed as if I was born with that sort of nature. She turned it down, and I was heartbroken. I had been associated with alcohol when I was younger. My father was always letting me sip his beer. It made me feel grown up. This night was different. My feelings were hurt. I drank on my own. I enjoyed it. It made me feel good, and it helped me to forget.

It wasn't for another year that I became independently high. This time, it was beer and marijuana. I enjoyed the feeling that this substance gave me. I always felt inferior before, but now, under the influence, I felt superior to the people around me. I came from a broken home, and both of my adoptive parents were alcoholic. I had been surrounded by drinking all of my life.

When I was eight, we moved to California. My mother had gotten together with a man whom I hated. He treated me unfairly. He had caught me stealing, and he never gave me a chance for amends. I felt neglected. I never had any friends and I was always lonely. I started smoking more marijuana and drinking more alcohol. I became involved in "breaking and entering" and a lot of fighting. This all gave me a feeling of superiority.

My mother and I moved to Michigan when I was thirteen. I really felt like somebody there. I could smoke more marijuana than any of the "home town boys." I started growing my own pot.

A short time later, I moved to Florida with my father. There, I started dealing barbiturates. I built up a large tolerance to them. They were not working as well as they used to.

At age sixteen, I was working in a pool hall. I had quit school and left home. I was living on the streets. Even in the gutter I felt superior. A lot of runaways hung around this place known as the "scum hole," and it was raided by the police at least once a day. Hookers, hustlers and dealers made their living there. I was one of the leaders of this group. I became interested in cocaine and hallucinogens. As usual, I went overboard. I started pimping and dealing. I was looked up to by the runaways. I felt like I was "it." There was no one better. We traveled in packs like wolves, and we lived in pickup trucks. I remember going into stores in groups of 20 or 30 and doing our shopping without any money. We were the scum of the town.

Many times I could pass for eighteen. I spent a lot of time in bars, which caused periods of loss of memory and blackouts. Later I overdosed on barbituates, but it didn't stop me. I started using more chemicals than my wallet could afford. I was offered a job "breaking bones" for a living. I accepted it on the spot. This was satisfactory for awhile, but I started requiring more substance. My disease was still progressing.

I hit my first and worst bottom when I started selling my body for drugs. I accommodated men as well as women. I would have accommodated lower orders if it had been necessary. I felt as if my life was not worth living. Many times I had strong suicidal feelings. My moral standards were shot. I felt defeated. Chemicals, marijuana and alcohol were worth more to me than my own life. I needed them to sustain myself. One night I started thinking about what I was doing to myself. I couldn't handle it. Once again, I resorted to prostituting to obtain cocaine. A "friend" of mine pumped my veins full of it. Wow! I couldn't believe it. I was never so happy in my life. I was kicked out of the house where I had been living and was told that, "no junkie was wanted in this house." When I came down, I was really in trouble. I was in a deep depression. I was thinking about my near past, and it made me nauseous. All I wanted was another fix, and that really scared me. I was afraid of becoming a human pin cushion. I had too many friends who were, so I hopped on the next plane to California. I thought I could start over. I was leery of drugs for awhile, and I couldn't get any. I didn't know anyone and I was very lonely. For about five months I turned to alcohol. I drank about one quart of alcohol per day. When I finally found a cocaine and acid connection, I started stealing for money to support my habit. My drug of choice was acid. I could not stop. I got a job at a doughnut shop and began stealing from $20 to $200 per day from the cash register. Every cent was spent on drugs. I took about one hundred hits of acid a month for two and one-half to three months. I couldn't live without it.

My girlfriend moved in with me. This was a mistake on her part. She had a good job and was supporting ninety percent of my habit. After about three months, that situation was at bottom. She moved out and so did my funding. I went into heavy withdrawals. I started working with a band, and I hit my second bottom. I was stealing from my mother to support my addiction. I was a human garbage disposal. I would have done anything that altered my mind. I once stayed awake for two weeks. I didn't eat any solid food at all. I was living on cocaine, acid, alcohol and amphetamines. I dropped down to 115 pounds. When that period passed, I got my old job back and started stealing money again. I was living and selling drugs from my hotel room!

Shortly after this, my recovery started. My girlfriend was admitted to a drug hospital by her parents. I couldn't believe this. Who were they to say that either of us were drug addicts? She found out about all of my lies and confronted me about them. My cover was blown, and my life was ruined. I again felt like life was not worth living. I wanted to die, but I believed that I should make myself suffer for all of the things that I had done. She threatened to leave me if I did not get clean. I had no choice. I loved her. I went to meetings and couldn't hear anything, because I was too high. I tried to stay clean for someone else. After one and one-half months, she told me that she never wanted to see me again. That was really a blow. I stayed clean that night, but the next day I had another relapse. For two months I couldn't seem to stay clean for more than a week at a time. I was confused. I didn't know which way to turn. I started using acid again. Nothing had changed. We were both caught in a progressive downward spin. We almost fixed cocaine one night but couldn't find a needle. So, we snorted it instead. This went on for another two months. It seemed like we just could not stop, that our recovery depended on each other.

Soon, we came back to the Program of N.A. The first thirty days were confusing. My feelings were scrambled. I couldn't tell up from down. Then, one night at a meeting, it was like someone hit me in the head with a two by four. I realized what was happening. I realized where I was coming from and where I was trying to go. I started going to more meetings. I was attending an average of ten meetings per week. I became active by becoming a secretary of one group. I got a sponsor and a lot of phone numbers. I started writing down how I felt about given situations. A Higher Power was becoming clearer in my mind. I started taking the steps seriously. It seemed as if the program was the only way to go on living.

My feelings started to surface. Life slowly became better. I finally realized that I was not a bad person trying to become a good person — I was a sick person trying to get well. And the program was the key to this problem and many others in my life. I had reached sixty-six days of clean time. My life was great. Things were starting to make sense. It was like a large jigsaw puzzle slowly being put together. The picture was beginning to appear. I started feeling good about being clean and having a complete abstinence of all mind or mood-altering chemicals.

Then, the impossible — at least that's what I thought. I had a compulsion to use, and I had the most frightening and humiliating relapse in my recovery. I took some acid, snorted cocaine, smoked pot and drank beer all in one night. It took me three days to come down. I was scared, because I thought that I was going to end up in a mental institution. I couldn't believe what I had done. I had proved myself to be powerless over my addiction and felt like a failure. I experienced so much humility. I was afraid to look into a mirror. I was embarrassed to face the other members of the Program. I fought with the help of people who cared, people in N.A. I regained confidence. I started working a better program and obtained a new sponsor. He had me write out my First Step. I worked my First Step for approximately one month. I embedded that step on my forehead. I took my time on my steps. My girlfriend had a relapse about two weeks later. I went to a party and she was there. I sat on my hands and watched the mood changes in the people I used to party with. I don't suggest a situation like that for anyone. But that's what it took for me. I had to prove to myself that I could do it. I watched my old friends get obnoxious and loud. I decided that night that I was going to live. I was tired of being a walking dead man, mentally and spiritually.

The only chance I had to live was by the Program of Narcotics Anonymous. I must admit that I still have my off days like anyone else, but the big problems in life aren't so big anymore. I am slowly gaining back my ambitions in life. I started putting an effort into school in order to obtain my high school diploma. I lived with my sponsor for three months, working for my room and board. I performed everyday chores, which would never have been considered during my period of addiction. I did everything that my sponsor suggested. If he said jump, I asked, "how high?" I was willing to go to any lengths. I did nothing but work my program. It was no bed of roses. In fact, some parts of my recovery were living hell. It was worth it. The picture started to come into focus once again. Things improved with life in general. I had learned to live on life's terms. I also learned to live a day at a time. I did it the hard way, but today is what counts. It took me six months to grasp this remarkable recovery program. It took everything I did to get to where I am now. I enjoy my life now, a day at a time. I can work the 12 Steps of N.A. on any given situation at any given moment. I enjoy working with others and giving them the same chance that was given to me. I owe my life to the Program of N.A. I owe special thanks to the loving people that helped me and gave me a chance to become a new person with a new life. And the ultimate thanks to my Higher Power — God.

Chapter Forty-Two

IT WON'T GET ANY WORSE

There were a lot of reasons why I first started using. I felt different from my peers. I went to a private school. The kids in private school didn't like me because I hung around with the kids on my street who went to public school. I was a misfit. The public school kids would pick on me, too. I couldn't leave the block, so I had to hang around with them. I grew up feeling different. I had a lot of fights with my parents because I felt very restricted. I really didn't like myself and I wanted to change so that the other kids would think I was cool. I was afraid of girls and thought they wouldn't like me. My first encounter with using was when I was about 12 or 13, with a bunch of girls who were huffing glue. They were real friendly to me and asked me to join them. I didn't even have to think about it. I just did it. Huffing became very compulsive with me. I started doing it all the time, by myself and anywhere I wanted. I remember feeling guilty, thinking, "God's watching me," and feeling wrong. All the guys on the block could drink on the weekends and I wanted to be a part of it, so I wanted to drink. I had to be in when it got dark so I had to wait until my parents went somewhere on a Saturday. I wanted to be able to say that I got drunk, so I stole a fifth of booze from my father and drank the whole thing. I got really sick and did a lot of weird things in my neighborhood, and everyone knew that I was drunk. I couldn't wait until I got to school the next day to see what all the kids would say. I didn't care that they thought I was a fool. It just felt really good to know that they were all talking about me. It enabled me to say things that I was afraid to, do whatever I wanted to, and I could say, "Well, I couldn't help it, I was drunk." Soon after, I started smoking dope and I loved it. I also remember the paranoia, thinking that God was going to strike me dead. I started smoking compulsively soon after I tried it. Dope made me feel really hip and like I had a lot of friends. I remember feeling that God was bull and that I didn't need him. All I needed was to get high, do nothing. I was just going into ninth grade and my grades were going downhill. I was fighting with my parents all the time, and I was unhappy at home. All I wanted was for people to leave me alone and just let me get high. I started burglarizing houses to get booze and money to get high on. Although I made eighty dollars a week and had seven hundred in the bank, I was draining that quickly. I got caught ripping off houses and my parents couldn't believe it. I got put on probation and I felt like it was a big joke. While I was on probation, dope was dry, so I bought three pints a day. I needed to get high and tried THC. I was told it was from pot. I remember hating it. As soon as I came down, and was able to stand up, I wanted more. This became my drug of choice. I soon found it was PCP, but it was too late and I didn't care. I was soon doing acid and everything else I could get and I remember stealing medicine from my mother and doing it in school and being sent to the hospital because I could not wake up. They were downs and I took too much. I thought I'd just have to take less the next time. I started seeing a psychologist because my parents didn't know what to do. I told this shrink that I just used socially. I had it together in my head. He stuck up for me and told my parents not to put it down until they had tried it. He gave me a new license to use. He helped me to get my parents off my back. My father knew I was dealing dope and was going to put me away, so I partied it up and overdosed. I told my parents that I wouldn't use like that if they wouldn't threaten me like that. My shrink still stuck up for me. I conned that guy into thinking I was his friend and I really cared for him. It was me and him against my parents. We convinced them that I was responsible because I paid all of my drinking fines and disorderly conducts. I usually owed money on three of them, and I was just one step ahead of the constables. I was always ripping houses off and people (other addicts). I stole money from my mother twice a week, usually twenty dollars at a shot.

Things kept getting worse for me. I had a girlfriend who did not show up for a party with me, so I did her share of drugs as well as mine that night and I overdosed five minutes after taking it. My brother found me chasing cars and barking at them and he dragged me home and my parents took me to the hospital. I woke up in a strait jacket that was tied to a bed that was soaked in piss and sweat. I was fifteen years old then. I remember a psychiatrist asking me why I wanted to kill myself and I couldn't understand what he was saying. I just wanted to get high. After this, I saw this shrink for a week and he convinced me that if I took acid (or PCP) again I would lose my mind. When I was in the hospital part of me died. I was pale, and slow talking and thinking. I was physically, mentally, and emotionally beat. I tried at this point to just drink three beers a day and just smoke one joint. I really tried but it only lasted three days, and I dropped and smoked as much as I wanted. I didn't use chemicals for awhile. The progression was tamed for the time being. When I graduated from this shrink, he told me I could function in society if I stayed off of hard drugs. After a couple of weeks, I was with a girl who had some pot sprinkled with PCP. After I smoked it, I wanted to do more. Two days later I was out to do anything I could get my hands on. My master plan was being formed. I had just turned 17 and I was planning to set up this big dealing operation. I started getting paranoid, afraid of being busted or killed. I was afraid to go out in the daytime or to talk to anyone on the phone. I had quit school and I wasn't working. I knew it was the drugs and I figured I would just stop using and clean up my act so I could use again. When I stopped using, the walls started breathing, flashes of lights, sirens, friends plotting to kill me, shakes, sweating, crying, and I felt like I was losing my mind. God, how I hurt! I paid friends not to kill me. They told me I was crazy and I offered them more dope. I didn't know what was real and what wasn't. In a last

253

desperate effort to find the answer in drugs, I bought five dollars worth of pot and smoked it to get to sleep for a day or two. I was halfway done smoking when I realized that I wasn't getting tired. I was getting more spaced out. It made all of those things I was feeling worse and I took the pot and pipe and threw it as far as I could. I ran home and begged for help from my father. I had never heard of a rehab before. I had only heard of the methadone program and I wasn't a junkie. They wanted me to join an inpatient and I wouldn't buy it. They asked if I wanted to go into an outpatient rehab, and I was willing to try it. I just wanted to stop hurting, and an addict told me that I might not get any better — meaning that walls breathing, flashes of light, shakes and sweating might never stop. If I did not use today, they wouldn't get any worse. I went for forty days and one morning I got up and it was all gone: the pain, the hallucinations, the paranoia. I had prayed so hard for God to remove these and He did. That was all I really needed God for — when I felt better I stopped praying. I attended a few meetings and really felt I didn't need them. The steps mentioned God and I had nothing to do with that. I got better and I tried to be a very honest person. I had a hard time staying clean. It was a constant battle. My old friends hung in front of my neighbor's house all the time. I turned down drugs a lot. My brother and I shared a room together, and he was still using. He stashed dope in the room and I knew where it was. I used a lot of people for support and I started recovering. I was always being told by my brother that my friends said "Hi," and the fact that I couldn't really be rid of them made it really hard.

I stayed in touch with people constantly and things at home got some better; trust gradually developed. After going through the rehab, I had a lot of clean friends. I had a girlfriend who I moved in with. So much had been going really good. I had a diploma, a brand new car, a driver's license and a good relationship with my parents. My girlfriend was seeing a therapist who told her we should get involved in something together like starting an N.A. meeting in our area. The closest N.A. meeting was over an hour away, and there were only two a month at that. After we started the meeting, she got high and moved out. My best friend had been getting high for awhile and they started going out together, and that really ripped me up inside. I had a dog who I cried to every night, and he couldn't even stand it and ran away. My girlfriend moved out of the apartment and I felt like nothing. The two friends I had left were still friends of hers and spent a lot of time with her. I was lonely, isolated, depressed, and I needed help.

Since I had started this N.A. meeting, I continued to go and the meeting grew. Here I was with two years, crying in the meeting, feeling sorry for myself and depressed and having newcomers with 30 days clean telling me it would be better; be grateful for what you have, and keep coming back. People who were new in the fellowship would come over to my house and 12-Step me. They kept me coming back. They told me that they loved me. I was depressed for two months like that and during that time, two more meetings started. I was making three meetings a week and I started working the steps. I was getting involved in our area service and I started being grateful for everything I had. I was so grateful to be alive and I believed that that was the cause of the N.A. fellowship. It was time for me to get up off my butt and start doing something for others. I started doing public information work in my area and started accepting God's will for me. I attended a lot of meetings, and spoke very often, trying to carry the message of recovery through N.A. I tried "giving away" what I had to other persons, especially the newcomers. I prayed very often and that hollow feeling of being different didn't apply any more. I attended conventions and conferences. At one of these, I had a spiritual awakening! I saw a tiny glimpse of God's will for me, and I prayed for the courage to carry that out. Through service, I can make it possible for many addicts who seek recovery to find it in N.A. Today in meetings, I try to carry a message of hope, and I let everyone know that if they want to recover from addiction, they can through Narcotics Anonymous.

At one point, I realized I needed a little more than meetings. I heard people being told to get a sponsor and work the steps, but this was to new people. I tried to work the steps, but I really didn't know how. I didn't have a sponsor and wasn't sure if I needed one. Finally, I came to a point where I was ready for total surrender; that meant that the things that were good for newcomers—sponsor, meetings, steps—would be good for me. I finally asked someone and he said he would sponsor me and I started and couldn't come out with the words but he said, "okay."

We moved away from each other two months later and I had to ask someone else, and I did. It's been working out real good. He guides me through the steps and helps me to think for myself. That aimless wondering I had done all my life has finally subsided. I learned to enjoy living a day at a time. I try to enjoy my struggle through the steps. I used to think that when I got to the end of the road I would be happy, but today I learned to experience the road I'm walking on—not becoming self-obsessed with where I want to be. I'm happy where I am today and feel I'm making progress in life. Today, I work the steps with the guidance of my sponsor, and I attend three or four meetings every week. I attend meetings to share my experience, strength and hope. Other members learn from me in this way, and I learn from them when they share. It is important for me to always remain teachable. I pray every day and thank God for each day, and the Twelve Steps and this Fellowship of Narcotics Anonymous.

Chapter Forty-Three

MY GRATITUDE SPEAKS

I was born in Atlanta, Georgia in 1960. The son of a doctor and a mother from an affluent family. All my life I have had food, clothes and shelter. I had a lot physically; I was an athlete.

As I grew up, however, I noticed the other kids developing hobbies. I kept to myself and my little fantasy world. Soon, I became uncomfortable around other kids. I could fight well and was respected for it. In 1969, I moved to a nicer neighborhood. I felt the other kids were snobs. I stopped fighting so much and became a class clown. In 1972, I went to a school where the bussing project was being implemented. I met tough kids and we fought every day. I loved it.

I could not relate to my six brothers and sisters. They had hobbies or studies on their minds. I had mischief on my mind. I went to a private school in the eighth grade where I was expelled for stealing pocketbooks and undermining the morale of the entire eighth grade. I was a tough guy conman.

I went to high school determined to grow my hair to my waist and be a tough guy. Doing drugs came naturally. At first I smoked pot. Then after only three months, I was dealing it and hooked. My first year in high school I went from doing nothing to getting loaded every day. I could not go without drugs. I was hooked from the start. I made straight "F's."

Appalled by my conduct, my parents sent me to a military high school. I stayed loaded on MDA for the four weeks I was there, after which I was expelled for possession of drugs. So I went back to the other high school. At first everyone was glad to see me, but soon they would only shake their heads and lecture me on how drugs were taking the color out of my face and making me a vegetable. I resented their judgmental attitudes and rebelled. These were freaks telling me this.

After doing 16 hits of purple haze (LSD) on my 16th birthday, I was never the same. Drugs were not fun again. At best I had been aware of what I could be and the pain of what I was kept me doing drugs, but drugs made it worse.

After flunking the 10th grade, I was sent to a six thousand dollar-year tutoring school for hard cases like me. I was going to clean up my act, take karate and live spiritual or die. I lasted two weeks that time and went back to using. The suffering was overwhelming, as was the alienation. After doing over-the-counter diet pills each day for five months I went into a mental institution. I stayed there eleven months and nineteen days. It was there I first attended meetings. I was not ready, however, and I continued to use the speed I snuck in. The doctor had me on 1,000 milligrams of Thorazine a day. I was a zombie.

The pain I felt that year was beyond words. I felt like an animal in the zoo. I would pace the floors. I would think of dope day and night. I was treated like a subhuman life form. I hated being locked up. I hated being treated like a madman. I ran away three times. Once a policeman caught me running. He pulled out his gun and said if I did not stop, I'd make him shoot me. In my mind I hoped if he shot, he'd kill me. I thought of suicide often.

On the day I got out of the hospital, I got loaded and wrecked a car. The next day I stole a pound and a half of marijuana. I maintained on marijuana, alcohol and pills for the next four month. My condition got worse. I could not work or do anything productive, so I stole and was lonely. I wanted to be with others; I was getting afraid to be alone, but I really did not want to die. I hated the hospital so much but I felt "at least you're out." I would rather die than go back.

After a dope deal fell through and I was ripped off for $105.00, I had no more resources. I went with a group of young people on a religious retreat. It smacked of Christianity and I felt I was destined to burn in hell, but the women looked good and I needed some people to take care of me. During that weekend, I met a member of a 12-Step Program and I turned my will and my life over to the care of God. With Him, I got grateful for the material things I had. I determined to go take a last chance at getting clean.

I found a card with an N.A. member's number on it from when I was locked up and called him. I ended up at my first N.A. meeting. I really felt sorry for the folks there. I had been "straight" five days except for 300 mgs. of Thorazine, the 10 mgs. of Haldol, and the 100 mgs. of Benedril I was taking each day. As you see, I was not serious.

I went to meetings for a month loaded like that; then I used street drugs again. At first, I maintained on marijuana then it ran out and I overdosed, eating forty capsules of speed. That was my last usage. I realized that it is a serious disease and it could kill me. I had overdosed plenty and ended up in emergency rooms, but never like that speed. My heart would go faster and faster and then stop then start again and repeat the process. I knew how to handle bad trips on drugs. I was a veteran of bad trips, but that load of amphetamine should have killed me. I did not even know what I was taking.

I came back to N.A., this time gravely serious. I sat in the first N.A. meeting where I felt the total seriousness of the N.A. Program. I looked around the room; the speaker was telling of how he used to plan to kill himself. I could really relate and I saw other people relating as well. I felt good about that but it was like leaving home. I had had to go through everything to get there, but now I had a new home and I was going to stay. A voice in my head, however, had different plans. It suggested that I get high after the meeting to celebrate my new home. I knew it was insane, yet the thought was so overwhelming I knew I could not fight it. Desperately, I glanced around the room. These people could stay clean! I could not. They were not like me. I was going to get loaded. "No!" I thought. "No! God, help me, God ... God, restore me to sanity," I cried in my mind. When I said that I tingled and the compulsion left. I was overwhelmed. I tried it again. It worked! It worked! Now, I really could stay clean! Even *me*.

I did everything you told me to do. I was as willing as only the dying can be. I made 90 meetings in 90 days. I got a sponsor and I called him twice a day and we talked for hours. At the N.A. meetings I felt an awareness between us addicts. I felt N.A. was really solid and it was the rock on which I would surrender my life. I did something very important. I stuck with the people who were serious about staying clean. We were into service work: emptying ash trays, setting up and cleaning up meeting halls. We would get there early and leave late; then I would call my sponsor at midnight and we would talk until two in the morning. I would take hot baths at night, and pray and write down my concept of God until 4 a.m. Then I would get to sleep. My parents supported me and I tried to show my gratitude and love for them. They paid fifty-thousand dollars a year for hospitals. They knew N.A. worked. It is the only thing that ever worked, but I had to be beaten to the very end. I did as much as I could do. If I had used any more, I know I would be dead.

I feel my disease is progressive. Today if I used it would be even worse than when I stopped. It has subtle ways of trying to get me to use, like luster and lust, anger and pride, but I always remember what my last one did for me and say, "No thanks, not today."

Going to any lengths to stay clean is a big part of the N.A. Program in my opinion. I would work the steps or tunnel to China to stay off drugs. I feel I have found in N.A. the way to the daylight and freedom. If I ever use again, I will die and lose everything. So, I just don't use today.

I do not remember the good times using; that is not a good First Step. I remember the mental hospital, the suicidal thoughts, and the times when I was hurting very badly. I do not want that. So, I came to believe in a loving God who can restore me to sanity. I pray for God to reveal Himself to me in ways that I can understand. I pray, "God, genuine faith." Then I turned my will and life over to the *care* of God. I know that my way did not work so I have to surrender to God's will for me which I do not understand, but which turns out better than anything I had planned. I just prayed to the same God to write my inventory through me; in this way, I sat at a desk for two or three hours and did write down some defects of character and some assets. I began to see my "inner nature." I did not share my inventory with another human being for a week or so. During that week I was frustrated and hurt. I would go back and work on my Fourth Step and get nowhere. Then I learned a very important thing; to go back and read the inventory. When I did that, I saw it was time for a Fifth Step. Next was getting ready to have the defects removed. Of course, I had a good sponsor take me through these steps and I learned to be gentle to myself and be my own friend. When I became my own friend, God added a woman to my life. That has been a learning and growing experience. The relationship forced me to work the steps and call my sponsor. I learned I was still insecure and had to make amends and demonstrate my good will. By working the Eleventh Step, I feel protected from turbulent emotions. I can stay more calm and rational in busy days or hard times, like when my girlfriend is playing games.

In relationships, I have learned that I have to be my own best friend and work on myself. Then I have something that the woman wants. I think women give beautiful gifts and are great teachers.

Nothing has been so rewarding as working with other addicts. No matter what is happening in my life, I know I can get out of my self-centered trip by simply becoming interested in the welfare and recovery of a newcomer or an oldtimer in pain. My story, by the grace of God has a happy ending, thanks to N.A. I would like to thank them in my words and in my deeds.

Chapter Forty-Four

NO EXCUSE FOR LONELINESS

Like everyone else, I started my life as a baby, and later became a child. And, like everyone else, I grew up one day and discovered that I had an adult body. But, unlike most people, I was still a child when I made this discovery. I am an addict. Drugs, in whatever form, were my primary addiction. Self-destructive behavior, obsessive and compulsive thinking were symptoms that lived with me, before I ever used chemicals, and stayed with me after I let go of drugs.

When I was a little girl, I started to look for a substitute for Papa. I had a father, but he wasn't the father I wanted. He had a domineering, compulsive personality. He was intellectual, but very bigoted and negative, and above all, violent and unpredictable. I believe that he had a drinking problem. His job required that he spend a good deal of time away from home, so there were months out of every year that I didn't see him at all. He was my Higher Power, when I was small. He was big, strong and frightful. When he did take the time out to play with my older brother and me, he was so much fun! But, even when we were playing together, he could not be trusted. The slightest thing could send him into a rage. Yes, I was a battered child. It was not uncommon for me to go to school with bruises on my face, along with instructions as to what lie my parents wanted me to tell the teacher on how I got those bruises. I had an older brother. He and I were very competitive. Although he was two years older than I, we were always about the same size growing up. He was popular in school, both with the teachers and with the other kids. All his life, people told him what a genius he was. I worshipped him also.

When I was eleven, my little brother was born. I didn't like that at all, because my status as the "baby" was gone. He represented my first responsibility around the house. Now, there was much more work to be done around the house, and I was expected to help with it. Mama didn't have the time to spend with me that I had been used to. He was a lovely baby, but deep down inside I resented him for being born.

Mama worked all my life. The black maids that raised us kept the radio on the rock and roll stations all the time, and kept the atmosphere pretty loose around the house during the day. I liked the way they seemed to live and think much better than the lifestyle my parents were trying to teach me.

What I seemed to want most in life was attention. I usually got it. I was bright, pretty and wild, with a tough little spirit. I decided early on that I would grow up to be either a singer, a writer or an artist. By the time I was fourteen, I had chosen singing as a career.

In the late sixties, there was very little of the "subculture" trickling into our community, compared to some of the larger cities. But, eventually, through the mass media, a little "hippie" movement was starting to blossom in our city. I had seen people like that in movies, and I really thought they were neat. The men all looked like rock stars, and I wanted what they had. When my older brother discovered pot, I was close on his heels. He found out where all the flower children hung out, and joined them. To his embarrassment, so did I. He was witty and handsome, so older kids in the street scene liked him right from the start. I didn't feel like I had anything to offer these wonderful people, so I donated my body to the "cause." I donated it to any guy that looked the way I wanted him to look, especially if there were drugs available.

I had my first taste of illicit drugs at fourteen, when I was sent out of town for an illegal abortion, and the doctor gave me morphine. I liked most of the effects. I had been experimenting with alcohol since early childhood, and was quickly becoming a partier. And, any time anyone suggested a new kick, like cough syrup or glue, I tried it.

Once I found the right sources, I began taking all kinds of goodies. I really liked smoke, in all its forms, especially hashish. I had my first hit of acid when I was fifteen, and I dropped speed in pill form every chance I got. Downers never really agreed with me, but I took them. Even back then, I can remember a real sense of desperation in trying to find drugs when none were around. The drugs I took gave me the first real freedom I had ever known. I depended on them to expand my mind, to relax me, and to mix with my "hip" buddies.

When I was sixteen, our family moved to South America. I was four months pregnant (again), and I'd been eating acid every other day or so for the first three months of the baby's gestation. The premature baby I gave birth to died in less than five hours. Its little insides were deformed, and it was blue. For a couple of months after that, my parents kept me under lock and key, but they couldn't hold me for long. The pot in Columbia was strong, and it drew me like a magnet.

After a year, we returned to the States, and I was enrolled in school. It had been a long time since I had been in school, so I didn't adjust to the discipline well at first. During my first couple of months back, I continued to use and to fool around with a lot of guys, but that changed when I came down with hepatitis. School got better for me without the drugs. I made good grades, and I even won medals and superlatives. Unfortunately, I had been working on a correspondence course for my junior year, and I never did finish it. I skipped Graduation Day, in order to avoid the embarrassment of being the only senior to walk away with no diploma. I lied about that fact for years.

When my eighteenth birthday arrived, I tried to get out of the house as soon as possible. I had run away from home once before, and the legal aspects of it had brought me back. Now, I was free to go. Of course, it never occurred to me that I had no idea where I was going. First, I hitch-hiked out of the state to visit a lover, only to return brokenhearted when his mother threw me out of their house. Then, I moved in with my brother's rock band, until they kicked me out too, for playing "head games" with three of the musicians, at once. From then on, I used people, in order to have a place to sleep. Believe me, they used me too. I had never worked in my life, so when it dawned on me that I would be supporting myself, it came as a shock. I had several jobs. The first job I had was slinging beer in our town's first "hippie bar." After that, I went from one thing to another, until I landed a really easy "gig" minding shop in a health food store. For awhile, I stayed away from most drugs because I was on a "health kick." Unfortunately, I still had my compulsive personality, and I blew up like a balloon. I might have looked healthy and serene, but deep down inside, I hated myself. It became obvious to me that something was terribly wrong with me. Here I was, clean from drugs, and all I could do with myself was eat like a pig, and hole up in my room.

Music was the only thing I had going for me. There was a piano player that moved in with me, and we went everywhere together, even to the bathroom. Both of us had very high ideals about spirituality, which we tried out on one another, and found to be impossible. Of course, that was the kind of thing that called for organic drugs, like peyote, mushrooms, pot and such, so I started using again.

Right before my nineteenth birthday, I left town, heading west. I didn't have a dime. I didn't bother to tell my mother and father where I was going. I didn't even give an hour's notice at work. I just left. Once I got out there I got weird. The street scene there reminded me of the one in South America, and I fell into it immediately. The first people that took me in were the "guru" type. They were pretty interesting, but I got restless. The next group I fell in with was more down to earth. There was a street gang in the town that ruled the block. One of the members took a liking to me, so I moved in with him. We loved each other as much as either of us was capable of loving anyone, but we sure had funny ways of showing it. We screwed around on each other all the time, and when he wasn't throwing me out or taking me back, I was running out the door, with my thumb outstretched. We were lovers for about six months before his death. One night, when he was out on the strip peddling "MDA," the police searched him. Before they could find anything, he ate the entire "stash" which was enough to intoxicate ten people. His mother came to the funeral, and she gave me a ring that had been taken off his dead finger. I still wear it.

This man's death was the turning point for me. It was the excuse I wanted to just let go of all sense of dignity, and just stay loaded and filthy. Before his death, I had been living however and wherever I could. I hadn't really been staying stoned all the time; I'd tried to be useful and kind to people, and I was even creative at times. But, once my lover was gone, I was free to let everything slide. I went on a drunk for about six months, traveling around the country. I supported myself by panhandling, and I stayed drunk and stoned on anything I could find, all the time. There was usually a man in my life, whose main function was to protect me from the evils of the road. Sometimes, though, the men I chose were the evils. During that time, I changed my outlook and my behavior drastically. In earlier years, I was so peaceful that I didn't even eat meat. Now, I was violent and hostile. There were several instances of rape, which went unreported to the authorities. A woman hitchhiking is considered easy prey to sexual abuse, and I knew that I'd get no sympathy from them. I sobered up a time or two when I found myself in jail, and I made several jails all over the country. Rape and arrest were just part of the package of living the way I was living, so I accepted them without question.

After almost a year of living on the road, in and out of jail, in and out of scrapes, I returned to my hometown, broke, sick, and beaten. Of course, my old friends from high school were still around, so I figured that I'd be taken care of. They didn't respond to me the way I'd anticipated. Frankly, they didn't seem to want to have anything to do with me, so I switched crowds. Humiliated, I ended up moving in again with my family, because they were the only people that would claim me. That's when I reached my bottom. It took a couple of months for me to really let go of the drugs and the booze, but I did come to a realization of how unmanageable my life was. I had to at least try to clean up my act a little bit. A little bit just wasn't enough. During the day, I was too hungover to work, so I couldn't function out in the world. I hated the way I felt about myself; I hated being frightened and sick all the time, and I hated having to drink and use drugs to just get through the night. A few months earlier, I had gone into delirium tremens, and I was deathly frightened of going into them again. But I started really thinking about the danger my family was in with me living right there in the house. I couldn't be trusted, once I took the first drink or drug, because I had a tendency to get violent and obscene when I'd black out. Blackouts were becoming an everyday occurrence for me. There was no way my body or mind could function without taking in at least enough booze and barbiturates to knock me out every night. With my back against the wall, I paid a visit to the local university clinic and begged an intern to prescribe a bottle of tranquilizers for me. He did, and I actually followed his instructions to take just a small number of them each day, and withdrew from them gradually. That was in the summertime. I continued to take pills and smoke marijuana for another four months after that, but my attitude and pattern had changed. On sheer intuition, I started to realize that I'd better let go of all mood-altering chemicals. I knew that I would jump from one drug to another, if I didn't. That idea must have been planted in me by a Higher Power, because I certainly hadn't been given any information that would cause me to believe it.

I stayed clean for almost a year with no outside help. This is not something I recommend to other addicts. During that year, I really developed some serious emotional illnesses. It has taken me years of living the N.A. way to get over that first year with "my own program." For one thing, I became an anorexic, suffering from a disease just as devastating as all of my other addictions put together. When I wasn't starving myself, I was compulsively gorging myself and vomiting. I also went into a three-month depression, when I didn't even have enough faith to walk outside, because I didn't trust the sidewalk to be there. I lived in constant paranoia, and I lost control over my emotions, crying at the drop of a hat.

One day, I woke up so upset that I just had to have help. I wanted to get my hands on some drugs, any drugs! The only help I could find in the phone book was a program that helps people with drinking problems. I knew I had a drinking problem, when I drank, so, I figured they'd let me slide in under the wire. I also knew that if I didn't call someone to keep me from using, I would call someone that would get me high. The day I walked into that clubhouse, shaking and crying, nobody had any reason to believe that I hadn't had any booze or any drugs for almost a year. I was a wreck. After all those months of clean time, I was just as jumpy, just as lost, as a person who'd been on a drunk the night before. The people in that fellowship took me in like a sick child, nursing me and feeding me. I was twenty-one years old, and I'd lived a completely different lifestyle than anyone I met there, but at least these new friends were staying away from drugs and booze. Most of them believed, like I did, that all drugs were off limits for them, but that was a burning issue, and nobody really had any answers. I felt love, and I felt better, but I still wasn't home.

A lot happened to me in the next four years. I stayed clean from drugs, and I continued to attend meetings, wherever I was, and whatever else I did. I was introduced to the Twelve Steps, and I made several attempts to work them. I read and memorized the literature I was given and I did several inventories. I started to develop a relationship with a Higher Power. I never missed a day asking God to help me stay clean each morning, and thanking Him each night. I talked about my feelings sometimes, and when I did, I felt better. But, I usually felt like a little kid around the others in the meetings. There was still something terribly wrong with me. I had not really gotten honest about my strange food-related addiction, and I continued to indulge it, and to wallow in selfobsession and self-pity for four years. It was never really clear to me about what to do with my feelings, my obsessions and my dishonesty. I didn't make any connection between the feelings and the chemicals, so it never made sense to me that all of it went together, as symptoms of an illness.

After my fourth birthday, some of the people I had used with as a kid started coming around, trying to clean up from drugs. Then, a songwriter blew into town from another city. He seemed to be a nice guy, but he kept asking me when we were going to start Narcotics Anonymous. I had heard of N.A. a few years before, but I really didn't know anything about it. After some prodding on his part, a couple of us got started on the project of forming a chapter of Narcotics Anonymous in our town. We had to wait awhile for the literature to come from the West Coast, and I don't know how many conferences I had with the preacher that agreed to let us meet in his church, but in the spring of that year, we held our first N.A. meeting. There were three people there and we felt very close. Now, there are six N.A. meetings in my city.

I have personally gone through a lot of changes since then. In my service work for this fellowship, I have found a feeling of accomplishment and belonging that is beyond belief. I have had to do a lot of growing up though, because now I am surrounded by my peers, and they can see through me more quickly than anyone else ever could. I no longer feel like a child among giants. My relationships within the N.A. Fellowship are very deep and loving. I have close friends, brothers and sisters all over the country, and I hope to have more all over the world.

A couple of months before my introduction to Narcotics Anonymous, I let go of my self-destructive behavior. I started to recognize it as part of the same basic problem that I'd had with the drugs. Once I saw the First Step of N.A., all my questions were answered, and I understood what to do with my feelings, and what to call my insanity. I admitted that I was powerless over my addiction; that my life was unmanageable. The addiction was that feeling of isolation, that unnatural desire to hurt myself, that feeling of insatiability, that selfobsession. Now, I could talk about these things. Now, I could turn them over to the care of my Higher Power. I really started to get in touch with my Higher Power. My concept of a God is different from most of the concepts I've heard outside N.A., but similar to some of the concepts I've heard in meetings. I don't really know what God is, but I do attempt to communicate with Him several times each day. I only call Him "God" or "Him" so that things will stay simple, but I think of Him more as a force or an underlying intelligence than anything else. There is no way I could begin to tell you all the miracles I've been shown. I do know that this Power kept me alive for years, even when I was out to destroy myself. Now, the most obvious way I can see and feel God is through nature, and through the communication I have with my brothers and sisters in N.A.

I have many interests, hobbies and talents now. I sing rock music; I draw portraits; I run, walk and swim. I plan to attend an art college next fall, and develop a career in commercial art. I date men, and I no longer feel as if I owe them something for taking me out. For almost three years, I held the same job, and that's a record for me. My life is well-rounded, and I am becoming a more comfortable version of myself, not the neurotic, boring person that I had thought I'd be without drugs. None of my outside interests and relationships are as important to me as my relationship to Narcotics Anonymous. I have learned plenty since I found this program, and gained many things that I can't even put into words. The most obvious things I've learned are that I don't know much, and that I can't make it alone. I need my brothers and sisters in N.A., because I now know that I am powerless over my addiction; not over my substance, but over an isolating, sickening, frightening illness that is inside me. In the Twelve Steps, I have a way to live clean, honest, and comfortable. With the love that I'm shown in Narcotics Anonymous, I have no excuse for loneliness. I have all I need.

Chapter Forty-Five

RELAPSE AND RETURN

My marriage was on the rocks. My wife had sworn out a warrant on assault charges and had confronted me about my addiction. Although I admitted it to her, I was not ready to accept it myself. She told my other family members I was addicted and asked me to accept help. I was not ready for help, but during the hearing she told the judge she would drop charges if I would agree to go into a treatment program. Needless to say, I was more willing to go to treatment than to jail, so I did—for all the wrong reasons.

While in treatment, I decided to listen to what they had to say. I was soon admitting my addiction but had difficulty embracing the concepts of a Higher Power. Because of a series of spiritual experiences, I finally began to accept the idea of God. This enabled me to become very involved in my treatment effort and I tried to put aside all outside problems, investing myself totally in my recovery.

Treatment went by quickly and I really believed I was equipped to go back into society and pick up where I left off. It only took three days for my security and confidence to be shaken. Three days after my discharge my wife entered treatment. In the beginning I was happy she was admitting her own addiction. Soon she was requesting that we have no contact and I resented that. I became jealous when she told me she had been advised to get rid of her problem and that I was it. The feelings of rejection were a deep kind of pain and I was resentful over not having been given my second chance to put my family back together. The pain was unbearable and the only way I remembered to relieve it was to return to my immediate reliever — drugs.

In much less time than I thought possible, the reality of progression of the disease, as I had been taught in treatment, came true. In a period of five months I lost my family, all my material possessions except the clothes on my back, my job and all of my friends, and most certainly any control over my drug usage. I had married again, was heavily in debt and resorted to something I had never done before — stealing. The bottom I had hit before treatment was really nothing compared to this. I felt alone and desperate. I realized that I was no longer comfortable with the drug life.

I isolated myself in my apartment and withdrew myself to be rid of the drugs in the physical self. The mental craving was still there after withdrawal. I finally decided I couldn't make it by myself. I began to pray again and make conscious contact with the Higher Power. For the first time, I got honest about my powerlessness and reached out for help. I called old acquaintances in the Fellowship and asked for help in getting transportation to meetings.

In the beginning of my return to the Fellowship, only the body was present, but at least I had the willingness to get the body there. I felt so hopeless and helpless that I considered going into treatment again. After a lengthy conversation with a member of the Fellowship, (who told me I knew what to do), my mind finally caught up with my body and I began to work the steps.

I went to every meeting available, each week, and soon I began to feel differently. I was aware of a sense of peace. Some of the fear left and for the most part I had been relieved of the craving. Although my material world was still nonexistent, I began to distinguish my needs from my wants and got comfortable with what I didn't have. The Higher Power seemed to be taking care of business for me, and many of my problems disappeared or resolved themselves.

I became involved in the Fellowship, spending all my time with recovering addicts. I knew I was getting clean and that I wanted to be clean. I became aware of how people cared about me and that if I listened to them, God would speak to me through them. Without any effort on my part, my world began to fall into place. I was soon employed again, reconciled with my parents and sister and was able to cope with the outside world just as it was.

My feelings of gratitude spilled over. I finally felt I had something to share with other recovering addicts and I couldn't wait to "give it away." I became heavily involved in Twelve Step work and returned to the treatment center, where it all began, to offer myself as a volunteer for anything they needed me for. I drove van loads of patients to meetings, shared with the patients about my experience, strength and hope and became willing to be God's instrument to speak to others in any way He chose.

My life has taken on new meaning and I am able today, with the help of the Higher Power, to feel feelings I never allowed myself to feel before. I am more confident, but I know it is God-confidence. I am more reliant, but I know it is God-reliance. I am more independent, but I know it is God-dependency. Today I am free to be exactly who I am because I know "whose" I am.

Recognizing my dependency on God as I understand Him, continuing to work the steps of the program and my sincere desire to "give away" what I have, I can truthfully say I am a Happy Drug Addict!

Chapter Forty-Six

SICK AND TIRED AT EIGHTEEN

I started drinking and using drugs when I was 13. From that point on, my whole life revolved around drugs and the people I used with. I went to any lengths to use. I slept with men for drugs, stole from my family and friends, lied to and conned everyone and anyone I could. Within a year, I was a prostitute.

At sixteen, I got married. We went to New York, to San Francisco and to Maine, but no geographics worked. Things only got progressively worse. My husband and I split up after ten months — he didn't want to use.

The next year of my life revolved around a series of bad relationships and a lot of drugs. I became a junkie. I used everything I could beg, borrow or steal in one day; sometimes it was a lot, sometimes, it was nothing. I was deep into using and soon found myself deep into a new relationship. This is when my using was at its worst. We tried to clean up time after time, with no success. We got arrested a lot. He was doing burglaries and robberies, and when he was out, I was turning tricks and getting loaded. He was shot and killed. All my friends were either dead or in jail. I was completely alone. I was still seventeen, and had been getting released to my father every time I was arrested. My last arrest was one week before my eighteenth birthday. My family didn't want anything to do with me anymore. I had nothing and no one left.

I hated myself for what I had become. I had attempted suicide, and even that didn't work. I was sick and tired of being sick and tired. I wanted to die. I wanted to live. I couldn't seem to do either.

I was on an outpatient program, and my probation officer sent me to N.A. with a court card. I started with one meeting a week, and went to five, after four "dirty" tests.

My probation officer wanted me to make it. She was on another "anonymous" program, and she had the faith that I didn't have. I remember how hard it was to stay clean. I had the "I wanna-want-to's."

I continued to associate with people who were using. I was still dealing pharmaceuticals, because I had the idea that heroin was my problem. I didn't use the pills, but the dealing put me in the position to be around heroin—and I still didn't know why I couldn't stay clean.

Eventually, I succeeded in staying clean for about eighty days. I had been in a bar, dealing again, and found myself loaded again. I sat there with my head on my chest, knowing this just wasn't any good anymore. Nothing had changed out there.

Something had happened; I had finally hit that "bottom" I had heard so much about. I just couldn't do it anymore. The next morning, I surrendered, totally with no reservations.

Shortly after that, I ran into an old connection at a meeting. She had about nine months of clean time. She gave me a lot of hope; she became my friend; she gave me love. I got a sponsor and followed directions. We went to two, three and sometimes four meetings everyday for my first six months. I started working, and continued to go to at least one meeting a day. I was the secretary of two N.A. meetings, and the G.S.R. of another. I took people to meetings, and got involved with the people in recovery houses. I made the program my life.

It hasn't been all easy for me, since I've been here. There have been some real hard times. I wasn't one of those people who walked in the doors of N.A., and the obsession was immediately removed. I can remember sitting in my bathtub once (it seemed like forever), because it was all I could to to keep myself from getting loaded. I prayed for the obsession to be removed. I kept telling myself, "Just for today, I won't get loaded, this too shall pass, just for today, just for today. . ." It passed.

After a year clean, I lost my job, my roommate, my car, and my apartment, all in one week. I had the faith that God wasn't going to bring me that far just to drop me. God won't give me more than I can handle. I believed that anything taken away would be replaced by something better. They were.

The fellowship has never failed to give me the support I've needed, even if it meant a phone call at 3:00 a.m. They've always been there for me. You keep what you have by giving it away, so I've been there for others too.

I work the steps and use the principles of this program in all my affairs. They work. I know that the steps will work on anything. All of my experiences just reinforce that. Turning my will and my life over to the care of God today gives me such peace inside. Watching how the steps work in my life, and watching someone I knew when they first came in grow into a beautiful individual is such a good feeling. Passing down what was given to me, and watching them pass it along is great. The love and caring in this program is something that you will never find anywhere else — one addict helping another addict.

I have learned to live life on life's terms. Through the meetings, the fellowship, and the steps, I have learned how to accept myself, and even love myself. I continually grow through the program. I have found a Power greater than myself who is a loving God, not the punishing God that I grew up with. I have faith today. Complete faith that "my" God is taking care of me. All of my life I sought answers through my adventures; I finally found peace from within.

I no longer have to feel that total pitiful and incomprehensible demoralization. I never have to hate myself, or be alone and unwanted. Today I enjoy my life: program functions, picnics, parties, dances, campouts and conventions. I have outside interests I never dreamed I'd be doing: skiing, racquetball and horseback riding. I have a good job doing what I want to do. I go to school and do well. I drive the car I always dreamed of owning. Things are good in my life today. My worst day clean is always better than my best day using. I'm 23 years old and I'll have 5 years of clean time this December.* I found that is really isn't what we used, how much we used, or how long we used that gets us here. It's the feeling — the hopelessness and helplessness we felt. The Third Tradition states: "The only requirement for membership is a desire to stop using." People loved me into this program. They held my hand and told me it was okay, and they gave me that hard love of telling me to sit down, shut up, and listen when I needed that too. Narcotics Anonymous is a way of life for me today. I wouldn't give it up for anything, for without it I'd have nothing. Narcotics Anonymous gave me back my life, and for this I am eternally grateful.

*Written in 1981.

Chapter Forty-Seven

THE WAR IS OVER

For me, it all started a long time ago. I was an abuser and user, and 17 years old. I got kicked out of my folks' house and I was staying with my brother. I was going nowhere in a hurry. So, I did what all American kids do, I joined the service. From the first day in, I felt different even though we all dressed alike and walked alike. I went gung-ho and all that there was to do, I did. I made squad leader in basic training, and went to Jump School. While there, I trained to be an Airborne Ranger. It was 1968, and when I finished I got orders to Vietnam. I wasn't scared, as I was a part of "America's Finest." I had a cause and a reason to live. I believed I was protecting my country, but after being there, I soon forgot that belief. It was not like on T.V. I felt fear; raw-gut fear. People all around me were dying, so I was scared and lonely. I wouldn't make friends because the next day they would be dead or wounded. One day a guy said, "Here, try this, it's a cigarette with heroin in it." I never wanted to do heroin because I saw junkies in the States, and I disliked them. I liked downers, speed and booze.

After that introduction, I found a new friend. It replaced my parents, girlfriend and buddies. It never let me down. I used on a daily basis and loved it. The Army gave us downers and speed. I was soon caught up in the insanity. I no longer cared about living. In fact, I had a death wish. I volunteered for all high-risk missions; I thought that if I came home a hero, dead in a box, I would show my family that I was somebody.

I remember asking God to watch over "the kid" one day. I don't know why. I was in Vietnam 28 months when I had a nervous breakdown and was sent home. One day I was in Southeast Asia, 23 hours later I was in California. I didn't know how to act. I was sent to Alaska, 60 below zero, after being in Vietnam, 115 degrees.

Well, the Army there was different. I was an Arctic-Airborne Ranger, 22 years old, scared and different. The Vietnam experiences that I had glorified in my mind were sickening to the men in the unit. They couldn't relate or understand: I was a baby killer and a drug-crazed animal. That hurt my pride and ego. I got no "hero's welcome" and I wasn't crippled. I wanted to lose an arm or a leg because all my friends in Nam had. I was "odd man" again.

I took to drinking heavily. The career men hated me, and my peer group resented my authority. I was an E-5 Sarge, so I drank alone and used alone. The town people disliked the servicemen and I wanted to die. I fought for 28 months for them to remain free and safe and they treated me like a dog.

I got busted and went to Washington and learned brick-laying. A marketable skill was the answer, as I had to deal drugs to live. On the construction site, there were as many drugs and alcohol as in the streets, so I was off and running. I never knew there was another way of life. I thought this is me. I didn't want to live, but God saw fit that I get a break.

I was busted again and sent to a drug program for a year. When I got out I had no outside support. I believe "An addict alone is in bad company."

My bubble burst and I was using harder than ever. I was ready to kill myself. I had an M-2 Automatic weapon and a voice in my head said, "Call for help. You deserve to live, you are worth it." I thought, who should I call? The Army caused my problem, so I thought, and I called their hospital. A man on the program said "God loves you and so do I."

In all the years of my life I never heard that before. No one ever said: "I love you, your life is worth living, you are somebody." I went into their program which is N.A.-oriented. I learned that all Vets have the same problem. It wasn't the service that was at fault, but dealing with life on life's terms was my problem. I found out about myself and that I wasn't alone anymore.

At meetings, there were people just like me. It wasn't easy, but I went to meetings there and listened. I used to think I had all the answers, but today I am glad that I don't. N.A. taught me a new lifestyle. How to love myself and how to feel love. I owe all the gifts that I have received to this program and to God. Today, I can be responsible and productive. I am forever grateful; I used to hear bells ring in my head and have nighmares that would keep me awake. I was very antisocial. I had an attitude of, "who cares."

Today, I know someone cares for me. I work the steps and I have become a part of the N.A. Program. I used to be a taker, I have learned that I can now be as much, a giver. That's what is in this program for me now. It hasn't been all "hearts and flowers" for me, and to tell the truth, if it was, I probably wouldn't want it. TODAY THE WAR IS OVER.

Chapter Forty-Eight

UP FROM DOWN UNDER

My name is Melvyn, and I am an addict. I believe that I was born an addict, and that whatever I did, it was not with the intention of becoming addicted to drugs. I was brought up in Cheshire, England, of working-class parents, and went to school like everyone else. But I wasn't like everyone else; I felt different. It is a hard feeling to describe, but as far back as I can remember in my childhood, I had always felt out of it. Somehow I didn't belong. At school I soon realized that I was not going to be successful. So I stopped trying, set my expectations to zero, and was at the bottom of the class from when I started in grammar school to when I finished. But as long as I didn't try, then in my mind, I couldn't fail. I spent my class time inside my head, living in a fantasy world of my own making. There, I was always feeling good. Even on holidays I stayed in my world of fantasy, not getting up until lunch time each day. By the time I started to look for other kids, they were already off somewhere, and I was left alone to make believe by myself.

I left school having failed all my examinations, not having a clue to what I should do with my life. At this time, I tried two things which I thought might help me — I became a probationary local preacher with a protestant church, and I started drinking. I soon realized that preparing the Sunday sermon in the pub Saturday night was not really the right kind of action for a budding local preacher. So I gave away preaching and did more drinking. But life still wasn't working out, so I joined the Royal Navy, starting a geographical that was to last for over 10 years and 40 different countries.

I joined the Royal Navy for nine years and lasted three. The first drink had me beat. No matter what I resolved, after my tot of rum at lunch time, I was looking for more. I was always borrowing money and clothes so I could get ashore (I was always broke and my uniform was always still dirty from the night before). When I went ashore, I never knew where I would end up, when I would get back to ship, or what I had done. Blackouts were with me from the start.

After I was kicked out of the Navy at the age of 20, I wandered around Europe for many months, working where I could, sleeping out, begging, picking up cigarette butts, and still drinking whenever I could. I remember once getting drunk in Moscow, smashing a toilet bowl (it rocked when I sat on it), and getting lost on the Underground. If there was a drug scene in Europe in those days (1963), I didn't come across it. In fact, I didn't come across drugs until five years later in Singapore. I had spent the previous two years in Australia, travelling around, working in mining camps and city offices. My drinking had gotten me into such a state that I could no longer use public transportation to work; I had to travel by taxi. I was frightened of everyone. I sometimes trembled so much I could not walk or hold things. I was in a mess. Whatever a man was supposed to be, and I wasn't quite sure what a man was, I obviously wasn't one. So in my sickness, I decided to prove that I was a man by going to Vietnam. I had already tried to get to Vietnam in 1966, by applying to join the Australian Army, but because of my record in the Navy, they rejected me.

In Singapore, I was introduced to marijuana, and I liked it. It distorted my perception of time, space and hearing, not aggressively like alcohol, but gently. When I got to Saigon, I managed to get a job with the British Medical team working at a children's hospital in Cholon. There I continued drinking and smoking dope and eventually my sanity got somewhat affected. For kicks, I used to drive my ex-Army truck out into the countryside surrounding Saigon in the middle of the night. One night when I was stoned, I took an English reporter with me, and he was terrified the whole trip. I figured it was great fun and that nothing could hurt me. One night I drove past the presidential palace, didn't stop when told to, and ended up with a barbed wire barricade wrapped around my back axle, leaving some ARVN soldiers some explaining to do. I lasted six months in Saigon. Then one night I drove my truck into a jeep, pushed it into the side of a house and squashed it. The side of the house collapsed, and I didn't stop. The following morning the British Embassy, the British Medical team, the owner of the house I'd smashed, the owner of the jeep I'd smashed and the American pilots who lived in the house, were all looking for me. As a result I stopped drinking for life, which lasted five weeks, when one drink set me off again.

At the end of 1969, I was in England, broke as usual, no money and no job. I decided to try and get back to Australia, and got enough money together so that, provided I slept out and didn't spend any money on food or drugs, I might make it. My thinking was so off by this time that I decided to go via North Africa, a place I had never been to before. So off I set, and made it to Spain all right, not spending any money but getting drunk a few times. Just south of Barcelona the compulsion to drink hit me, and I went off on a bender that lasted about a week, leaving me in a little room in Algeciras. There I dried out, or tried to, but was very lonely and miserable. For the first time in my life, by my standards, I had failed. I knew I wasn't going to Australia. They wouldn't even let me buy a ticket for the Tangier ferry, because I smelled so badly. (At this period I went for a month without washing. When I was in Asia I always made sure I was clean when getting tickets and visas; now I was unable even to do this.) I managed to get off the booze, but then went on to the dope. I arranged with some guys to smuggle hashish from Morocco, but the dope was freaking me out so much I shot through. I'll never forget that journey back through Europe — complete failure and depression — I couldn't even be successful as a bum, and that really hurt.

I eventually managed to get to Australia, but I could never keep a job very long because of my drinking. There came the time when I literally couldn't move because of all the unknown fears that I had. So I went to see a doctor, and as a result I got on the alcohol and pills way of life — pills during the day at work, and rum at night at home. This was great for awhile, but as usual, the good times didn't last. I found that I still couldn't keep a job, and the fears started coming back as well. My mother had been saying for years, "Why don't you get married and settle down?" So, in a last desperate measure to sort myself out, I decided to get married. I didn't even have a girlfriend at the time; my drug use had always taken a priority over girls, and my sex life was a fantasy. So I got married, and my life immediately got worse. Ever since I had left home at 17, I had had only myself to think about. Now I had a wife, and it was a responsibility that I could not handle. My lies and cheating got worse, and it was all reflected back at me by my wife. When I got married, I thought that at least my sex problems would be resolved. They weren't — they got worse. I still preferred using drugs to going to bed with my wife. I thought perhaps I was homosexual. So I decided to seduce a friend that I knew was homosexual. I did, and discovered that I wasn't homosexual. So in the end, I couldn't make it with women, and I certainly couldn't make it with men. I was more screwed up than ever before.

It was now 1974, and I had a good job as a computer programmer/analyst, I had a house and a car. In spite of all this, I was mentally, emotionally and spiritually finished. I could go down no further. I hit my rock bottom one afternoon in November 1974, in a forest near me. During a quiet afternoon's drinking I had gone berserk, and tried to run off the edge of the world. I had had enough. I wanted to get off. Eventually, I collapsed and passed out. When I came to, I knew that I had to stop drinking and using drugs. Since Vietnam, I sometimes drove on the right-hand side of the road when intoxicated. In Australia one drives on the left-hand side of the road. That night I drove on the right again, and had cars going everywhere, tried to run over a policewoman twice, and ended the night in cells.

There was no Narcotics Anonymous in Melbourne at that time, but I got myself to another Twelve Step Prgram which dealt with alcohol. To me, alcohol was just another drug, so I didn't have any problems identifying with that program. I was told that if I put my recovery before everything else, then I could stay clean for the rest of my life. That was what I wanted. In my withdrawal, I was violent, and my wife left me. All this did was to clear the way for me to go to as many meetings as possible and concentrate on my recovery without being concerned about her.

I did not pick up the first drug, and I listened to the people who had recovered. I did not associate with people who had come into the program at the same time or later than me; they could not help me. I only talked to those who had been in the program for years, and had something I wanted. I learned to listen and be guided by others, something I had never done before. I remember being told there was no value in a sick mind consulting a sick mind about a sick mind. During my first weeks in the program, I was told to stay away from the first drink or drug, to stay away from the old environment, to contact other members daily, and be constantly aware that I was an addict. I used to walk around, from getting up to going to bed, with the words "I am an addict" circulating in my head.

I learned that when the compulsion to use something hit me, I should take steps in the opposite direction; that I shouldn't dwell upon the compulsion, but that if I did something positive, its hold on me would be lessened. I think someone once said that "you can't stop a bird from crapping on your head, but you can stop it from building a nest there!" In the same way, I can't stop the thought of using coming into my mind, but I can stop it from dwelling there and taking charge of me.

My wife came back after a few months, but it still didn't work out. I was very sick, not only from my addiction, but I also had tuberculosis, which the doctors didn't diagnose until I had been coughing up blood for six months. When I went into the hospital, my wife left me for good. Since I came out of the hospital in 1976, I have continued to concentrate on my recovery. I was involved in the starting of N.A. in Melbourne, and as a result I have been able to relate to addicts, and not just alcoholics.

For two years, I didn't go out with a girl. I just worked the steps and did what I could about my defects of character. I found that I had problems of sexual fantasy, impotence and compulsive eating, and television-watching to get over. I learned to talk to girls and not be frightened of them. I learned to handle rejection, knowing that it is okay to be rejected. I found that I could accept myself, defects and all, and that is a wonderful thing.

After a couple of years in the program, I started to cry spontaneously. All of a sudden, tears would come streaming down my face and I would start sobbing. I discovered that the emotional barriers that I had built over the years to protect myself were coming down—simply by me working the program. I was learning to really feel, and I found that I could handle my feelings.

My spiritual progress has been somewhat different from what I expected. As I have matured in the program, and learned to think for myself, I have examined the principles upon which I base my life. In doing this, I found out that I do not believe in any kind of God, and that my Higher Power is the power of the program. Today I am an atheist. I still concentrate on my own recovery, because if I am well, then I can be of value to others, but if I am sick, then I am of no use to anyone, not even myself.

Being an atheist does not stop me from working the program. The only thing I do not do, of course, is pray. The main thing is that I do what is possible with what I have got. No one can do more. The advice that I was given at my first meeting still holds good today — "don't pick up the first drink or drug, go to meetings and work the steps."

—NOTES—